Expert Twisted

Event-Driven and Asynchronous Programming with Python

Mark Williams

Cory Benfield

Brian Warner

Moshe Zadka

Dustin Mitchell

Kevin Samuel

Pierre Tardy

Apress®

Expert Twisted

Mark Williams
Pasadena, CA, USA

Cory Benfield
London, UK

Brian Warner
New York, USA

Moshe Zadka
New York, USA

Dustin Mitchell
New York, USA

Kevin Samuel
Nice, France

Pierre Tardy
Toulouse, France

ISBN-13 (pbk): 978-1-4842-3741-0
https://doi.org/10.1007/978-1-4842-3742-7

ISBN-13 (electronic): 978-1-4842-3742-7

Library of Congress Control Number: 2018965166

Managing Director, Apress Media LLC: Welmoed Spahr
Acquisitions Editor: Jonathan Gennick
Development Editor: James Markham
Coordinating Editor: Jill Balzano

Cover image designed by Freepik (www.freepik.com)

Distributed to the book trade worldwide by Springer Science+Business Media New York, 233 Spring Street, 6th Floor, New York, NY 10013. Phone 1-800-SPRINGER, fax (201) 348-4505, e-mail orders-ny@springer-sbm.com, or visit www.springeronline.com. Apress Media, LLC is a California LLC and the sole member (owner) is Springer Science + Business Media Finance Inc (SSBM Finance Inc). SSBM Finance Inc is a Delaware corporation.

For information on translations, please e-mail rights@apress.com, or visit http://www.apress.com/rights-permissions.

Apress titles may be purchased in bulk for academic, corporate, or promotional use. eBook versions and licenses are also available for most titles. For more information, reference our Print and eBook Bulk Sales web page at http://www.apress.com/bulk-sales.

Any source code or other supplementary material referenced by the author in this book is available to readers on GitHub via the book's product page, located at www.apress.com/9781484237410. For more detailed information, please visit http://www.apress.com/source-code.

Printed on acid-free paper

Dedicated to AZ, NZ, and TS: Twisted prevails, and we're looking forward to the next generation of maintainers.

—Moshe Zadka

Table of Contents

About the Authors

Mark Williams works on Twisted. At eBay and PayPal, he worked on high-performance Python web services (over a billion requests a day!), application and information security, and porting enterprise, Java-only libraries to Python.

Cory Benfield is an open source Python developer heavily involved in the Python HTTP community. He's a Requests core contributor, a urllib3 core contributor, and the lead maintainer of the Hyper Project, a collection of HTTP and HTTP/2 tools for Python. For his sins, he also helps out with the Python Cryptographic Authority on PyOpenSSL.

Brian Warner is a security engineer and software developer, having worked at Mozilla on Firefox Sync, the Add-On SDK, and Persona. He is co-founder of the Tahoe-LAFS distributed secure filesystem, and develops secure storage and communication tools.

Moshe Zadka has been part of the open source community since 1995, made his first core Python contributions in 1998, and is a founding member of the Twisted open source project. He also loves to teach Twisted and Python, having given tutorials at several conferences as well as regularly blogging.

Dustin Mitchell has contributed to Buildbot and is a member of the TaskCluster team at Mozilla, having also worked on the Release Engineering, Release Operations, and Infrastructure teams.

Kevin Samuel has been a Dev and trainer since Python 2.4 and has been putting his skills to work in East Europe, North America, Asia, and West Africa. He has been working closely with the Crossbar.io team and is an active member of the French Python community.

Pierre Tardy is a continuous integration specialist with Renault Software Labs, and he is currently the lead committer for Buildbot.

About the Technical Reviewers

Julian Berman is a New York-based software developer and open source contributor. He is the author of the jsonschema Python library, an occasional contributor to the Twisted ecosystem, and an active member of the Python community.

Shawn Shojaie lives in the clement chaparral of California's Bay Area, where he works as a back-end software engineer. He has worked at Intel, NetApp, and now SimpleLegal, where he happily builds web-based applications for legal services. He spends weekdays writing Django and tuning PostgreSQL, and his weekends contributing to open source projects like django-pylint, occasionally editing technical essays. Find out more at him at shawnshojaie.com.

Tom Most is a software engineer in the telecommunications industry. He is a Twisted committer with 10 years of experience of applying Twisted to web services, client libraries, and command-line applications. He is the maintainer of Afkak, the Twisted Kafka client. He can be found online at freecog.net and reached at twm@freecog.net.

Acknowledgments

Thanks to my wife, Jennifer Zadka, without whose support I could not have done it.

Thanks to my parents, Yaacov and Pnina Zadka, who taught me how to learn.

Thanks to my advisor, Yael Karshon, for teaching me how to write.

Thanks to Mahmoud Hashemi, for inspiration and encouragement.

Thanks to Mark Williams, for always being there for me.

Thanks to Glyph Lefkowitz, for teaching me things about Python, about programming, and about being a good person.

—Moshe Zadka

Thanks to Mahmoud Hashemi and David Karapetyan for their feedback. Thanks to Annie for putting up with me while I wrote

—Mark Williams

The original version of this book was revised. A correction to this book is available at https://doi.org/10.1007/978-1-4842-3742-7_13

Introduction

Twisted has recently celebrated its sweet sixteen birthday. It has been around for a while; and in that time, it grew to be a powerful library. In that time, some interesting applications have been built on top of it. In that time, many of us learned a lot about how to use Twisted well, how to think about networking code, and how to architect event-based programs.

After going through the introductory materials that we have on the Twisted site, a common thing to hear is "What now? How can I learn more about Twisted?" The usual way we answered that question is with a question: "What do you want to do with Twisted?" This book shows how to do interesting things with Twisted.

Each of the contributors to this book has done slightly different things with Twisted and learned different lessons. We are excited to present all of these lessons, with the goals of making them common knowledge in the community.

Enjoy!

PART 1

Foundations

CHAPTER 1

An Introduction to Event-Driven Programming with Twisted

Twisted is a powerful, well-tested, and mature concurrent networking library and framework. As we'll see in this book, many projects and individuals have used it to great effect for more than a decade.

At the same time, Twisted is large, complicated, and old. Its lexicon teems with strange names, like "reactor," "protocol," "endpoint," and "Deferred." These describe a philosophy and architecture that have baffled both newcomers and old hands with years of Python experience.

Two fundamental programming paradigms inform Twisted's pantheon of APIs: *event-driven programming* and *asynchronous programming*. The rise of JavaScript and the introduction of `asyncio` into the Python standard library have brought both further into the mainstream, but neither paradigm dominates Python programming so completely that merely knowing the language makes them familiar. They remain specialized topics reserved for intermediate or advanced programmers.

This chapter and the next introduce the motivations behind event-driven and asynchronous programming, and then show how Twisted employs these paradigms. They lay the foundation for later chapters that explore real-world Twisted programs.

We'll begin by exploring the nature of event-driven programming outside of the context of Twisted. Once we have a sense of what defines event-driven programming, we'll see how Twisted provides software abstractions that help developers write clear and effective event-driven programs. We'll also stop along the way to learn about some of the unique parts of those abstractions, like *interfaces*, and explore how they're documented on Twisted's website.

© Mark Williams, Cory Benfield, Brian Warner, Moshe Zadka, Dustin Mitchell, Kevin Samuel, Pierre Tardy 2019
M. Williams et al., *Expert Twisted*, https://doi.org/10.1007/978-1-4842-3742-7_1

By the end of this chapter you'll know Twisted terminology: protocols, transports, reactors, consumers, and producers. These concepts form the foundation of Twisted's approach to event-driven programming, and knowing them is essential to writing useful software with Twisted.

A Note About Python Versions

Twisted itself supports Python 2 and 3, so all code examples in this chapter are written to work on both Python 2 and 3. Python 3 is the future, but part of Twisted's strength is its rich history of protocol implementations; for that reason, it's important that you're comfortable with code that runs on Python 2, even if you never write it.

What Is Event-Driven Programming?

An *event* is something that causes an event-driven program to perform an action. This broad definition allows many programs to be understood as event-driven; consider, for example, a simple program that prints either Hello or World! depending on user input:

```
import sys
line = sys.stdin.readline().strip()
if line == "h":
    print("Hello")
else:
    print("World")
```

The availability of a line of input over standard input is an event. Our program pauses on sys.stdin.readline(), which asks the operating system to allow the user to input a complete line. Until one is received, our program can make no progress. When the operating system receives input, and Python's internals determine it's a line, sys.stdin.readline() resumes our program by returning that data to it. This resumption is the event that drives our program forward. Even this simple program, then, can be understood as an *event-driven* one.

Multiple Events

A program that receives a single event and then exits doesn't benefit from an event-driven approach. Programs in which more than one thing can happen at a time, however, are more naturally organized around events. A graphical user interface implies just such a program: at any moment, a user might click a button, select an item from a menu, scroll through a text widget, and so on.

Here's a version of our previous program with a Tkinter GUI:

```python
from six.moves import tkinter
from six.moves.tkinter import scrolledtext

class Application(tkinter.Frame):
    def __init__ (self, root):
        super(Application,self). __init__ (root)
        self.pack()
        self.helloButton = tkinter.Button(self,
                                    text="Say Hello",
                                    command=self.sayHello)
        self.worldButton = tkinter.Button(self,
                                    text="Say World",
                                    command=self.sayWorld)
        self.output = scrolledtext.ScrolledText(master=self)
        self.helloButton.pack(side="top")
        self.worldButton.pack(side="top")
        self.output.pack(side="top")
    def outputLine(self, text):
        self.output.insert(tkinter.INSERT, text+ '\n')
    def sayHello(self):
        self.outputLine("Hello")
    def sayWorld(self):
        self.outputLine("World")
```

Application(tkinter.Tk()).mainloop()

This version of our program presents the user with two buttons, either of which can generate an independent click event. This differs from our previous program, where only `sys.stdin.readline` could generate the single "line ready" event.

We cope with the possible occurrence of either button's event by associating *event handlers* with each one. Tkinter buttons accept a callable `command` to invoke when they are clicked. When the button labeled "Say Hello" generates a click event, that event drives our program to call `Application.sayHello` as shown in Figure 1-1. This, in turn, outputs a line consisting of `Hello` to a scrollable text widget. The same process applies to the button labeled "Say Hello" and `Application.sayWorld`.

Figure 1-1. *Our Tkinter GUI application after a series of clicks of "Say Hello" and "Say World"*

`tkinter.Frame`'s `mainloop` method, which our `Application` class inherits, waits until a button bound to it generates an event and then runs the associated event handler. After each event handler has run, `tkinter.Frame.mainloop` again begins waiting for new events. A loop that monitors event sources and dispatches their associated handlers is typical of event-driven programs, and is known as an *event loop*.

These concepts are the core of event-driven programming:

1. *Events* represent that something has occurred and to which the program should react. In both our examples, events correspond naturally to program input, but as we'll see, they can represent anything that causes our program to perform some action.

2. *Event handlers* constitute the program's reactions to events. Sometimes an event's handler just consists of a sequence of code, as in our `sys.stdin.readline` example, but more often it's encapsulated by a function or method, as in our `tkinter` example.

3. An *event loop* waits for events and invokes the event handler associated with each. Not all event-driven programs have an event loop; our `sys.stdin.readline` example did not because it only responds to a single event. However, most resemble our `tkinter` example in that they process many events before finally exiting. These kinds of programs use an event loop.

Multiplexing and Demultiplexing

The way event loops wait for events affects the way we write event-driven programs, so we must take a closer look at them. Consider our `tkinter` example and its two buttons; the event loop inside `mainloop` must wait until the user has clicked at least one button. A naive implementation might look like this:

```
def mainloop(self):
    while self.running:
        ready = [button for button in self.buttons if button.hasEvent()]
        if ready:
            self.dispatchButtonEventHandlers(ready)
```

`mainloop` continually *polls* each button for a new event, dispatching event handlers only for those that have an event ready. When no events are ready, the program makes no progress because no action has been taken that requires a response. An event-driven program must suspend its execution during these periods of inactivity.

The while loop in our `mainloop` example suspends its program until one of the buttons has been clicked and `sayHello` or `sayWorld` should run. Unless the user is supernaturally fast with a mouse, this loop spends most of its time checking buttons that haven't been clicked. This is known as a *busy wait* because the program is actively busy waiting.

A busy wait like this pauses a program's overall execution until one of its event sources reports an event, and so it suffices as a mechanism to pause an event loop.

The inner list comprehension that powers our implementation's busy wait asks a critical question: Has anything happened? The answer comes from the `ready` variable, which contains all buttons that have been clicked in a single place. The truthiness of `ready` decides the answer to the event loop's question: when `ready` is empty and thus falsey, no buttons have been clicked and so nothing has happened. When it's truthy, however, at least one has been clicked, and so something *has* happened.

The list comprehension that constructs `ready` coalesces many separate inputs into one. This is known as *multiplexing*, while the inverse process of separating different inputs out from a single coalesced input is known as *demultiplexing*. The list comprehension multiplexes our buttons into `ready` while the `dispatchButtonEventHandlers` method demultiplexes them out by invoking each event's handler.

We can now refine our understanding of event loops by precisely describing how they wait for events:

- An *event loop* waits for events by *multiplexing* their sources into a single input. When that input indicates that events have occurred, the event loop demultiplexes it into its constituent inputs and invokes the event handler associated with each.

Our `mainloop` multiplexer wastes most of its time polling buttons that haven't been clicked. Not all multiplexers are so inefficient. `tkinter.Frame.mainloop`'s actual implementation employs a similar multiplexer that polls all widgets unless the operating system provides more efficient primitives. To improve its efficiency, `mainloop`'s multiplexer exploits the insight that computers can check a GUI's widgets faster than a person can interact with them, and inserts a `sleep` call that pauses the entire program for several milliseconds. This allows the program to spend part of its busy-wait loop passively rather than actively do nothing, saving CPU time and energy at the expense of negligible latency.

While Twisted can integrate with graphical user interfaces, and in fact has special support for tkinter, it is at its heart a networking engine. *Sockets*, not buttons, are the fundamental object in networking, and operating systems expose efficient primitives for multiplexing socket events. Twisted's event loop uses these primitives to wait for events. To understand Twisted's approach to event-driven programming, we must understand the interaction between these sockets and these multiplexing networking primitives.

The select Multiplexer

Its History, Its Siblings, and Its Purpose

Almost all modern operating systems support the select multiplexer. select gets its name from its ability to take a list of sockets and "select" only those that have events ready to be handled.

select was born in 1983, when computers were capable of far less. Consequently, its interface prevents it from operating at maximum efficiency, especially when multiplexing a large number of sockets. Each operating system family provides its own, more efficient multiplexer, such as BSD's kqueue and Linux's epoll, but no two interoperate. Luckily their principles are similar enough to select that we can generalize their behavior from select's. We'll use select to explore how these socket multiplexers behave.

select and Sockets

The code that follows omits error handling and will break on many edge cases that occur in practice. **It is intended only as a teaching tool. Do not use it in real applications. Use Twisted instead.** Twisted strives to correctly handle errors and edge cases; that's part of why its implementation is so complicated.

With that disclaimer out of the way, let's begin an interactive Python session and create sockets for select to multiplex:

```
>>> import socket
>>> listener = socket.socket(socket.AF_INET, socket.SOCK_STREAM)
>>> listener.bind(('127.0.0.1', 0))
>>> listener.listen(1)
>>> client = socket.create_connection(listener.getsockname())
>>> server, _ = listener.accept()
```

A full explanation of the socket API is beyond the scope of this book. Indeed, we expect that the parts we discuss will lead you to prefer Twisted! The preceding code, however, contains more fundamental concepts than irrelevant details:

1. `listener` - This socket can *accept* incoming connections. It is an internet (`socket.AF_INET`) and TCP (`socket.SOCK_STREAM`) socket accessible by clients on the internal, local-only network interface (which conventionally has an address of `127.0.0.1`) and on a port randomly assigned by the operating system (`0`). This listener can perform the setup necessary for one incoming connection and enqueue it until we're reading for it (`listen(1)`).

2. `client` - This socket is an outgoing connection. Python's `socket.create_connection` function accepts a (`host, port`) tuple representing the listening socket to which to connect and returns a socket connected to it. Because our listening socket is in the same process and named `listener`, we can retrieve its host and port with the `listener.getsockname()`.

3. `server` - The server's incoming connection. Once `client` has connected to our host and port, we must accept the connection from `listener`'s queue of length 1. `listener.accept` returns a (`socket, address`) tuple; we only need the socket, so we discard the address. A real program might log the address or use it to track connection metrics. The listening queue, which we set to 1 via the socket's `listen` method, holds this socket for us before we call accept and allows `create_connection` to return.

`client` and `server` are two ends of the same TCP connection. An established TCP connection has no concept of "client" and "server"; our `client` socket has the same privileges to read, write, or close the connection as our `server`:

```
>>> data = b"xyz"
>>> client.sendall(data)
>>> server.recv(1024) == data
True
>>> server.sendall(data)
>>> client.recv(1024) == data
True
```

The How and Why of Socket Events

Under the hood, the operating system maintains read and write buffers for each TCP socket to account for network unreliability and clients and servers that read and write at different speeds. If `server` became temporarily unable to receive data, the `b"xyz"` we passed `client.sendall` would remain in its write buffer until `server` again became active. Similarly, if we were too busy to call `client.recv` to receive the `b"xyz" server.sendall` sent, `client`'s read buffer would hold onto it until we got around to receiving it. The number that we pass `recv` represents the maximum data we're willing to remove from the read buffer. If the read buffer has less than the maximum, as it does in our example, `recv` will remove *all* the data from the buffer and return it.

Our sockets' bidirectionality implies two possible events:

1. A *readable event*, which means the socket has something available for us. A connected server socket generates this event when data has landed in the socket's receive buffer, so that calling `recv` after a readable event will immediately return that data. A disconnection is represented by `recv`ing no data. By convention, a listening socket generates this event when we can `accept` a new connection.

2. A *writable event*, which means space is available in the socket's write buffer. This is a subtle point: as long as the socket receives acknowledgment from the server for the data it's transmistted across the network faster than we add it to the send buffer, it remains writable.

`select`'s interface reflects these possible events. It accepts up to four arguments:

1. a sequence of sockets to monitor for *readable events*;

2. a sequence of sockets to monitor for *writable events*;

3. a sequence of sockets to monitor for "exceptional events." In our examples, no exceptional events will occur, so we will always pass an empty list here;

4. An optional *timeout*. This is the number of seconds `select` will wait for one of the monitor sockets to generate an event. Omitting this argument will cause `select` to wait forever.

We can ask select about the events our sockets have just generated:

```
>>> import select
>>> maybeReadable = [listener, client, server]
>>> maybeWritable = [client, server]
>>> readable, writable, _ = select.select(maybeReadable, maybeWritable, [], 0)
>>> readable
[]
>>> writable == maybeWritable and writable == [client, server]
True
```

We instruct select not to wait for any new events by providing a timeout of 0. As explained above, our client and server sockets might be readable or writable, while our listener, which can only accept incoming connections, can only be readable.

If we had omitted the timeout, select would pause our program until one of the sockets it monitored became readable or writable. This suspension of execution is analogous to the multiplexing busy-wait that polled all buttons in our naive mainloop implementation above.

Invoking select *multiplexes* sockets more efficiently than a busy wait because the operating system will only resume our program when at least one event has been generated; inside the kernel an event loop, not unlike our select, waits for events from the network hardware and dispatches them to our application.

Handling Events

select returns a tuple with three lists, in the same order as its arguments. Iterating over each returned list *demultiplexes* select's return value. None of our sockets have generated readable events, even though we've written data to both client and server; our preceding calls to recv emptied their read buffers, and no new connections have arrived for listener since we accepted server. Both client and server have generated a writable event, however, because there's space available in their send buffers.

Sending data from client to server causes server to generate a readable event, so select places it in the readables list:

```
>>> client.sendall(b'xyz')
>>> readable, writable, _ = select.select(maybeReadable, maybeWritable, [], 0)
>>> readable == [server]
True
```

12

The writable list, interestingly, once again contains our client and server sockets:

```
>>> writable == maybeWritable and writable == [client, server]
True
```

If we called select again, our server socket would again be in readable and our client and server sockets again in writable. The reason is simple: as long as data remains in a socket's read buffer, it will continuously generate a readable event, and as long as space remains in a socket's write buffer, it will generate a writable event. We can confirm this by recving the data client sent to server and calling select again for new events:

```
>>> server.recv(1024) == b'xyz'
True
>>> readable, writable, _ = select.select(maybeReadable, maybeWritable,
[], 0)
>>> readable
[]
>>> writable == maybeWritable and writable == [client, server]
True
```

Emptying server's read buffer has caused it to stop generating readable events, and client and server continue to generate writable events because there's still space in their write buffers.

An Event Loop with select

We now know how select multiplexes sockets:

1. Different sockets generate readable or writable events to indicate that an event-driven program should accept incoming data or connections, or write outgoing data.

2. select multiplexes sockets by monitoring them for readable or writable events, pausing the program until at least one is generated or the optional timeout has elapsed.

3. Sockets continue generating readable and writable events until the circumstances that led to those events changes: a socket with readable data emits readable events until its read buffer

is emptied; a listening socket emits readable events until all
incoming connections have been accepted; and a writable socket
emits writable events until its write buffer is filled.

With this knowledge, we can sketch an event loop around select:

```python
import select

class Reactor(object):
    def __init__ (self):
        self._readers = {}
        self._writers = {}
    def addReader(self, readable, handler):
        self._readers[readable] = handler
    def addWriter(self, writable, handler):
        self._writers[writable] = handler
    def removeReader(self, readable):
        self._readers.pop(readable,None)
    def removeWriter(self, writable):
        self._writers.pop(writable,None)
    def run(self):
        while self._readers or self._writers:
            r, w, _ = select.select(list(self._readers), list
            (self._writers), [])
            for readable in r:
                self._readers[readable](self, readable)
            for writable in w:
                if writable in self._writers:
                    self._writers[writable](self, writable)
```

We call our event loop a *reactor* because it reacts to socket events. We can request
our Reactor call readable event handlers on sockets with addReader and writable event
handlers with addWriter. Event handlers accept two arguments: the reactor itself and
the socket that generated the event.

The loop inside the run method multiplexes our sockets with select, then
demultiplexes the result between sockets that have generated a read event and sockets
that have generated a write event. The event handlers for each readable socket run
first. Then, the event loop checks that each writable socket is still registered as a writer

before running its event handler. This check is necessary because closed connections are represented as read events, so a read handler run immediately prior might remove a closed socket from the readers and writers. By the time its writable event handler runs, the closed socket would be removed from the _writers dictionary.

Event-Driven Clients and Servers

This simple event loop suffices for implementing a client that continually writes data to a server. We'll begin with the event handlers:

```python
def accept(reactor, listener):
    server, _ = listener.accept()
    reactor.addReader(server, read)

def read(reactor, sock):
    data = sock.recv(1024)
    if data:
        print("Server received", len(data),"bytes.")
    else:
        sock.close()
        print("Server closed.")
        reactor.removeReader(sock)

DATA=[b"*",  b"*"]
def write(reactor, sock):
    sock.sendall(b"".join(DATA))
    print("Client wrote", len(DATA)," bytes.")
    DATA.extend(DATA)
```

The accept function handles a readable event on a listening socket by accepting the incoming connection and requesting the reactor monitor it for readable events. These are handled by the read function.

The read function handles a readable event on a socket by attempting to receive a fixed amount of data from the socket's receive buffer. The length of any received data is printed – remember, the amount passed to recv represents an *upper bound* on the number of bytes returned. If no data is received on a socket that has generated a readable event, then the other side of the connection has closed its socket, and the read

15

function responds by closing its side of the socket and removing it from the set of sockets monitored by the reactor for readable events. Closing the socket deallocates its operating system resources, while removing it from the reactor ensures the select multiplexer does not attempt to monitor a socket that will never be active again.

The write function writes a sequence of asterisk (*) to a socket that generated a write event. After each successful write, the amount of data is doubled. This simulates the behavior of real network applications that do not consistently write the same amount of data to a connection. Consider a web browser: some outgoing requests contain a small amount of form data typed in by a user, while others upload a large file to a remote server.

Note that these are module-level functions and not methods on our Reactor class. They're instead associated with the reactor by registering them as readers or writers because TCP sockets are only one kind of socket, and the way we must handle their events differs from the way we would handle other sockets' events. select, however, works the same way no matter what sockets it's given, so the logic that runs event handlers on the lists of sockets it returns should be encapsulated by the Reactor class. We'll look at how important encapsulation and the interfaces it implies are to event-driven programs later.

We can now establish a listener and a client and allow the event loop to drive the acceptance of a connection and the transmission of data from client to the server socket.

```
import socket
listener = socket.socket(socket.AF_INET, socket.SOCK_STREAM)
listener.bind(('127.0.0.1',0))
listener.listen(1)
client = socket.create_connection(listener.getsockname())

loop = Reactor()
loop.addWriter(client, write)
loop.addReader(listener, accept)
loop.run()
```

Running this shows both success and failure:

```
Client wrote 2 bytes.
Server received 2 bytes.
Client wrote 4 bytes.
Server received 4 bytes.
```

```
Client wrote 8 bytes.
Server received 8 bytes.
...
Client wrote 524288 bytes.
Server received 1024 bytes.
Client wrote 1048576 bytes.
Server received 1024 bytes.
^CTraceback (most recent call last):
  File "example.py", line 53, in <module>
    loop.run()
  File "example.py", line 25, in run
    writeHandler(self, writable)
  File "example.py", line 33, in write
    sock.sendall(b"".join(DATA))
KeyboardInterrupt
```

The success is clear enough: data passes from the client socket to the server. This behavior follows the path laid out by the accept, read, and write event handlers. As expected, the client begins by sending two bytes of b'*' to the server, which in turn receives those two bytes.

The simultaneity of client and server demonstrates the power of event-driven programming. Where our GUI application could respond to events from two different buttons, this small network server can now respond to events from a client or server, allowing us to colocate both in a single process. The multiplexing abilities of select provide a single point in our programs event loop where it can respond to either.

The failure is also clear: after a certain number of repetitions, our program freezes until it's interrupted via the keyboard. A clue to this failure lies in our program's output; after a while, the client sends many times the amount of data the server receives, and the KeyboardInterrupt's traceback leads right to our write handler's sock.sendall call.

Our client has overwhelmed our server, with the result that most of the data the client has attempted to send remains in its socket's send buffer. The default behavior of sendall is to pause or *block* the program when called on a socket that has no room left in its send buffer. Now, if sendall had *not* blocked and our event loop had been allowed to run, the socket would not have come up as writable, and the blocking sendall call would not have run; however, we cannot guarantee that a given send call will write enough just to fill up a socket's send buffer, so that sendall does not block, the write handler runs to completion, and select prevents further writes from occurring until the buffer has drained. The nature of networks is that we only know about an issue like this after it happens.

All of the events we've covered so far prompt our program to do something. None of them can prompt it to *stop* doing something. We need a new kind of event.

Non-blocking I/O

Knowing When to Stop

Sockets by default block a program that begins an operation that cannot be completed until the remote end does something. We can cause a socket to emit an event in this situation by requesting the operating system make it *non-blocking*.

Let's return to an interactive Python session and again construct a connection between a client and server socket. This time, we will make the client non-blocking and attempt to write an infinite stream of data to it.

```
>>> import socket
>>> listener = socket.socket(socket.AF_INET, socket.SOCK_STREAM)
>>> listener.bind(( '127.0.0.1',0))
>>> listener.listen(1)
>>> client=socket.create_connection(listener.getsockname())
>>> server, _ = listener.accept()
>>> client.setblocking(False)
>>> while True: client.sendall(b"*"*1024)
...
Traceback (most recent call last):
  File"<stdin>", line1, in <module>
BlockingIOError: [Errno11] Resource temporarily unavailable
```

We have again filled client's send buffer, but instead of pausing the process, sendall has raised an exception. The type of the exception varies between Python 2 and 3; here, we show Python 3's BlockingIOError, while on Python 2, it would be the more general `socket.error`. In both versions of Python, the exception's `errno` attribute will be set to `errno.EAGAIN`:

```
>>> import errno, socket
>>> try:
...     while True: client.sendall(b"*"*1024)
... except socket.error as e:
...     print(e.errno == errno.EAGAIN)
True
```

The exception represents an event generated by the operating system indicating that we should *stop* writing. This is almost enough to fix our client and server.

Tracking State

Handling this exception, however, requires we answer a new question: How much of the data we attempted to write made it into the socket's send buffer? We cannot know what data we actually sent without answering this question, and without knowing that we cannot write correct programs with non-blocking sockets. A web browser, for example, must track how much of a file it has uploaded, or it risks corrupting the contents in transit.

`client.sendall` could have placed any number of bytes in its write buffer before generating the EAGAIN event that became our exception. We must switch from the `sendall` method of socket objects to the `send` method, which returns the amount of data written to the socket's send buffer. We can demonstrate this with our `server` socket:

```
>>> server.setblocking(False)
>>> try:
...     while True: print(server.send(b"*" * 1024))
... except socket.error as e:
...     print("Terminated with EAGAIN:", e.errno == errno.EAGAIN)
1024
1024
...
1024
952
Terminated with EAGAIN:True
```

We mark `server` as non-blocking, so that it generates an `EAGAIN` event when its send buffer is full. The `while` loop then calls `server.send`. Calls that return 1024 have written all the provided bytes to the socket's send buffer. Eventually the socket's write buffer fills up, and an exception representing the `EAGAIN` event terminates the loop. The last successful `send` call before the loop's termination, however, returns 952, and here send has simply discarded the remaining 72 bytes. This is known as a *short write*. This happens with blocking sockets as well! Because they block when no space is available in their send buffer instead of raising an exception, `sendall` can and does contain a loop that checks the return value of the underlying `send` call and re-invokes it until all data has been sent.

In this case, the socket's send buffer was not a multiple of 1024, so we were not able to fit an even number of `send` calls' worth of data in before hitting `EAGAIN`. In the real world, however, the socket's send buffer changes size in response to conditions within the network and applications send varying amounts of data across connections. Programs that use non-blocking I/O, like our hypothetical web browser, must regularly deal with short writes like this.

We can use `send`'s return value to make sure we write all our data to the connection. We maintain our *own* buffer that contains the data we want to write. Every time `select` emits a writable event for that socket, we attempt to `send` the data currently in the buffer; if the `send` call completes without raising `EAGAIN`, we note the amount returned and remove that number of bytes from the beginning of our buffer, because `send` writes data into the send buffer from the beginning of the byte sequence it's passed. If, on the other hand, `send` raises an `EAGAIN` exception indicating the send buffer is completely full and cannot accept more data, we leave the buffer as it is. We proceed this way until our own buffer is empty, at which point we know all our data has been placed in the socket's send buffer. After that it's up to the operating system to send it to connection's receiving end.

We can now fix our simple client-server example by splitting its `write` function into one that initiates writing the data and an object that manages the buffer on top of `send`:

```python
import errno
import socket

class BuffersWrites(object):
    def __init__ (self, dataToWrite, onCompletion):
        self._buffer = dataToWrite
```

```python
        self._onCompletion = onCompletion
    def bufferingWrite(self, reactor, sock):
        if self._buffer:
            try:
                written = sock.send(self._buffer)
            except socket.error as e:
                if e.errno != errno.EAGAIN:
                    raise
                return
            else:
                print("Wrote", written,"bytes")
                self._buffer = self._buffer[written:]
        if not self._buffer:
                reactor.removeWriter(sock)
                self._onCompletion(reactor, sock)
DATA=[b"*", b"*"]
def write(reactor, sock):
    writer = BuffersWrites(b"".join(DATA), onCompletion=write)
    reactor.addWriter(sock, writer.bufferingWrite)
    print("Client buffering", len(DATA),"bytes to write.")
    DATA.extend(DATA)
```

BuffersWrites's initializer first argument is the bytes it will write, which it uses as the initial value for its buffer, while its second argument, onCompletion, is a callable object. As its name implies, onCompletion will be called when the provided data has been completely written.

The bufferingWrite method's signature is what we expect from a writable event handler suitable for passing Reactor.addWriter. As described, it attempts to send any buffered data to the socket it's passed, saving the returned number that indicates the amount written. If send raises an EAGAIN exception, bufferingWrite suppresses it and returns; otherwise it propagates the exception. In both cases. self._buffer remains unchanged.

If send succeeds, a number of bytes equal to the amount written is sliced off the beginning of self._buffer and bufferingWrite returns. For example, if the send call wrote only 952 out of 1024 bytes, self_buffer would contain the final 73 bytes.

Finally, if the buffer's empty then all the requested data has been written, and there's no work left for the `BuffersWrites` instance left to do. It requests that the reactor stop monitoring its socket for writable events and then calls `onCompletion` because data it was provided has been completely written. Note that this check occurs in an `if` statement that's independent of the first `if self._buffer` statement. The preceding code might have run and emptied the buffer; if the final code were within an `else` block attached to the `if self._buffer` statement, it would not run until the next time the reactor detected a writable event on this socket. To simplify resource management, we perform the check within this method.

The `write` function looks similar to our previous version except now it delegates sending the data to `BuffersWrites` via its `bufferingWrite` method. Most notably, `write` passes *itself* to `BuffersWrites` as the `onCompletion` callable. This creates the same looping effect as the previous version via *indirect recursion*. `write` never calls itself directly, but instead passes itself to an object that our *reactor* eventually calls. This indirection allows this sequence to continue without overflowing the call stack.

With these modifications, our client-server program no longer blocks. Instead it fails for another reason: eventually, DATA becomes too large to fit inside your computer's available memory! Here's an example from the author's computer:

```
Client buffering 2 bytes to write.
Wrote 2 bytes
Client buffering 4 bytes to write.
Server received 2 bytes.
Wrote 4 bytes
...
Client buffering 2097152 bytes to write.
Server received 1024 bytes.
Wrote 1439354 bytes
Server received 1024 bytes.
Server received 1024 bytes.
....
Wrote 657798 bytes
Server received 1024 bytes.
Server received 1024 bytes.
....
```

```
Client buffering 268435456 bytes to write.
Traceback (most recent call last):
  File "example.py", line 76, in <module>
    loop.run()
  File "example.py", line 23, in run
    writeHandler(self, writable)
  File "example.py", line 57, in bufferingWrite
    self._onCompletion(reactor, sock)
  File "example.py", line 64, in write
    DATA.extend(DATA)
MemoryError
```

State Makes Programs Complex

Despite this problem, we have successfully written an event-driven network program that uses non-blocking IO to control socket writes. The code, however, is a mess: indirection from write through BuffersWrites, then the reactor, and finally back to write obscures the logical flow of outbound data, and it's clear that implementing anything more complicated than a simple stream of asterisks would involve extending ad hoc classes and interfaces beyond their breaking points. For example, how can we address the MemoryError? Our approach will not scale to real applications.

Managing Complexity with Transports and Protocols

Programming with non-blocking I/O is undoubtedly complicated. The UNIX authority W. Richard Stevens writes the following about the matter in volume one of his seminal *Unix Network Programming* series:

> But, is it worth the effort to code an application using non-blocking I/O, given the complexity of the resulting code? The answer is no.

> (*UNIX Network Programming, Volume 1. 2nd ed. p. 446*)

The complexity of our code seems to prove Stevens correct. The right abstractions, however, can encapsulate complexity within a manageable interface. Our example already has reusable code: any new unit of code that writes to a socket will need to

23

use the core logic of BuffersWrites. We have *encapsulated* the complexity of writing to a non-blocking socket. Building on this insight we can distinguish between two conceptual domains:

1. *Transports*: BuffersWrites manages the process of writing output to a non-blocking socket *regardless of the contents of that that output*. It can send photos, or music, or anything we can imagine, so long as it's expressible as bytes. BuffersWrites is a *transport* because it is *a means of transportation for bytes*. Transports encapsulate the process of reading data from a socket, as well as accepting a new connection. It represents the *cause* of actions in our program and it is the *recipient* of our program's own actions.

2. *Protocols*: Our example program generates data with a trivial algorithm and merely counts what it receives. More complicated programs might generate web pages or process voice phone calls into text. As long as they can accept and emit bytes, they can work in concert with what we described as a transport. They might also direct the behavior of their transport, such as closing an active connection upon receipt of invalid data. The field of telecommunications describes rules like this that define how data can be exchanged as a *protocol*. A *protocol*, then, *defines how to generate and process input and output*. It encapsulates the *effect* of our program.

Reactors: Working with Transports

We begin by changing our Reactor to work in terms of transports:

```python
import select
class Reactor(object):
    def __init__ (self):
        self._readers = set()
        self._writers = set()
    def addReader(self, transport):
        self._readers.add(transport)
```

```python
def addWriter(self, transport):
    self._writers.add(transport)
def removeReader(self, readable):
    self._readers.discard(readable)
def removeWriter(self, writable):
    self._writers.discard(writable)
def run(self):
    while self._readers or self._writers:
        r, w, _ = select.select(self._readers,self._writers, [])
        for readable in r:
            readable.doRead()
        for writable in w:
            if writable in self._writers:
                writable.doWrite()
```

Where our readable and writable events' handlers were previously functions, they are now methods on transport objects: doRead and doWrite. Furthermore, the reactor no longer tracks sockets – it directly selects transports. From the reactor's perspective, then, the transport's interface consists of:

1. doRead,

2. doWrite,

3. something that makes the transport's state visible to select: a fileno() method that returns a number that select understands as a reference to a socket.

Transports: Working with Protocols

Next, we will consider a protocol implementation by going back to our read and write functions. The read function had two responsibilities:

1. Counting the number of bytes received on the socket.

2. Responding to a closed connection.

The write function had one responsibility: enqueue data to be written.

From this we can sketch a first draft of a Protocol interface:

```
class Protocol(object):
    def makeConnection(self, transport):
        ...
    def dataReceived(self, data):
        ...
    def connectionLost(self, exceptionOrNone):
        ...
```

We've split read's two responsibilities into two methods: dataReceived and connectionLost. The former's signature is self explanatory, while the latter receives one argument: an exception object if the connection was closed because of that exception (e.g., because of ECONNRESET), or None if it was closed without one (e.g., with an empty read because of a passive close). Note that our protocol interface lacks a write method. That's because writing data, which involves transporting bytes, falls within the transport's domain. As a result, a Protocol instance must have access to a transport that represents the underlying network connection, and which will have a write method. The assocation between the two happens via makeConnection, which accepts a transport as its argument.

Why not pass the transport as an argument to Protocols initializer? A separate method might seem clumsier, but it affords us greater flexibility; for example, you can imagine how this method would allow us to introduce Protocol caching. Furthermore, we'll see that because a transport invokes a protocol's dataReceived and connectionLost methods, it too must be associated with a protocol. If both our Transport and Protocol classes required their peer in their initializer, we would have a circular relationship that prevented both from being instantiated. We choose to make our Protocol accept its transport via a separate method to break this cycle because of the flexibility it affords.

Playing Ping-Pong with Protocols and Transports

This is enough for us to write a more complicated protocol that exercises this new interface. Our previous client-server example simply had the client send larger and larger sequences of bytes to the server; we can augment this so that the two send bytes back and forth, up to an optional maximum, after which the sender that's exceeded the maximum closes the connection.

```python
class PingPongProtocol(object):
    def __init__ (self, identity, maximum=None):
        self._identity = identity
        self._received = 0
        self._maximum = maximum
    def makeConnection(self, transport):
        self.transport = transport
        self.transport.write(b'*')
    def dataReceived(self, data):
        self._received += len(data)
        if self._maximum is not None and self._received >= self._maximum:
            print(self._identity,"is closing the connection")
            self.transport.loseConnection()
        else:
            self.transport.write(b'*')
            print(self._identity,"wrote a byte")
    def connectionLost(self, exceptionOrNone):
        print(self._identity,"lost the connection:", exceptionOrNone)
```

The initializer accepts an `identity` string used to identify the protocol instance and the optional maximum amount of data to accept before terminating the connection. `makeConnection` associates the `PingPongProtocol` with its transport and begins the exchange by sending a single byte. `dataReceived` records the amount of data it's received; if the total amount exceeds the optional maximum, it tells the transport to lose its connection, or equivalently, to disconnect. Otherwise it continues the exchange by sending back a byte. Finally, `connectionLost` prints a message when the protocol's side of the connection has been closed.

`PingPongProtocol` describes a set of behaviors whose complexity is meaningfully beyond what our previous attempt at a non-blocking client-server application was able to do. At the same time, its implementation reflects the prose description that precedes it, without becoming mired in the particulars of non-blocking I/O. We have been able to increase the complexity of our application while decreasing the complexity of its unique I/O management. We'll return to explore the ramifications of this, but suffice it to say that narrowing our focus allows us to eliminate complexity in specific areas of our program.

We cannot use `PingPongProtocol` until we write `Transport`. We can, however, write a first draft of `Transport`'s interface:

```python
class Transport(object):
    def __init__ (self, sock, protocol):
        ...
    def doRead(self):
        ...
    def doWrite(self):
        ...
    def fileno(self):
        ...
    def write(self):
        ...
    def loseConnection(self):
        ...
```

The first argument to Transport's initializer is the socket the instance wraps. This enforces Transport's encapsulation of sockets on which the Reactor now relies. The second argument is the protocol whose dataReceived will be called when new data is available and whose connectionLost will be called when the connection has been closed. The doRead and doWrite methods match the reactor-side transport interface we enumerated above. The new method fileno is also part of this interface; an object with a properly implemented fileno method can be passed to select. We will proxy calls to our Transport's fileno down to the socket it wraps, making the two indistinguishable from select's perspective.

The write method provides the interface on which our Protocol relies to send outgoing data. We have also added loseConnection, a new Protocol-side API that initiates the closing of a socket and represents the active-close side of our passive-close connectionLost method.

We can implement this interface by absorbing BuffersWrites and the socket handling in our read function:

```python
import errno

class Transport(object):
    def __init__ (self, reactor, sock, protocol):
        self._reactor = reactor
        self._socket = sock
        self._protocol = protocol
```

```python
        self._buffer = b "
        self._onCompletion = lambda:None
    def doWrite(self):
        if self._buffer:
            try:
                written = self._socket.send(self._buffer)
            except socket.error as e:
                if e.errno != errno.EAGAIN:
                    self._tearDown(e)
                return
            else:
                print("Wrote", written,"bytes")
                self._buffer = self._buffer[written:]
        if not self._buffer:
            self._reactor.removeWriter(self)
            self._onCompletion()
    def doRead(self):
        data=self._socket.recv(1024)
        if data:
            self._protocol.dataReceived(data)
        else:
            self._tearDown(None)
    def fileno(self):
        return self._socket.fileno()
    def write(self, data):
        self._buffer += data
        self._reactor.addWriter(self)
        self.doWrite()
    def loseConnection(self):
        if self._buffer:
            def complete():
                self.tearDown(None)
            self._onCompletion = complete
        else:
            self._tearDown(None)
```

```
def _tearDown(self, exceptionOrNone):
    self._reactor.removeWriter(self)
    self._reactor.removeReader(self)
    self._socket.close()
    self._protocol.connectionLost(exceptionOrNone)
def activate(self):
    self._socket.setblocking(False)
    self._protocol.makeConnection(self)
    self._reactor.addReader(self)
    self._reactor.addWriter(self)
```

doRead and doWrite mirror the socket manipulations in previous examples' read and write functions as well as BuffersWrites. doRead also proxies any received data to the protocol's dataReceived method or calls its connectionLost method upon receiving an empty read. Finally, fileno rounds out the interface that Reactor requires by making Transports selectable.

The write method buffers writes as before, but instead of delegating the process of writing to a separate class, it invokes its sibling doWrite method to flush its buffer to the socket. If the buffer is empty, a call to loseConnection tears down the connection by:

1. removing the transport from the reactor;

2. closing the underlying socket to release its resources back to the operating system;

3. sending None to the protocol's connectionLost to indicate that the connection was lost due to a passive close.

If the buffer is *not* empty then there *is* data to write, so loseConnection overwrites _onCompletion with a *closure* that tears down the connection following the same process as described above. As with BuffersWrites, Transport._onCompletion is called only when all bytes in our write buffer have been flushed to the underlying socket. loseConnection's use of _onCompletion thus ensures that the underlying connection remains open until all data has been written. The default value of _onCompletion is set in Transport's initializer to a lambda with no effect. This ensures mulitple calls to write can reuse the underlying connection. Together these implementations of write and loseConnection implement the transport interface required by Protocol.

Finally, `activate` activates the transport by:

1. preparing the wrapped socket for non-blocking I/O;

2. passing the `Transport` instance to its protocol via `Protocol.makeConnection`;

3. and finally registering the transport with the reactor.

This completes the `Transport`'s encapsulation of its socket by wrapping the beginning of a connection's life cycle, where the end is already encapsulated by `loseConnection`.

Where `Protocol` allowed us to expand our focus and add behaviors to our application via `PingPongProtocol`, `Transport` has narrowed it around the input-ouput life cycle of sockets. The reactor – our event loop – detects and dispatches events from their originating sockets, while the protocol contains our desired event handlers. The `Transport` mediates by translating socket events to protocol method calls and enforcing *control flow* between these method calls; for example, it ensures that a protocol's `makeConnection` is called at the beginning of its life and `loseConnection` at the end. This is another improvement over our ad hoc client-server example; we have localized control flow around the sockets entirely within `Transport`, instead of spread out over unrelated functions and objects.

Clients and Servers with Protocols and Transports

We can show the generality of `Transport` by defining a subtype, `Listener`, that accepts incoming connections and associate them with a unique `PingPongProtocol` instance:

```
class Listener(Transport):
    def activate(self):
        self._reactor.addReader(self)
    def doRead(self):
        server, _ = self._socket.accept()
        protocol = PingPongProtocol("Server")
        Transport(self._reactor, server, protocol).activate()
```

A listening socket emits no writable events, so we override `activate` to only add the transport as a reader. Our readable event handler, `doRead`, must accept a new client connection and protocol, then tie the two together with an activated `Transport`.

The stage is now set for a client-server example powered by protocols and transports:

```
listenerSock = socket.socket(socket.AF_INET, socket.SOCK_STREAM)
listenerSock.bind(('127.0.0.1',0))
listenerSock.listen(1)
clientSock = socket.create_connection(listenerSock.getsockname())

loop = Reactor()
Listener(loop, listenerSock, None).activate()
Transport(loop, clientSock, PingPongProtocol("Client", maximum=100)).
activate()
loop.run()
```

The two will exchange single bytes until the client receives its maximum of 100, after which the client closes the connection:

```
Server wrote a byte
Client wrote a byte
Wrote 1 bytes
Server wrote a byte
Wrote 1 bytes
Client wrote a byte
Wrote 1 bytes
Server wrote a byte
Wrote 1 bytes
Client wrote a byte
Wrote 1 bytes
Server wrote a byte
Server wrote a byte
Client is closing the connection
Client lost the connection: None
Server lost the connection: None
```

Twisted and Reactors, Protocols, and Transports

We've come a long way: starting with `select`, we worked our way up to a set of interfaces around an event loop and its handlers that cleanly partition responsibilities. Our `Reactor` drives our program, with `Transports` dispatching socket events to application-level handlers defined on `Protocols`.

Our reactors, transports, and protocols are clearly toy implementations. For example, `socket.create_connection` blocks, and we haven't investigated any non-blocking alternative. In fact, the underlying DNS resolution that `create_connection` implies might itself block!

As concepts, however, they are ready for serious use. Reactors, transports, and protocols are the foundation of Twisted's event-driven architecture. As we've seen, their architecture in turn rests upon the realities of I/O multiplexing and non-blocking, enabling Twisted to operate efficiently.

Before we explore Twisted itself, however, we will consider our examples as a whole to evaluate the strengths and weaknesses of event-driven programming.

The Value of Event-Driven Programming

W. Richard Stevens's admonishment regarding the complexity of non-blocking I/O counts as an important criticism of the event-driven programming paradigm we've explored. It is not the only shortcoming, however: our event-driven paradigm does not perform well under high CPU loads.

The client-server example that wrote exponentially growing sequences of bytes naturally consumed large amounts of memory, but it also consumed a significant amount of CPU. The reason is the naivete of its buffer management: the socket simply cannot accept chunks of data larger than a certain size. Every time we call `send` with an amount as large or larger than that, the `send` call copies it into a memory location controlled by the kernel. Some portion of the data is then written, which we then slice off the buffer's front; because `bytes` is immutable in Python, this implies another copy. If we attempt to send N bytes, we will copy the buffer once, then twice, and again and again up to N. Because each copy implies a traversal of the buffer, this process has a time complexity of $O(n^2)$.

Twisted's own buffering mechanisms perform better at the expense of complexity beyond that appropriate to a readable introduction to event-driven programming. Not all computationally demanding tasks are as easily improved, however: Monte

Carlo simulation must repeatedly perform statistical analysis and random samples; a comparison-sorting algorithm must compare every pair of elements in a sequence; and so on.

Our event-driven programs all execute multiple logical behaviors – we have a client and a server communicating within one process. This communication happens *concurrently*: the client side of the connection makes a small amount of progress before pausing and allowing the server to make a small amount of progress. At no point are the client and server operating *in parallel,* as they would in separate Python interpreters, perhaps on separate computers linked by a network. When our naive buffer management executes a lengthy copy, no progress can be made until this completes, whereas if the client and server ran on separate computers, the server could accept new connections while the client laboriously shuffled bytes around. If we were instead running a computationally demanding algorithm in our process, our reactor could not call `select` to discover new events to which to react until after the completion of this algorithm.

Event-driven programming, then, is a poor match for computationally demanding tasks. Fortunately, many tasks make greater demands on input and output than computation. Network servers are a classic example of this; a chat server might have many thousands of users, but only a small portion are active at any time (and then usually not when you ask for help!). Event-driven programming consequently remains a powerful paradigm in networking.

Event-driven programming has a particular strength that more than makes up for this shortcoming: its emphasis on *cause* and *effect.* The generation of an event represents a cause, while that event's handler represents the desired effect.

We codified this division in `Transport` and `Protocol`: transports represent the *cause* of actions – some input or socket output – while protocols encapsulate *effects.* Our `PingPongProtocol` interacts with its transport via a clearly delineated interface that exposes handlers to higher-level events – causes – such as the arrival of incoming bytes or the end of a connection. It then produces *effects* from those causes, which might in turn result in new *causes*, such as writing data to the transport. The distinction between the two is enforced by the respective interfaces.

This means we can replace one transport with another and simulate the execution of our protocol by calling the methods representing expected effects. This changes the core of our client-server into a unit of testable code.

Consider a transport implementation built on BytesIOs that implements only the Protocol's side of the Transport interface:

```python
import io

class BytesTransport(object):
    def __init__ (self, protocol):
        self.protocol = protocol
        self.output = io.BytesIO()
    def write(self, data):
        self.output.write(data)
    def loseConnection(self):
        self.output.close()
        self.protocol.connectionLost(None)
```

We can use this to write a unit test suite for our PingPongProtocol:

```python
import unittest

class PingPongProtocolTests(unittest.TestCase):
    def setUp(self):
        self.maximum = 100
        self.protocol = PingPongProtocol("client", maximum=self.maximum)
        self.transport = BytesTransport(self.protocol)
        self.protocol.makeConnection(self.transport)
    def test_firstByteWritten(self):
        self.assertEqual(len(self.transport.output.getvalue()), 1)
    def test_byteWrittenForByte(self):
        self.protocol.dataReceived(b"*")
        self.assertEqual(len(self.transport.output.getvalue()), 2)
    def test_receivingMaximumLosesConnection(self):
        self.protocol.dataReceived(b"*" * self.maximum)
        self.assertTrue(self.transport.output.closed)
```

This test asserts the requirements we laid out for our PingPongProtocol without setting up any sockets or performing any actual I/O. We can test the *effect* of our program without the concrete *causes*. Instead, we simulate the readable event by calling our protocol instance's `dataReceived` method with bytes, while the protocol generates a writable event by calling `write` on our bytes transport and a close request by calling `loseConnection`.

Twisted strives to separate cause and effect. The most obvious benefit, as demonstrated, is testability. Writing comprehensive tests for event-driven Twisted programs is easier to do because of the fundamental division between protocols and transports. Indeed, Twisted takes this distinction between responsibilities as a deep lesson in design, resulting in its large and sometimes arcane lexicon. Making so many things explicitly separate objects requires a wealth of names.

We are now ready to write an event-driven program with Twisted. We will encounter the same design issues we did in our toy examples, and the experience of writing those toys will elucidate the strategies Twisted offers for addressing those issues.

Twisted and the Real World

We begin our exploration of Twisted with an implementation of our `PingPongProtocol` client and server:

```
from twisted.internet import protocol, reactor

class PingPongProtocol(protocol.Protocol):
    def __init__ (self):
        self._received = 0
    def connectionMade(self):
        self.transport.write(b'*')
    def dataReceived(self, data):
        self._received += len(data)
        if self.factory._maximum is not None and self._received >= self.
        factory._maximum:
            print(self.factory._identity, "is closing the connection")
            self.transport.loseConnection()
        else:
            self.transport.write(b'*')
            print(self.factory._identity,"wrote a byte")
```

```python
    def connectionLost(self, exceptionOrNone):
        print(self.factory._identity,"lost the connection:",
        exceptionOrNone)

class PingPongServerFactory(protocol.Factory):
    protocol = PingPongProtocol
    _identity = "Server"

    def __init__ (self, maximum=None):
        self._maximum = maximum

class PingPongClientFactory(protocol.ClientFactory):
    protocol = PingPongProtocol
    _identity = "Client"

    def __init__ (self, maximum=None):
        self._maximum = maximum

    listener=reactor.listenTCP(port=0,
                                factory=PingPongServerFactory(),
                                interface='127.0.0.1')
    address = listener.getHost()
    reactor.connectTCP(host=address.host,
                        port=address.port,
                        factory=PingPongClientFactory(maximum=100))
    reactor.run()
```

Our PingPongProtocol class is nearly identical to our toy implementation. There are three changes:

1. We inherit from twisted.internet.protocol.Protocol. This class provides useful default implementations of important functionality. At the time Twisted's transports and protocols were first designed, inheritance was a fashionable approach to code reuse. The difficulties around public and private APIs and separation of concerns have rightly led to a decline in its popularity. A complete discussion of inheritance's shortcomings is beyond the scope of this chapter, but we do not recommend writing new APIs that rely on inheritance!

2. We have replaced `makeConnection` with `connectionMade`, which is an event handler that Twisted calls when the underlying connection is ready. Twisted's `Protocol` class implements `makeConnection` for us and leaves `connectionMade` as a stub that we can fill in. In practice, we do not want to change the way a transport is associated with a protocol, but we do often want code to run as soon as a connection is ready. This handler provides a way to do so.

3. The maximum number of bytes and the protocol's identity are no longer instance variables; instead, they're attributes on a new `factory` instance variable.

Protocol factories mediate the creation of protocols and their binding to transports. This is our first example of how Twisted localizes responsibility to classes. Protocol factories come in two basic flavors: server and client. As their names imply, one manages the creation of server-side protocols, while the other manages the creation of client-side protocols. Both create protocol instances by calling their `protocol` attribute with no arguments. This is why `PingPongProtocol`'s initializer accepts no arguments.

`PingPongServerFactory` subclasses `twisted.internet.protocol.Factory` and sets its `_identity` attribute to `"Server."` Its initializer accepts the reactor as an argument and the optional maximum. It then relies on its superclass's implementation to create instances of its protocol – set at the class level to `PingPongProtocol` – and associate them with itself. This is why `PingPongProtocol` instances has a `factory` attribute: `Factory` creates it for us by default.

`PingPongClientFactory` subclasses `twisted.internet.protocol.ClientFactory` and sets its `_identity` attribute to `"Client."` It is otherwise identical to `PingPongServerFactory`.

Factories provide a convenient place to store state that is shared across all protocol instances. Because protocol instances are unique to connections, they cease to exist when the connections do, and cannot persist state on their own. Moving settings like our maximum permissible value and our protocol client or server identity strings to their factories thus follows a common pattern in Twisted.

The `reactor` exposes `listenTCP` and `connectTCP` methods that associate factories with server and client connections. `listenTCP` returns a `Port` object whose `getHost` method is analogous to `socket.getsockname`. Instead of returning a tuple, however, it returns an instance of `twisted.internet.address.IPv4Address`, which in turn has convenient `host` and `port` attributes.

Finally, we start the `reactor` by calling `run`, just like we did with our toy implementation. We're greeted with output that's similar to what our toy implementation printed:

```
Client wrote a byte
Server wrote a byte
Client wrote a byte
Server wrote a byte
Client wrote a byte
Server wrote a byte
Client wrote a byte
Server wrote a byte
Client is closing the connection
Client lost the connection: [Failure instance: ...: Connection was closed
cleanly.
]
Server lost the connection: [Failure instance: ...: Connection was closed
cleanly.
]
```

Leaving aside the `Failure` object passed to `connectionLost`, which we will cover in our discussion of asynchronous programming in Twisted, this output seems to demonstrate that our new implementation's behavior matches our old implementation's.

We can do better than comparing outputs, however, by adapting our protocol test:

```
from twisted.trial import unittest
from twisted.test.proto_helpers import StringTransportWithDisconnection,
MemoryReactor

class PingPongProtocolTests(unittest.SynchronousTestCase):
    def setUp(self):
        self.maximum = 100
        self.reactor = MemoryReactor()
        self.factory = PingPongClientFactory(self.reactor,self.maximum)
        self.protocol = self.factory.buildProtocol(address.IPv4Address(
            "TCP","localhost",1234))
```

```
        self.transport = StringTransportWithDisconnection()
        self.protocol.makeConnection(self.transport)
        self.transport.protocol = self.protocol
    def test_firstByteWritten(self):
        self.assertEqual(len(self.transport.value()), 1)
    def test_byteWrittenForByte(self):
        self.protocol.dataReceived(b"*")
        self.assertEqual(len(self.transport.value()), 2)
    def test_receivingMaximumLosesConnection(self):
        self.protocol.dataReceived(b"*" * self.maximum)
        self.assertFalse(self.transport.connected)
```

Twisted has its own test infrastructure that we will cover in our discussion of asynchronous programming; for now, we can treat SynchronousTestCase as equivalent to the standard library's unittest.TestCase. Our setUp method now constructs a MemoryReactor fake, which stands in place of our real reactor. It passes this to PingPongClientFactory and then constructs a PingPongProtocol client by calling the buildProtocol method inherited from ClientFactory. This, in turn, requires an address argument, for which we supply another fake. We then use Twisted's built-in StringTransportWithDisconnection, whose behavior and interface aligns with our toy BytesTransport implementation. Twisted calls this a StringTransport because at the time it was written, all released versions of Python had a default string type of bytes. In a world with Python 3, StringTransport has become a misnomer because it must still work in terms of bytes.

Our test methods adjust to StringTransportWithDisconnection's interface: value returns the written content, while connected becomes False when the protocol calls loseConnection.

The Twisted implementation of a PingPongProtocol client and server makes the similarities between Twisted and our example code clear: the reactor multiplexes events from sockets and dispatches them via transports to protocols, which can then create new events via their transports.

While this dynamic forms the heart of Twisted's event-driven architecture and informs its design decisions, it is relatively low level. Many programs never implement their own Protocol subclasses. We turn next to a kind of event that underlies patterns and APIs used directly in many Twisted programs.

Events in Time

All the events we've seen so far originate from inputs, such as a user clicking a button or new data arriving on a socket. Programs must often schedule actions to run at a point in the future, separate from any input. Consider a heartbeat: every 30 seconds or so, a network application will write a byte to its connections to ensure the remote end doesn't close them because of inactivity.

Twisted provides a low-level interface to schedule future actions via `reactor.callLater`. We usually do not call this API directly, but will do so now to explain how it works.

```
from twisted.internet import reactor

reactor.callLater(1.5, print,"Hello from the past.")
reactor.run()
```

`reactor.callLater` accepts a numeric delay and a callable. Any other positional or keyword arguments are passed to the callable when it's invoked. Running this program will produce no output until approximately 1.5 seconds have passed, at which point `Hello from the past` will appear.

`reactor.callLater` returns a `DelayedCall` instance that can be canceled:

```
from twisted.internet import reactor

call = reactor.callLater(1.5, print,"Hello from the past.")
call.cancel()
reactor.run()
```

This program emits no output, because the `DelayedCall` is canceled before the reactor can run it.

Clearly `reactor.callLater` emits an event that indicates the specified time has elapsed and runs the callable it receives as that event's handler. The mechanism by which this happens, however, is less clear.

Fortunately, the implementation is fundamentally simple and also makes it clear why the delay is only approximate. Recall that `select` accepts an optional timeout argument. When we wanted `select` to tell us immediately what events had been generated and not wait for new ones, we called it with 0 as a timeout. We can now use this timeout to multiplex time-based events in addition to socket-based ones: to ensure that our DelayedCalls run, we can invoke select with a timeout equal to the delay of the next DelayedCall that should be scheduled, that is, the one that is nearest in time.

Imagine a program that contains the following:

```
reactor.callLater(2, functionB)
reactor.callLater(1, functionA)
reactor.callLater(3, functionC)
reactor.run()
```

The reactor records the DelayedCall in a min-heap, sorted by the wall clock time it's scheduled to run:

```
def callLater(self, delay, f,*args,**kwargs):
    self._pendingCalls.append((time.time()+delay, f, args, kwargs)
    heapq.heapify(self._pendingCalls)
```

If the first reactor.callLater occurs at time *t*, and each call takes no time, then after all three calls, pendingCalls would appear as follows:

```
[
    (t+1, <DelayedCall: functionA>),
    (t+2, <DelayedCall: functionB>),
    (t+3, <DelayedCall: functionB>),
]
```

Adding an element to a heap has a time complexity of $O(\log n)$, so repeated callLater invocations have a total worst case time complexity of $O(n \log n)$. If the reactor instead sorted _pendingCalls, repeated callLater invocations would take $O(n)$ * $O(n \log n) = O(n^2)$.

Now, before the reactor enters select, it checks if there are any pending DelayedCalls; if there are, it extracts the top element of the heap and uses the difference between its target runtime and the current time as select's timeout. Then, before handling any socket events, it pops each element off the heap whose time has passed and runs it, skipping canceled calls. If there are no pending DelayCalls, the reactor calls select with a timeout of None, representing no timeout.

```python
class Reactor(object):
    ...
    def run(self):
        while self.running:
            if self._pendingCalls:
                targetTime, _ = self._pendingCalls[0]
                delay=targetTime-time.time()
            else:
                targetTime = None
            r, w, _ = select.select(self.readers,self.writers, [], targetTime)
            now = time.time()
            while self._pendingCalls and (self._pendingCalls[0][0] <= now):
                targetTime, (f, args, kwargs) = heapq.heappop()
                if not call.cancelled:
                    f(*args,**kwargs)
            ...
```

Of our three `reactor.callLater` calls, `functionA`'s has the shortest delay, and thus sits at the top of the the `pendingCalls` heap. If our reactor's `run` loop begins immediately afterwards (i.e., also at time t), the `delay` variable will then be $(t + 1) - t = 1$, and the `select` call will return no more than a second later. Now, `time.time` returns $t + 1$, so `functionA`'s `DelayedCall`, and thus `functionA`, runs. The `DelayedCalls` for both `functionB` and `functionC`, however, still remain in the future, so the inner `while` loop ends and the process begins again.

The implementation reveals why `DelayedCalls` do not run immediately after their delay has elapsed: their invocation depends on their position in the `pendingCalls` heap and how long the preceding `DelayedCalls` take to complete. If `functionA` took longer than a second to run, `functionB` would run later than its deadline. This is especially likely for `DelayedCalls` delayed for the same amount of time.

Repeated Events with **LoopingCall**

reactor.callLater suffices to implement our heartbeat. We can define a function that calls callLater with itself, and then start the indirection recursion by calling the function directly once:

```
def f(reactor, delay)
    reactor.callLater(delay, f, reactor, delay)
f(reactor,1.0)
```

This works but only awkwardly. We cannot access the DelayedCall representing the next call to f after the initial call to f, so we cannot easily cancel it if the other side terminates the connection. We could track these calls by hand, but fortunately, Twisted provides a convenient wrapper around callLater that handles all this for us: twisted. internet.task.LoopingCall. Here's a protocol that uses LoopingCall to implement its heartbeat:

```
from twisted.internet import protocol, task

class HeartbeatProtocol(protocol.Protocol):
    def connectionMade(self):
        self._heartbeater = task.LoopingCall(self.transport.write, b"*")
        self._heartbeater.clock = self.factory._reactor
        self._heartbeater.start(interval=30.0)
    def connectionLost(self):
        self._heartbeater.stop()

class HeartbeatProtocolFactory(protocol.Factory):
    protocol = HeartbeatProtocol
    def __init__ (self, reactor):
        self._reactor = reactor
```

The protocol creates a new LoopingCall instance that will write a single asterisk to the protocol's transport as the connection is established. It then replaces the LoopingCall's clock with its factory's reactor; as we'll see soon, this indirection aids testing. Finally, the protocol starts the LoopingCall with an interval of 30 seconds, so that approximately every 30 seconds it will call transport.write with a single asterisk. At what point does the LoopingCall begin counting 30 seconds? Does it count from 0, in which case it should call its function right away, or does it count from 1, in which case it should wait a full 30 seconds? The answer is up to the programmer. The second, optional now argument to LoopingCall.start dictates whether the function should be called as part of the call to start or after a full interval has passed. It defaults to True, so our heartbeater will immediately write a single asterisk to the transport.

Retrieving the reactor from its factory makes HeartbeatProtocol as easy to test as PingPongProtocol:

```python
from twisted.trial import unittest
from twisted.internet import main, task
from twisted.test.proto_helpers import StringTransportWithDisconnection

class HeartbeatProtocolTests(unittest.SynchronousTestCase):
    def setUp(self):
        self.clock = task.Clock()
        self.factory = HeartbeatProtocolFactory(self.clock)
        self.protocol = self.factory.buildProtocol(address.IPv4Address(
            "TCP","localhost",1234))
        self.transport = StringTransportWithDisconnection()
        self.protocol.makeConnection(self.transport)
        self.transport.protocol = self.protocol
    def test_heartbeatWritten(self):
        self.assertEqual(len(self.transport.value()), 1)
        self.clock.advance(60)
        self.assertEqual(len(self.transport.value()), 2)
    def test_lostConnectionStopsHeartbeater(self):
        self.assertTrue(self.protocol._heartbeater.running)
        self.protocol.connectionLost(main.CONNECTION_DONE)
        self.assertFalse(self.protocol._heartbeater.running)
```

HeartbeatProtocolTest.setUp is nearly identical to PingPongProtocolTests. setUp, except it uses twisted.internet.task.Clock instead of MemoryReactor. Clock, as its name implies, provides an implementation of a reactor's time-related interfaces. Most importantly, it has a callLater method:

```python
>>> from twisted.internet.task import Clock
>>> clock = Clock()
>>> clock.callLater(1.0, print,"OK")
```

Because they're intended to be used in unit tests, Clock instances naturally have no select loop of their own. We can simulate the expiration of a select timeout by calling advance:

```
>>> clock.advance(2)
OK
```

test_heartbeatWritten calls advance to cause its protocol's LoopingCall to write a single byte. This is analogous to PingPongProtocolTests.test_byteWrittenForByte's call to its protocol's dataReceived; both simulate the occurrence of events that the reactor would have managed outside of these tests.

Twisted's approach to event-driven programming depends on clearly delineated interfaces like Protocol's and Clock's. So far, however, we have taken the nature of each interface for granted: How can we know that Clock, or MemoryReactor, can replace the real reactor in a test suite? We can answer this by exploring the tools that Twisted uses to manage its interfaces.

Event Interfaces with zope.interface

Twisted uses a package called zope.interface to formalize its internal interfaces, including those that describe its event-driven paradigm.

Zope is a venerable but still active project that has produced several web application frameworks, the oldest of which was first publicly released in 1998. Many technologies originated in Zope and were factored out for use in other projects. Twisted uses Zope's *interface* package to define its interfaces.

A full explanation of zope.interface is beyond the scope of this book. However, interfaces play an important role in testing and documentation, so we introduce them by exploring the interfaces of the Twisted classes used in our preceding examples.

We begin by asking an instance of Clock what interfaces it *provides*:

```
>>> from twisted.internet.task import Clock
>>> clock = Clock()
>>> from zope.interface import providedBy
>>> list(providedBy(clock))
[<InterfaceClass twisted.internet.interfaces.IReactorTime>]
```

First, we create an instance of Clock. We then retrieve providedBy from the zope. interface package; because Twisted itself depends on zope.interface, it's available for us to use in an interactive session. Calling providedBy on our Clock instance returns an iterable of the *interfaces* it provides.

Unlike interfaces in other languages, zope.interface's interfaces can be *implemented* or *provided*. Individual objects that conform to an interface *provide* it, while things that *create* those interface-providing objects *implement* that interface. This subtle distinction matches Python's "duck typing." An interface definition might describe a call method and thus apply to a function object created with def or lambda. These syntactic elements cannot be marked as *implementers* of our interface, but the function objects themselves can be said to *provide* it.

An *interface* is a subclass of zope.interface.Interface that uses a special API to describe required methods and their signatures as well as attributes. Here's an excerpt from the twisted.internet.interfaces.IReactorTime interface provided by our Clock:

```
class IReactorTime(Interface):
    """

    Time methods that a Reactor should implement.
    """


def callLater(delay, callable,*args,**kw):
    """

    Call a function later.

    @type delay:  C{float}
    @param delay: the number of seconds to wait.

    @param callable: the callable object to call later.

    @param args: the arguments to call it with.

    @param kw: the keyword arguments to call it with.

    @return: An object which provides L{IDelayedCall} and can be used to
             cancel the scheduled call, by calling its C{cancel()} method.
             It also may be rescheduled by calling its C{delay()} or
             C{reset()} methods.
    """
```

Note that the `callLater` "method" has no `self` argument. This is a consequence of the fact that interfaces cannot be instantiated. It also lacks a body, and instead satisfies Python's function definition syntax by providing only a docstring. Unlike abstract classes, such as those provided by the standard library's `abc` module, they also cannot include any implementation code. Instead, they exist solely as markers that describe a subset of an object's functionality.

Zope provides a helper named `verifyObject` that throws an exception if an object does not provide an interface:

```
>>> from zope.interface.verify import verifyObject
>>> from twisted.internet.interfaces import IReactorTime
>>> verifyObject(IReactorTime, clock)
True
>>> verifyObject(IReactorTime, object())
Traceback (most recent call last):
  File"<stdin>", line1, in <module>
  ...
zope.interface.exceptions.DoesNotImplement: An object does not implement
interface<Interface
```

We can use this to confirm that the reactor provides the same `IReactorTime` interface as a `Clock` instance:

```
>>> from twisted.internet import reactor
>>> verifyObject(IReactorTime, reactor) True
```

We'll return to `verifyObject` later when we write our own interface implementations. For now, though, it's enough to know that we can replace the reactor with a `Clock` instance anywhere we depend on `IReactorTime.callLater`. In general, if we know *what* interface an object provides includes the methods or attributes we depend on, we can replace that object with any other that provides the same interface. While we can discover an object's provided interfaces interactively with `providedBy`, Twisted's online documentation has special support for interfaces. Figure 1-2 depicts the documentation for `Clock` on Twisted's website.

Figure 1-2. `twisted.internet.task.Clock` *documentation. The dashed box highlights the link to the IReactorTime interface.*

The interfaces implemented by the Clock class are highlighted in the dotted rectangle. Clicking on each one leads to that interface's documentation, which includes a list of all known implementers and providers. If you know what the object is, then you can determine its interfaces by visiting its documentation.

We turn next to a problem whose solution in Twisted involves defining implementers for interfaces.

Flow Control in Event-Driven Programs

PingPongProtocol differs from the streaming protocol we wrote for our last non-Twisted event-driven example: each side in PingPongProtocol writes a byte in response to a received byte, whereas the streaming protocol had the client send increasingly large sequences of bytes to the server, pausing its writes as the server became overwhelmed. Adapting the rate at which the sender writes to match the rate at the recipient reads is known as *flow control*.

When combined with event-driven programming, non-blocking I/O enables us to write programs that can respond to many different events at any given time. *Synchronous* I/O, as we saw with our streaming client protocol implemented in terms of sendall, pauses or *blocks* our program, preventing it from doing anything until the I/O operation completes. While this makes concurrency more difficult, it makes flow control much easier: a writer that outpaces its reader is simply paused by the operating system until the reader accepts pending data. In the case of our streaming client, this resulted in a deadlock, because the slow reader ran within the same process that was paused for writing too quickly, and thus could never run to catch up. The more common case has readers and writers run in separate processes, if not on separate machines, and their synchronous, blocking I/O naturally provides flow control.

It is rare, however, to encounter plain blocking I/O in network applications. Even the simplest must manage two things at once for each connection: the communication of data and timeouts associated with each I/O operation. Python's socket module allows programmers to set these timeouts on recv and sendall operations, but behind the scenes this is implemented by calling select with a timeout!

We have the events necessary to implement flow control. select informs us of writable events, while EAGAIN indicates that a socket's send buffer is full, and thus indirectly that the receiver is overwhelmed. We can compose these to pause and resume writers and achieve flow control comparable to what blocking I/O provides.

Flow Control in Twisted with Producers and Consumers

There are two components in Twisted's flow control system: *producers* and *consumers*. Producers write data to consumers by calling a consumer's write method. Consumers *wrap* producers; each consumer can be associated with a single producer. This relationship ensures the consumer has access to its producer, so that it can place *back pressure* on it by calling certain methods on the producer to regulate the flow of data. Common transports, such as the TCP transport bound to protocols like our PingPongProtocol, can be both consumers and producers.

We explore the interaction between producers and consumers by reimplementing our pre-Twisted streaming client example.

Push Producers

We begin with the client's producer:

```python
from twisted.internet.interfaces import IPushProducer
from twisted.internet.task import LoopingCall
from zope.interface import implementer

@implementer(IPushProducer)
class StreamingProducer(object):
    INTERVAL=0.001
    def __init__ (self, reactor, consumer):
        self._data = [b"*", b"*"]
        self._loop = LoopingCall(self._writeData, consumer.write)
        self._loop.clock = reactor
    def resumeProducing(self):
        print("Resuming client producer.")
        self._loop.start(self.INTERVAL)
    def pauseProducing(self):
        print("Pausing client producer.")
        self._loop.stop()
    def stopProducing(self):
        print("Stopping client producer.")
        if self._loop.running:
            self._loop.stop()
    def _writeData(self, write):
        print("Client producer writing", len(self._data),"bytes.")
        write(b"".join(self._data))
        self._data.extend(self._data)
```

Our producer, StreamingProducer, implements twisted.internet.interfaces.
IPushProducer. This interface describes producers that continuously write data to their
consumer until it pauses them. The following methods on StreamingProducer satisfy the
IPushProducer interface:

- resumeProducing: This resumes or initiates the process of writing
  data to the consumer. Because our implementation generates its
  data by doubling a sequence of bytes after every write, it requires

some kind of loop to feed a continuous stream to its consumer. A simple while loop would not work: without returning control to the reactor, the program could not process new events until the loop has terminated. An event-driven program such a web browser would effectively pause its execution during a large file upload. StreamingProducer avoids this by delegating the write loop to the reactor via a LoopingCall instance, and so its resumeProducing method starts that LoopingCall. The interval of one millisecond is arbitrarily low. Our producer cannot write data any faster than that, so the interval is a source of latency, and one millisecond minimizes it acceptably.

- pauseProducing: This pauses the process of writing data to the consumer. The consumer calls this to indicate it has been overwhelmed and cannot accept more data. It suffices in our implementation to stop the underlying LoopingCall. The consumer may call resumeProducing later when the underlying resource can accept more data. This cycle of resumeProducing and pauseProducing calls constitutes flow control.

- stopProducing: This terminates the production of data. This differs from pauseProducing because the consumer can never call resumeProducing to receive more data after calling stopProducing. Most obviously, it is called when a socket connection is closed. StreamingProducer's implementation only differs from its pauseProducing method in that it must first check if the looping call is running. This is because the consumer might request that no further data be written while the producer is already paused. More complicated push producers would perform additional clean up; for example, a producer that streams data from a file would need to close it here to release its resources back to the operating system.

Note that IPushProducer does not specify *how* its implementer writes data to a consumer or even gets access to it. This makes the interface flexible, but also makes it more difficult to implement. StreamingProducer follows a typical pattern by accepting the consumer in its initializer. We'll cover the full consumer interface shortly, but for now, it's enough to know that consumers must provide a write method.

We can test that StreamingProducer implements the intended behavior of an IPushProducer:

```python
from twisted.internet.interfaces import IPushProducer
from twisted.internet.task import Clock
from twisted.trial import unittest
from zope.interface.verify import verifyObject

class FakeConsumer(object):
    def __init__ (self, written):
        self._written = written
    def write(self, data):
        self._written.append(data)

class StreamingProducerTests(unittest.TestCase):
    def setUp(self):
        self.clock = Clock()
        self.written = []
        self.consumer = FakeConsumer(self.written)
        self.producer = StreamingProducer(self.clock,self.consumer)
    def test_providesIPushProducer(self):
        verifyObject(IPushProducer,self.producer)
    def test_resumeProducingSchedulesWrites(self):
        self.assertFalse(self.written)
        self.producer.resumeProducing()
        writeCalls = len(self.written)
        self.assertEqual(writeCalls,1)
        self.clock.advance(self.producer.INTERVAL)
        newWriteCalls = len(self.written)
        self.assertGreater(newWriteCalls, writeCalls)
    def test_pauseProducingStopsWrites(self):
        self.producer.resumeProducing()
        writeCalls = len(self.written)
        self.producer.pauseProducing()
        self.clock.advance(self.producer.INTERVAL)
        self.assertEqual(len(self.written), writeCalls)
```

```
def test_stopProducingStopsWrites(self):
    self.producer.resumeProducing()
    writeCalls = len(self.written)
    self.producer.stopProducing()
    self.clock.advance(self.producer.INTERVAL)
    self.assertEqual(len(self.written), writeCalls)
```

FakeConsumer accepts a list to which each write call appends the data it received. This allows the test suite to assert that StreamingProducer has called its consumer's write method when expected.

test_providesIPushProducer ensures that StreamingProducer defines the methods required by IPushProducer. If it did not, this test would fail with zope.interface. exceptions.DoesNotImplement. Tests like this that assert implementations satisfy their interfaces are a useful high-pass filter in development and refactoring.

test_resumeProducingSchedulesWrites asserts that calling resumeProducing implies writing data to the consumer, and that each time the specified interval has passed, more data is written. test_pauseProducingStopsWrites and test_ stopProducingStopsWrites both assert the opposite: calling pauseProducing and stopProducing prevent further writes from occurring after every interval has elapsed.

Consumers

StreamingProducer emits data but has nowhere to put it. To complete our streaming client, we need a *consumer*. StreamingProducer's initializer makes it clear that the consumer's interface must provide a write method, and the overview indicated that additional consumer methods managed interactions with producers. twisted. internet.interfaces.IConsumer requires that implementers implement three methods:

- write: This accepts data from a producer. This is the only method provided by FakeConsumer in our tests above, because it is the only part of the IConsumer interface IPushProducer calls.

- registerProducer: This associates a producer with the consumer, ensuring that it can call the producer's resumeProducing and pauseProducing to regulate the flow of data and stopProducing to terminate it. This accepts two arguments: the producer and a streaming flag. We will explain the purpose of this second argument later; for now, it is enough to know that our streaming client will set this to True.

- unregisterProducer: This dissociates a producer from the consumer. A consumer might accept data from multiple producers throughout its lifetime; consider again a web browser, which might upload multiple files over a single connection to a server.

It is no coincidence that both IConsumer implementers and transports both expose write methods; as mentioned above, the TCP transport bound to connected protocols is a consumer with which we can register a StreamingProducer instance. We can adapt our PingPongProtocol example to register StreamingProducer with its underlying transport upon a successful connection:

```
from twisted.internet import protocol, reactor
from twisted.internet.interfaces import IPushProducer
from twisted.internet.task import LoopingCall
from zope.interface import implementer

@implementer(IPushProducer)
class StreamingProducer(object):
    INTERVAL=0.001
    def __init__ (self, reactor, consumer):
        self._data = [b"*", b"*"]
        self._loop = LoopingCall(self._writeData, consumer.write)
        self._loop.clock = reactor
    def resumeProducing(self):
        print("Resuming client producer.")
        self._loop.start(self.INTERVAL)
    def pauseProducing(self):
        print("Pausing client producer.")
        self._loop.stop()
    def stopProducing(self):
        print("Stopping client producer.")
        if self._loop.running:
            self._loop.stop()
    def _writeData(self, write):
        print("Client producer writing", len(self._data),"bytes.")
        write(b"".join(self._data))
        self._data.extend(self._data)
```

```python
class StreamingClient(protocol.Protocol):
    def connectionMade(self):
        streamingProducer = StreamingProducer(
            self.factory._reactor,self.transport)
        self.transport.registerProducer(streamingProducer,True)
        streamingProducer.resumeProducing()

class ReceivingServer(protocol.Protocol):
    def dataReceived(self, data):
        print("Server received", len(data),"bytes.")

class StreamingClientFactory(protocol.ClientFactory):
    protocol = StreamingClient
    def __init__ (self, reactor):
        self._reactor = reactor

class ReceivingServerFactory(protocol.Factory):
    protocol = ReceivingServer

listener = reactor.listenTCP(port=0,
                             factory=ReceivingServerFactory(),
                             interface='127.0.0.1')
address = listener.getHost()
reactor.connectTCP(host=address.host,
                   port=address.port,
                   factory=StreamingClientFactory(reactor))
reactor.run()
```

The StreamingClient protocol creates a StreamingProducer that it then registers with its transport. As promised, the second argument to registerProducer is True. Registering a producer does not automatically resume it, however, so we must begin StreamingProducer's write loop by calling resumeProducing. Note that StreamingClient never calls stopProducing on its producer: transports calls this on behalf of their protocols when the reactor signals a disconnection.

Running this produces output like the following:

```
Resuming client producer.
Client producer writing 2 bytes.
Server received 2 bytes.
```

```
Client producer writing 4 bytes.
Server received 4 bytes.
Client producer writing 8 bytes.
Server received 8 bytes.
...
Client producer writing 524288 bytes.
Pausing client producer.
Server received 65536 bytes.
Server received 65536 bytes.
Server received 65536 bytes.
Server received 65536 bytes.
Resuming client producer.
Client producer writing 1048576 bytes.
Pausing client producer.
...
```

Eventually the program will consume all available memory, constituting a successful experiment in flow control.

Pull Producers

A second producer interface exists: `twisted.internet.interfaces.IPullProducer`. Unlike `IPushProducer`, it only writes to its consumer when its `resumeProducing` method is called. This is the purpose of the second argument to `IConsumer.registerProducer`: `IPullProducers` require that `streaming` be `False`. Don't write `IPullProducers`! Most transports behave like sockets and generate writable events that obviate the need for a write loop like `StreamingProducer`'s. When data must be manually pumped out of a source, it is easier to write and test a `LoopingCall` instead.

Summary

We've seen how event-driven programming divides programs into *events* and their *handlers*. Anything that happens to a program can be modeled as an event: input from a user, data received over a socket, or even the passage of time. An *event loop* uses a *multiplexer* to wait for any of the possible events to occur, running the appropriate handlers for those that did. Operating systems provide low-level interfaces, such as `select`, to multiplex network socket I/O events. Event-driven network programming with `select` is most effective with *non-blocking*, which generates events for operations like `send` and `recv` that indicate the program should stop running an event handler.

The stop event – `EAGAIN` – emitted by non-blocking sockets results in complex code without the right abstractions. *Protocols* and *transports* divide the program's code between *causes* and *effects*: transports translate read, write, and stop events into higher-level causes that protocols can respond to, generating new events in turn. This division of responsibility between protocols and transports allows implementing event handlers that are easily tested by replacing transports with in-memory fakes. Later on, we'll see other practical benefits of the protocol-transport split.

Protocols, transports, and reactors – its name for event loops – are fundamental to Twisted's operation and inform its overall architecture. Twisted's reactor can react to non-I/O events, such as the passage of time. Testing these is no more difficult than testing protocols because reactors, like transports, have in-memory fakes. Twisted formalizes the interfaces that reactors and other objects must implement by means of `zope.interface`. By determining what interfaces an object provides, it's possible to select a replacement suitable for testing that's guaranteed to be equivalent because it provides the same interfaces. Twisted's online documentation makes discovering interfaces easier than inspecting live objects in a Python session.

A practical use for interfaces comes in Twisted's solution to something that event-driven network programming makes difficult: flow control. `IPushProducer` and `IConsumer` define a set of behaviors that allow the receiver of streaming data to pause the source when it's overwhelmed.

This introduction suffices to explain the core principles of event-driven programming in Twisted. There's much more, however: in the next chapter, we'll learn how Twisted eases event-driven programming further by allowing programs to work with values that have yet to be computed.

CHAPTER 2

An Introduction to Asynchronous Programming with Twisted

The previous chapter derived Twisted's event-driven architecture from first principles. Twisted programs, like all event-driven programs, make concurrency easier at the expense of making data flow control more difficult. An event-driven program does not automatically have its execution suspended by blocking I/O when it sends more data than a receiving party can handle. It is the program's responsibility to determine when this occurs and how to deal with it.

The way data flows between communicating parties also affects the way that it flows within a single program. As a result, the strategies for *composing* different components of an event-driven applications differ from those used in blocking programs.

Event Handlers and Composition

Consider a program that is not event-driven and uses blocking I/O to perform a network operation:

```
def requestField(url, field):
    results = requests.get(url).json()
    return results[field]
```

© Mark Williams, Cory Benfield, Brian Warner, Moshe Zadka, Dustin Mitchell, Kevin Samuel, Pierre Tardy 2019
M. Williams et al., *Expert Twisted*, https://doi.org/10.1007/978-1-4842-3742-7_2

requestField retrieves a URL with the requests HTTP library, decodes the response's body as JSON, and then returns the value of the requested field property from the resulting dictionary. requests uses blocking I/O, so a call to requestField pauses the entire program until the network operations required by the HTTP request complete. The function can thus assume that before it returns, results will be available for manipulation. Callers of this function can make the same assumption because requestField will block them until it has computed its result:

```
def someOtherFunction(...):
    ...
    url = calculateURL(...)
    value = requestField(url, 'someInteger')
    return value + 1

x = someOtherFunction(...)
```

Neither someOtherFunction nor the top-level x assignment can finish until requestField has retrieved the URL and extracted the value for the someInteger property from the JSON response. This is a kind *composition*: someOtherFunction invokes requestField to complete part of its own execution. We can make this clearer with explicit function composition:

```
def someOtherFunction(value):
    return value + 1

x = someOtherFunction(requestField(calculateURL(...), 'someInteger'))
```

This code replaces someOtherFunction's local variables with nested function calls, but is otherwise equivalent.

Function composition is a fundamental tool for organizing programs. It allows a program to be *factored*, or split into separate units that form a whole whose behave exactly matches the non-factored version. This improves readability, reusability, and testability.

Unfortunately, event handlers cannot be composed like someOtherFunction, requestField, and calculateURL. Consider a hypothetical, non-blocking version of requestField:

```
def requestField(url, field):
    ??? = nonblockingGet(url)
```

What could replace the ??? in a non-blocking version of requestField? This is a difficult question to answer because nonblockingGet does not suspend the program's execution to complete the network operations that constitute an HTTP request to url; instead, an event loop *outside* requestField multiplexes readable and writable events, calling event handlers to send and receive data as soon as it becomes possible to do so. There is not an obvious way to return the event handlers' value from our hypothetical nonblockingGet function.

Fortunately, by representing event handlers as functions, we can use the generality of function composition to factor an event-driven program into separate components. Let's assume that the hypothetical nonblockingGet function itself accepts an event handler function as an argument that it invokes when the request's completion event occurs. This higher-level event would be synthesized out of lower-level events, analogous to the way that we saw transports emit a connectionLost event for the sake of their protocols in Chapter 1. We can then rewrite requestField to take advantage of this new argument:

```
def requestField(url, field):
    def onCompletion(response):
        document = json.loads(response)
        value = response[field]

    nonblockingGet(url, onCompletion=onCompletion)
```

onCompletion is a *callback*, or a callable object passed as an argument to some other callable that performs some desired operation. When that operation completes, the callback is called with some pertinent argument or arguments. In this case, nonblockingGet invokes its onCompletion callback when its HTTP request resolves to a complete response object. We saw an equivalent onCompletion callback in the previous chapter's BuffersWrites implementation; there, it was invoked when all buffered data had been written to the socket.

Callbacks compose *internally* where other functions, like our someOtherFunction example above, compose *externally*; values are made available to callbacks within the execution of the callable that achieves the desired result, instead of being returned from that callable.

In the same way that nonblockingGet factors out the event-driven HTTP request code, requestField can factor out the way the extracted field is used by accepting its own callback. We'll have requestField accept a useField callback, and then have the onCompletion callback invoke it:

```
def requestField(url, field, useField):
    def onCompletion(response):
        document = json.loads(response)
        value = response[field]
        useField(value)

    nonblockingGet(url, onCompletion=onCompletion)
```

We can pass someOtherFunction as the useField callback to write an event-driven program that's equivalent to our blocking I/O version:

```
def someOtherFunction(useValue):
    url = calculateURL(...)
    def addValue(value):
        useValue(value + 1)
    requestField(url,"someInteger", useField=addValue)
```

someOtherFunction in turn must also compose internally by accepting its *own* callback, in contrast to calculateURL that composes externally as before. This callback-driven approach suffices to write any program; in fact, in the study of computer science, callbacks can be refined into control-flow primitives called *continuations* and used in a technique called *continuation-passing style*, in which functions terminate by invoking their continuations with a result. Continuation-passing style has been used in various language compilers to enable program analyses and optimizations.

Despite the theoretical power of continuation-passing style, it is awkward to read and write. Furthermore, external composition – as with requestField and calculateURL – and internal composition – as with requestField and useField – do not obviously compose with each other. It is difficult, for example, to imagine how calculateURL could be passed as a callback. Finally, error handling is a critical causality; imagine how we would handle exceptions in continuation-passing style! We have intentionally omitted any error handling in this example to keep the code short enough to read.

Fortunately, *asynchronous programming* provides a powerful abstraction that eases the composition of event handlers and addresses these problems.

What Is Asynchronous Programming?

Our initial implementation of `requestField` is *synchronous* because the entire program's execution linearly progresses with the passage of time. For example, given two calls to `request.get`, the first will complete before the second. Synchronous programming is a common paradigm that is congruent with blocking I/O. Most programming languages, including Python, default to synchronous operations that are enabled by blocking I/O.

The continuation-passing style of our event-driven `requestField` is a kind of *asynchronous programming*: while the logical flow through `nonblockingGet`'s callbacks is paused until the necessary data becomes available, the overall program's execution continues. The executions of two separate `nonblockingGet` invocations will interleave without any guaranteed order to their completion; beginning one earlier than the other does not ensure that it will finish first. This is the definition of concurrency.

An event-driven program that utilizes non-blocking I/O is necessarily asynchronous, because *all* I/O operations proceed on the basis of events that can arrive at any time and in any order. It's important to note that an asynchronous program does not require event-driven I/O; different platforms provide I/O and scheduling patterns based on fundamentally different primitives. Windows, for example, provides I/O Completion Ports (IOCP), which inform programs of the *completion* of a requested operation, not the opportunity to perform an operation. For example, a program that requests the IOCP infrastructure perform a read on a socket will be notified when and with what data the read completes. Twisted has some support for this in the form of its IOCP reactor, but for our purposes, we can understand asynchronous programming as a consequence of the event-driven paradigm's disjointed and piecemeal execution in the same way that synchronous programming is a consequence of blocking I/O.

Placeholders for Future Values

Callbacks in event-driven programs obscure control flow because they compose *internally*; rather than returning a value to their caller, they forward results to callbacks they received as arguments. This results in a mix of application logic and control flow that makes refactoring difficult, and a disconnection between the point where errors occur and the code that is interested in them.

Introducing an object that represents a value that has yet to be calculated allows callbacks to be composed *externally*. Consider how our non-blocking `requestField` example changes when it's allowed to return this kind of placeholder:

```
def requestField(url, field):
    def onCompletion(response):
        document = json.load(response)

    return jsonDoc[field]
placeholder = nonblockingGet(url)
return placeholder.addCallback(onCompletion)
```

nonblockingGet now returns a *placeholder* that is not the response, but rather a container into which the response will be placed when it's ready. A container with no operations would not provide much benefit, so this placeholder accepts *callbacks* it invokes when its value is ready. Instead of passing the onCompletion directly to nonblockingGet, we attach it as a callback to the placeholder nonblockingGet returns. The internal onCompletion callback's implementation can now return a value – the extracted field from the JSON document – which will become available as the argument to subsequent callbacks.

requestField can now transitively eliminate its own callback argument and return the placeholder to someOtherFunction, which can add its own callback:

```
def someOtherFunction(...):
    url = calculateURL(...)
    def addValue(value)
        return value + 1
    placeholder = requestField(url,"someInteger")
    return placeHolder.addCallback(addValue)
```

Our placeholder value has not eliminated callbacks entirely. Instead, it provides a control-flow abstraction that localizes callbacks to their originating scope, so that they can be composed *externally*. This becomes clearer when multiple callbacks process an asynchronous result. Consider the following internally composed callbacks:

```
def manyCallbacks(url, useValue, ...):
    def addValue(result):
        return divideValue(result + 2)
```

```
def divideValue(result):
    return multiplyValue(result // 3)
def multiplyValue(result):
    return useValue(result * 4)
requestField(url, "someInteger", onCompletion=addValue)
```

Control flows from addValue to divideValue and finally exits from multiplyValue into the useValue callback provided by manyCallbacks's caller. Changing the order of the three internal callbacks would require rewriting each one. A placeholder object, however, moves that order out of each callback:

```
def manyCallbacks(url, ...):
    def addValue(result):
        return result + 2
    def divideValue(result):
        return result // 3
    def multiplyValue(result):
        return result * 4
placeholder = requestField(url, "someInteger")
placeholder.addCallback(addValue)
placeholder.addCallback(divideValue)
placeholder.addCallback(multiplyValue)
return placeholder
```

divideValue no longer depends directly on multiplyValue, so it can be moved before multiplyValue or even removed without changing it or multiplyValue.

The actual composition of callbacks happens within the placeholder object, the core implementation of which is fundamentally simple. We'll name our placeholder class Deferred because it represents a *deferred* value – one that is not yet ready:

```
class Deferred(object):
    def __init__ (self):
        self._callbacks = []
    def addCallback(self, callback):
        self._callbacks.append(callback)
    def callback(self, result):
        for callback in self._callbacks:
            result = callback(result)
```

The creator of the Deferred instance invokes callback with the result when it becomes available. Each callback is invoked with the current result, and its return value becomes the result passed to the next callback. This is how the onCompletion above can change the HTTP response into only JSON field of interest.

The control flow imposed by Deferred's for loop suffices to invoke each callback in turn, but cannot handle exceptions any better than internally composed callbacks. Addressing this requires adding some kind of branching logic to detect and reroute exceptions to their destinations.

Asynchronous Exception Handling

Synchronous Python code handles exceptions with try and except:

```python
def requestField(url):
    response = requests.get(url).content
    try:
        return response.decode('utf-8')
    except UnicodeDecodeError:
        # Handle this case
```

A callback added to a Deferred via its addCallback method runs when no exception occurs, and thus is the asynchronous equivalent of the try block. We can add error handling by introducing an analogous callback for the except block that accepts the exception raised as its argument. A callback like this that is invoked with an exception is known as an *errback*.

Synchronous code can choose to let an exception travel upward to its caller by omitting try and except. Deferred's control flow, however, would allow an exception raised by a callback to move up from the for loop and back to the invoker of Deferred.callback. That would be the wrong place to put exception handling because the code that provides the Deferred with a value cannot know the error handling behavior intended by the code that added its callbacks. Encapsulating this error handling inside errbacks that we pass to Deferreds allows those Deferreds to invoke them at the right time instead of troubling the invoker of Deferred. callback.

At each step in the callback chain, then, the loop must catch any exception and forward it to the next errback. Because each step may call either a callback or an errback, our `callbacks` list will change to contain (`callback`, `errback`) pairs:

```python
def passthrough(obj):
    return obj

class Deferred(object):
    def __init__ (self):
        self._callbacks = []
    def addCallback(self, callback):
        self._callbacks.append((callback, passthrough))
    def addErrback(self, errback):
        self._callbacks.append((passthrough, errback))
    def callback(self, result):
        for callback, errback in self._callbacks:
            if isinstance(result,BaseException):
                handler = errback
            else:
                handler = callback
            try:
                result = handler(result)
            except BaseExceptionas e:
                result = e
```

Each iteration of the loop inspects the current result. Exceptions are passed to the next errback, while everything else is passed to the next callback as it was before. Any exception raised by either an errback or callback becomes a result to be handled by the errback that comes next in the chain. This makes the following Deferred code:

```python
someDeferred = Deferred()
someDeferred.addCallback(callback)
someDeferred.addErrback(errback)
someDeferred.callback(value)
```

equivalent to this synchronous code:

```
try:
    callback(value)
except BaseExceptionas e:
    errback(e)
```

Errbacks propagate exceptions by returning them and suppress them by returning any value that is *not* an exception. The following Deferred code filters out ValueErrors while letting all other exceptions propagate to the next errback:

```
def suppressValueError(exception):
    if not isinstance(exception, ValueError):
        return exception

someDeferred.addErrback(suppressValueError)
```

suppressValueError implicitly returns None when isinstance(exception, ValueError) evaluates to True, so the exception check in Deferred's callback loop passes None to the next callback. Every other exception returns out of suppressValueError, into the for loop, and on to the next errback. The total effect is equivalent to the following synchronous code:

```
try:
    callback(value)
except ValueError:
    pass
```

A convenient consequence of Deferred's new control flow becomes apparent when we consider the two places it can encounter exceptions:

1. Any callback in a Deferred's list of callbacks might raise an exception. For example, a bug in our manyCallback function's sequence of callbacks might result in addValue returning None, in which case divideValue would raise a TypeError.

2. The code that would pass the actual value to a Deferred's callback method might instead raise an exception. Imagine, for example, that nonblockingGet attempts to decode the HTTP response's body as UTF-8 and call back a Deferred with

the result. If the body contains non-UTF-8-byte sequences, a
UnicodeDecodeError would be raised. Such an exception means
that the actual value can never be computed, an error condition of
which the Deferred's errbacks should be aware.

Deferred now handles both cases; the first is clearly addressed by running each
callback and errback inside a try block, while the second can be handled by catching
and forwarding the exception to Deferred.callback. Consider an HTTP protocol
implementation that attempts to invoke a Deferred's callback with a UTF-8 decoded
response body:

```
class HTTP(protocol.Protocol):
    def dataReceived(self, data):
        self._handleData(data)
        if self.state == "BODY_READY":
            try:
                result = data.decode('utf-8')
            except Exceptionas e:
                result = e
            self.factory.deferred.callback(e)

class HTTPFactory(protocol.Factory)
    protocol = HTTP
    def __init__ (self, deferred):
        self.deferred = deferred

def nonblockingGet(url):
    deferred = Deferred()
    factory = HTTPFactory(deferred)
    ...
    return deferred
```

This works because Deferred's for loop begins each iteration by checking the nature
of the current result. The first time through the loop, the result is whatever the caller
provided callback; in the event of encoding Exception, the above code provides that
exception to callback instead.

Exception handling can now be localized in errbacks just as application logic was localized in callbacks. This allows us to translate from synchronous to asynchronous exception control flow. This code:

```python
def requestField(url, field):
    results = requests.get(url).json()
    return results[field]

def manyOperations(url):
    result = requestField(url, field)
    try:
        result += 2
        result //= 3
        result *= 4
    except TypeError:
        return -1
    return result
```

becomes this code:

```python
def manyCallbacks(url):
    def addValue(result):
        return result + 2
    def divideValue(result):
        return result // 3
    def multiplyValue(result):
        return result * 4
    def onTypeError(exception):
        if isinstance(exception,TypeError):
            return -1
        else:
            return exception
    deferred = requestField(url, "someInteger")
    deferred.addCallback(addValue)
    deferred.addCallback(divideValue)
    deferred.addCallback(multiplyValue)
    deferred.addErrback(onTypeError)
    return deferred
```

Twisted provides a `Deferred` implementation whose API is a superset of the one shown here; as we'll see in the next section, the real `Deferred` composes with itself and provides additional features such as timeouts and cancellation. At its core, however, its behavior matches our toy implementation.

An Introduction to Twisted's Deferred

The best way to get to know Twisted's `Deferred` is to play with it in a Python session. We'll begin by importing it from `twisted.internet.defer`:

```
>>> from twisted.internet.defer import Deferred
```

Callbacks

Like our toy implementation, `twisted.internet.defer.Deferred`'s `addCallback` method accepts a callback to add to the instance's callbacks list. Unlike our implementation, Twisted's also accepts positional and keyword arguments that will be passed to the callback:

```
>>> d = Deferred()
>>> def cbPrint(result, positional, **kwargs):
...     print("result =", result, "positional =", positional,
...           "kwargs =", kwargs)
...
>>> d.addCallback(cbPrint, "positional", keyword=1) is d
True
>>> d.callback("result")
result = result positional = positinal, kwargs = {'keyword': 1}
```

We create a `Deferred` named d, add `cbPrint` as a callback, then call back d with `"result"`. d passes this through to `cbPrint` as its first positional argument, while the additional arguments to `d.addCallback` are passed as its remaining arguments.

Note that `d.addCallback` returns d itself, which allows chained expressions like

```
d.addCallback(...).addCallback(...).addCallback(...).
```

71

Now that d has now been called back with a value, it cannot be called back again:

```
>>> d.callback("whoops")
Traceback (most recent call last):
  File "<stdin>", line 1, in <module>
  File "site-packages/twisted/internet/defer.py", line 459, in callback
    self._startRunCallbacks(result)
  File "site-packages/twisted/internet/defer.py", line 560,
  in _startRunCallbacks
    raise AlreadyCalledError
twisted.internet.defer.AlreadyCalledError
```

This is because Deferreds remember the value with which they've been called back:

```
>>> d2 = Deferred()
>>> d2.callback("the result")
<Deferred at 0x12345 current result: 'the result'>
```

The fact that Deferreds store results raises a question: What happens when a Deferred with a result has a callback added to it?

```
>>> d2.addCallback(print)
the result
```

The print runs as soon as it's added as a callback to d2. A Deferreds that has a result *immediately runs callbacks added to it*. It's tempting to imagine that Deferreds always represent a value that is not yet available. Code that assumes this, however, is wrong and a source of frustrating bugs. Consider the following:

```
class ReadyOK(twisted.internet.protocol.Protocol):
    def connectionMade(self):
        someDeferred = someAPI()
        def checkAndWriteB(ignored):
            self.transport.write(b"OK\n")
        someDeferred.addCallback(checkAndWriteB)
        self.transport.write(b"READY\n")
```

As its name implies, this ReadyOK protocol should greet new connections with a READY line, only writing OK and disconnecting when someAPI calls back its Deferred. READY will appear before OK when someDeferred has not been called back until after connectionMade returns, but this is not guaranteed; if someAPI returns someDeferred with a result, then OK appears before READY. This reversal of the expected order of lines would break clients that correctly required READY be sent first.

The solution in this case is to move self.transport.write(b"READY\n") *before* someDeferred = someAPI(). You might need to similarly reorganize your own code to ensure Deferreds with results do not violate invariants.

Errbacks and Failures

Deferreds also have errbacks that handle exceptions raised by callbacks and the code that calls provide Deferred.callback. We consider the first case first:

```
>>> d3 = Deferred()
>>> def cbWillFail(number):
...     1 / number
...
>>> d3.addCallback(cbWillFail)
<Deferred at 0x123456>
>>> d3.addErrback(print)
<Deferred at 0x123456>
>>> d3.callback(0)
[Failure instance: Traceback: <class 'ZeroDivisionError'>: division by zero
<stdin>:1:<module>
site-packages/twisted/internet/defer.py:459:callback
site-packages/twisted/internet/defer.py:567:_startRunCallbacks
--- <exception caught here> ---
site-packages/twisted/internet/defer.py:653:_runCallbacks
<stdin>:2:cbWillFail
]
```

The d3 Deferred has a callback that divides 1 by its argument and the built-in print function as an errback, so any exception raised by the callback will appear in our interactive session. Calling d3 back with 0 naturally produces a ZeroDivisionError, but produces something else as well: a *Failure* instance. Note that Failure string representation is wrapped in brackets ([. . .]). The errback printed a single failure, not a list with one Failure!

Exception objects in Python 2 do not contain tracebacks or other information about their origin. In an attempt to provide as much context as possible, Twisted introduced Failures as a container type for asynchronous exceptions that records tracebacks. A Failure constructed in an except block absorbs the active exception and its traceback:

```
>>> from twisted.python.failure import Failure
>>> try:
...     1 /0
... except:
...     f = Failure()
...
>>> f
<twisted.python.failure.Failure builtins.ZeroDivisionError: division by
zero>
>>> f.value ZeroDivisionError('division  by  zero',)
>>> f.getTracebackObject()
<traceback object at 0x1234567>
>>> print(f.getTraceback())
Traceback (most recent call last):
--- <exception caught here> ---
  File "<stdin>", line 2, in <module>

builtins.ZeroDivisionError: division by zero
```

The Failure instance stores the actual exception object under its value attribute and makes the traceback itself available in several different ways.

Failures also have convenience methods that ease interacting with them in errbacks. The check method accepts multiple exception classes and returns the one belonging to Failure's exception or None:

```
>>> f.check(ValueError)
>>> f.check(ValueError, ZeroDivisionError)
<class 'ZeroDivisionError'>
```

Failure.trap behaves like check, except that it re-raises the Failure's exception if it does not match any provided exception class. This allows errbacks to replicate the behavior of filtering except clauses:

```
>>> d4 = Deferred()
>>> def cbWillFail(number):
...     1 / 0
...
>>> def ebValueError(failure):
...     failure.trap(ValueError):
...     print("Failure was ValueError")
...
>>> def ebTypeErrorAndZeroDivisionError(failure):
...     exceptionType = failure.trap(TypeError, ZeroDivisionError):
...     print("Failure was", exceptionType)
...
>>> d4.addCallback(cbWillFail)
<Deferred at 0x12345678>
>>> d4.addErrback(ebValueError)
<Deferred at 0x12345678>
>>> d4.addErrback(ebTypeErrorAndZeroDivisionError)
<Deferred at 0x12345678>
>>> d4.callback(0)
Failure was <class 'ZeroDivisionError'>
```

ebValueError and ebTypeErrorAndZeroDivisionError together function like the two except blocks in this synchronous code:

```
try:
    1/0
except ValueError:
    print("Failure was ValueError")
except (TypeError,ZeroDivisionError) as e:
    exceptionType = type(e)
    print("Failure was", exceptionType)
```

Finally, Deferreds can be provided a Failure or can synthesize one from the current exception.

Calling back a Deferred with a Failure instance begins executing its errbacks. someDeferred.callback(Failure()) is thus analogous to passing our toy implementation's callback an exception.

Deferreds also expose an errback method. Passing this a Failure instance has the same effect as passing callback one; however, calling Deferred.errback with no arguments constructs a failure, making it easy to capture an exception for asynchronous handling:

```
>>> d5 = Deferred()
>>> d5.addErrback(print)
<Deferred at 0x12345678>
>>> try:
...     1/0
... except:
...     d.errback()
...
[Failure  instance:  Traceback:<  class 'ZeroDivisionError'>:  division
by  zero
---<exception caught here>---
<stdin>:2:<module>
]
```

Composing Deferreds

Deferreds are a control-flow abstraction that enable the composition of callbacks and errbacks. They also compose with themselves, so that a Deferred can wait on a Deferred.

Consider a Deferred named outerDeferred with the following sequence of callbacks, one of which returns innerDeferred, which has its *own* callbacks:

```
>>> outerDeferred = Deferred()
>>> def printAndPassThrough(result, *args):
...     print("printAndPassThrough",
...             " ".join(args), "received", result)
...     return result
...
>>> outerDeferred.addCallback(printAndPassThrough, '1')
<Deferred at 0x12345678>
>>> innerDeferred = Deferred()
>>> innerDeferred.addCallback(printAndPassThrough,  '2',  'a')
<Deferred at 0x123456789>
>>> innerDeferred.addCallback(printAndPassThrough,  '2',  'b')
<Deferred at 0x123456789>
>>> def returnInnerDeferred(result, number):
...     print("returnInnerDeferred #", number, "received", result)
...     print("Returning innerDeferred...")
...     return innerDeferred
...
>>> outerDeferred.addCallback(returnInnerDeferred, '2')
<Deferred at 0x12345678>
>>> outerDeferred.addCallback(printAndPassThrough, '3')
<Deferred at 0x12345678>
>>> outerDeferred.addCallback(printAndPassThrough, '4')
<Deferred at 0x12345678>
```

Calling back outerDeferred clearly invokes the printAndPassThrough callback with an identifier 1, but what happens when control reaches returnInnerDeferred?

We can answer this with a visual representation of flow of execution in Figure 2-1.

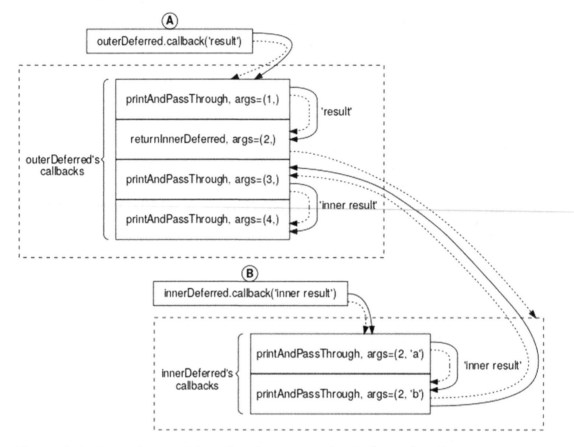

Figure 2-1. *Execution and data flow between* outerDeferred *and* innerDeferred. *Execution follows the dotted arrows, while the data flow follows the solid arrows.*

The box labeled **A** represents the outerDeferred.callback('result') call that starts outerDeferred's callback loop, while the dotted and solid arrows show the flow of execution and data respectively.

The first callback – printAndPassThrough with an identifier of 1 – receives 'result' as its first argument and prints out a message. Because it returns 'result', outerDeferred calls the next callback with that same object. returnInnerDeferred prints its identifier and a message that it's returning innerDeferred before doing so:

```
>>> outerDeferred.callback("result")
printAndPassThrough 1 received result
returnInnerDeferred 2 received result
Returning innerDeferred...
```

The callback loop inside `outerDeferred` detects that `returnInnerDeferred` has returned a `Deferred` instead of an actual value, and *pauses* its own callback loop until `innerDeferred` resolves to a value. The dotted arrow in Figure 2-1 shows that execution has transferred to `innerDeferred`, as does `outerDeferred`'s repr:

```
>>> outerDeferred
<Deferred at 0x12345678 waiting on Deferred at 0x123456789>
```

The box labeled **B** represents the `innerDeferred.callback('result')` call that resumes execution. Naturally, `innerDeferred`'s own callbacks, `printAndPassThroughs` with identifiers 2 a and 2 b, now run.

Once `innerDeferred` has run all its callbacks, execution returns to `outerDeferred`'s callback loop, where `printAndPassThroughs` 3 and 4 execute with the value returned by `innerDeferred`'s last callback.

```
>>> innerDeferred.callback('inner result')
printAndPassThrough 2 a received inner result
printAndPassThrough 2 b received inner result
printAndPassThrough 3 received inner result
printAndPassThrough 4 received inner result
```

In effect, then, `printAndPassThrough` 3 and 4 became `innerDeferred`'s callbacks. If any `innerDeferred`'s own callbacks returned `Deferreds`, its callback loop would pause in the same way `outerDeferred`'s did.

The ability to return `Deferreds` from callbacks (and errbacks as well) allows externally composing functions that return `Deferreds`:

```
def copyURL(sourceURL, targetURL):
    downloadDeferred = retrieveURL(sourceURL)
    def uploadResponse(response):
        return uploadToURL(targetURL, response)
    return downloadDeferred.addCallback(uploadResponse)
```

`copyURL` uses two hypothetical APIs: `retrieveURL`, which retrieves the contents of a URL; and `uploadToURL`, which uploads data to a target URL. The `uploadResponse` callback added to the `Deferred` returned by `retrieveURL` invokes `uploadResponse` with the data from the source URL and returns the resulting `Deferred`. Remember that a `Deferred`'s `addCallback` returns that same instance, so `copyURL` returns `downloadDeferred` to its caller.

Users of copyURL wait first for the download and then for the upload as intended. copyURL's implementation composes the functions that return Deferreds in the same way it composes callbacks without any special-purpose APIs.

The basic interface of Twisted's Deferreds allows its users to compose callbacks, errbacks, and Deferreds externally, easing the construction of asynchronous programs.

Deferreds are not the only way that asynchronous programs can externally compose their event handlers. In the nearly two decades since Twisted's Deferreds were introduced, Python has developed language-level mechanisms to suspend and resume special types of functions.

Generators and InlineCallbacks
yield

Python has supported *generators* since version 2.5. Generators are functions and methods that use a yield expression in their body. Calling a generator returns an iterable *generator object*. Iterating over this executes the body of the generator until the next yield expression, at which point execution pauses and the iterator evaluates to the yield expression's operand.

Consider the execution of the following generator:

```
>>> def generatorFunction():
...     print("Begin")
...     yield 1
...     print("Continue")
...     yield 2
...
>>> g = generatorFunction()
>>> g
<generator object generatorFunction at 0x12345690>
>>> result = next(g)
Begin
>>> result
1
```

generatorFunction returns a new generator object when called. Note that no part of generatorFunction's body has run yet. The built-in next function advances an iterator; advancing the generator object g begins executing generatorFunction's body, outputting Begin into our interactive Python session. Execution pauses upon reaching the first yield expression, and the value provided to yield becomes the next call's return value. Calling next again resumes executing the generator until it reaches the second yield:

```
>>> nextResult = next(g)
Continue
>>> nextResult
2
```

Another call to next resumes the generator. This time its entire body has executed. There are no further yields at which to pause so the generator object cannot provide another value to a subsequent next call. In according with Python's iteration protocol, calling next on the generato object raises StopIteration to indicate that it has been exhausted:

```
>>> next(g)
Traceback (most recent call last):
  File "<stdin>", line 1, in <module>
StopIteration
```

Generators thus follow the same API as any other iterator: values are returned either by explicit calls to next like the ones above or by implicit ones like those in for loops, while a StopIteration exception indicates that no more values can be returned. However, generators implement more than just the iteration API.

send

Generators can *accept* values as well as emit them. The yield operand can appear as the right-hand side of an assignment statement. The yield expression at which a generator is paused can be made to evaluate to something by passing that value to the generator's send method. Given the following yield expression in a generator gPrime:

```
def gPrime():
    a = yield 4
```

gPrime.send(5) causes the yield on the right-hand side of the assignment to evaluate to 5, so that the code within the generator becomes equivalent to this:

```
def gPrime():
    a = 5
```

As a result, the generator-local variable a takes on the value 5. At the same time, the gPrime().send(5) call advances the generator and evaluates to 4. Let's explore send's control flow in more detail by examining a fully worked example and its visualization in Figure 2-2.

```
>>> def receivingGenerator():
...         print("Begin")
...         x = 1
...         y = yield x
...         print("Continue")
...         z = yield x + y
...         print(x + y + z)
...
>>> g = receivingGenerator()
>>> result = next(g) # A Begin
>>> result
1
>>> nextResult = g.send(2) # B
Continue
>>> nextResult
3
>>> g.send(3) # C
6
Traceback (most recent call last):
  File "<stdin>", line 1, in <module>
StopIteration
```

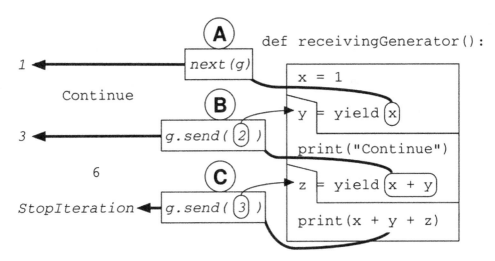

Figure 2-2. *Execution of and data flow into and out of* receivingGenerator. *Execution moves downward, while the data flow follows the solid arrows.*

We begin execution of receivingGenerator with next, the same way that we began execution of generatorFunction; generators must always be started by iterating over them once. The box marked **A** in Figure 2-2 indicates this initial call to next. As before, g runs until pausing on its first yield expression, and this next call evaluates to that yield's operand. Because that operand is the local variable x, which was assigned 1, the next call evaluates to 1. The black arrow out from yield x, through box **A**, traces the value 1 as it leaves the generator through next.

Now that the generator has started we can resume it again with send, as indicated by box **B**. g.send(2) passes the value 2 into the generator, which assigns it to the variable y. Execution continues, past print("Continue"), until pausing on the next yield. The operand here is the expression x + y, which evaluates to 3 and returns back through g.send(2). The black arrow that travels from x + y through box **B** shows the exit path taken by the result 3.

Calling g.send(3), represented by box **C**, sends 3 into the generator and resumes execution again, printing x + y + z = 6 to the session. However, the generator cannot pause its execution as it did before, because there are no further yield expressions in receivingGenerator. Because generators follow the iteration protocol, they raise StopIteration when exhausted; g.send(3) thus raises StopIteration instead of evaluating to a value, as indicated in Figure 2-2 and demonstrated in the example code.

throw

Just as send allows passing values into generators, throw allows raising exceptions within them. Consider the following code:

```
>>> def failingGenerator():
...     try:
...         value = yield
...     except ValueError:
...         print("Caught ValueError")
...
>>> tracebackG = failingGenerator()
>>> next(tracebackG)
>>> tracebackG.throw(TypeError())
Traceback (most recent call last):
  File "<stdin>", line 1, in <module>
  File "<stdin>", line 3, in failingGenerator
TypeError
>>> catchingG = failingGenerator()
>>> next(catchingG)
>>> catchingG.throw(ValueError())
Caught ValueError
Traceback (most recent call last):
  File "<stdin>", line 1, in <module>
StopIteration
```

failingGenerator wraps its yield expression in a try block whose except catches ValueError and then prints a message. All other exceptions pass back to the caller.

We create a new generator by calling failingGenerator and naming it tracebackG. We start things as usual with a call to next. Note that failingGenerator's yield lacks an operand; Python represents the *absence* of a value with None, so next evaluates to None (interative Python sessions do not print None when it's returned by a function). Inside the generator the first yield itself evaluates to None, because next cannot not send any value into the generator. As a result, g.send(None) is equivalent to next(g). This equivalence will become significant when we look into *coroutines*.

Next, we throw `TypeError` into `tracebackG` via its `throw` method. The generator is resumed at its `yield` expression, but instead of evaluating to a value, that `yield` *raises* the `TypeError` passed by `throw`. The resulting traceback terminates inside `failingGenerator`. What's less clear from the traceback is that the `TypeError` rises back up from `tracebackG.throw`. This makes sense: the `throw` call caused the resumption of the generator, which in turn raised `TypeError`, and it's natural that unhandled exceptions return up the call stack.

A new generator named `catchingG` demonstrates what happens when `failingGenerator`'s except block encounters a `ValueError`. As expected, the `yield` raises the exception passed to `throw`, and as expected from Python's exception handling, the except block catches the `ValueError` and prints its message. However, there are no further `yields` on which to pause the generator, so this time `throw` raises a `StopIteration` indicating the exhaustion of `failingGenerator`.

Asynchronous Programming with inlineCallbacks

Generators' suspension and resumption of execution corresponds to `Deferred`'s execution of callbacks and errbacks:

- A generator pauses its execution when it reaches a `yield` expression, while a `Deferred` pauses its callbacks and errbacks when one returns another `Deferred`;

- A paused generator can be resumed with a value via its `send` method, while a `Deferred` waiting on another `Deferred` resumes executing its callbacks when that `Deferred` resolves to a value;

- A paused generator can receive and catch an exception via its `throw` method, while a `Deferred` waiting on another `Deferred` resumes executing its errbacks when that `Deferred` resolves to an exception.

We can see these equivalences in action by comparing the following two code examples:

```python
def requestFieldDeferred(url, field):
    d = nonblockingGet(url)

    def onCompletion(response):
        document = json.load(response)
        return jsonDoc[field]
```

```python
    def onFailure(failure):
        failure.trap(UnicodeDecodeError)

    d.addCallack(onCompletion)
    d.addErrback(onFailure)

    return d

def requestFieldGenerator(url, field):
    try:
        document = yield nonblockingGet(url)
    except UnicodeDecodeError:
        pass

    document = json.load(response)
    return jsonDoc[field]
```

requestFieldDeferred attaches a callback to nonblockingGet's response Deferred that decodes the response as JSON and extracts a property, and an errback that suppresses only UnicodeDecodeErrors.

requestFieldGenerator instead yields nonblockingGet's Deferred. The generator can then be resumed with the response when it becomes available, or an exception if one occurs instead. Both the callback and errback have been moved into the same scope that calls nonblockingGet. Moving a function's body into its caller is known as *inlining*.

We cannot use requestFieldGenerator as it is written: Python 2 does not allow generators to return values, and we need a wrapper that accepts the yielded Deferred and arranges to call the generator's send or throw when that Deferred resolves to a value or exception.

Twisted provides this wrapper in twisted.internet.defer.inlineCallbacks. It decorates callables that return generators and invokes send and throw as each yielded Deferred resolves to a value or Exception. In turn, callers that invoke the decorated generator function or method receive a Deferred in lieu of a generator object. This ensures that existing APIs that expect Deferreds work seamlessly with inlineCallbacks.

Here's our requestFieldGenerator decorated with inlineCallbacks:

```python
from twisted.internet import defer

@defer.inlineCallbacks
def requestFieldGenerator(url, field):
```

```
    try:
        document = yield nonblockingGet(url)
    except UnicodeDecodeError:
        pass

    document = json.load(response)
    defer.returnValue(jsonDoc[field])
def someCaller(url, ...):
    requestFieldDeferred = requestFieldGenerator(url,"someProperty")
    ...
```

The `returnValue` function throws a special exception that contains its argument; `inlineCallbacks` catches this and arranges to call back `requestFieldGenerator` with that value. A `return` statement in Python 3 raises an equivalent exception that `inlineCallbacks` also catches, so `returnValue` is not necessary in code that will only run under Python 3.

By bringing code back from callbacks and errbacks into a single local scope, generators make asynchronous Twisted programs read as though they were synchronous. Short programs especially benefit from the consequent reduction in function definitions and clearer control flow.

Generators exchange familiarity for new difficulties. Most critically, it is impossible for the caller of a generator function or method to know if the returned generator object will use the value sent into it with `send` or silently ignore it. These two generators, for example, offer the same interface:

```
def listensToSend():
    a = 1
    b = yield a
    print(a+b)

def ignoresSend():
    a = 1
    yield a
    print(a)
```

Accidentally replacing `listensToSend` with `ignoreSend` will lead to a subtle bug that's difficult to diagnose. Both are valid Python code that are appropriate in distinct circumstances: `listensToSend` allows resumption with a value, making it suitable for `inlineCallbacks`, while `ignoreSend` simply yields a value, as would befit a processing pipeline that operates on lines in a file. These two distinct use cases are blurred by the Python generator API.

Fortunately, recent versions of Python 3 provide new syntax tailor-made for `inlineCallbacks`-style generators.

Coroutines in Python

In computer science, generators are a special case of *coroutines*, which can suspend themselves and pass execution on to any other coroutine, resuming when they receive back a value. Our `inlineCallbacks` decorated generator resembles a coroutine in that it can yield and receive values, but it unlike a coroutine, it cannot directly invoke another generator as it would any other function. Instead, it needs the machinery inside `inlineCallbacks` to hand off execution to another generator on its behalf. That machinery, which manages requests to execute code and routes results back to their requester, is known as a *trampoline*. To understand why, imagine execution as though it were bouncing off `inlineCallbacks` between different generators.

Coroutines with yield from

Python 3.3 introduced a new syntax that allows a generator to directly delegate its execution to another generator: `yield from`. The following Python 3.3+- only code demonstrates the behavior of a generator that yields from another generator:

```
>>> def e():
...     a = yield 1
...     return a + 2
...
>>> def f():
...     print("Begin f")
...     c = yield from e()
...     print(c)
...
>>> g = f()
>>> g.send(None)
```

```
Begin f
1
>>> g.send(2)
4
Traceback (most recent call last):
  File "<stdin>", line 1, in <module>
StopIteration
```

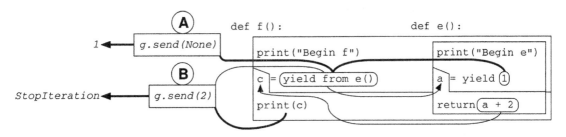

Figure 2-3. _Execution of and data flow into and out of e and f. Execution moves downward, while the data flow follows the solid arrows._

The generator e behaves exactly as the generator functions described in the previous section: if we called it, we would then start the returned generator by calling next on it (or passing its send method None), which would return 1, the operand to its yield; we could then pass values back into the generator with send, which would return either the operand to the next yield expression or to the return statement (remember that generators can return values in Python 3).

The generator g returned by f _yields from_ a generator returned by e, pausing to allow that sub-generator to execute. next, send, and throw calls issued against g are proxied through to the underlying e generator, so that generator g appears to be an e generator. In Figure 2-3, box **A** indicates the initial g.send(None) that begins execution of g. Execution moves through f()'s yield from to a generator returned by e(), pausing on the yield expression inside e's body that sends 1 back to g.send(None).

A generator that delegates execution to another generator with yield from regains control when that sub-generator terminates. Box **B** in Figure 2-3 represents the second call to g.send(2) that passes the value 2 through the suspended f generator into the sub-generator e, which resumes and assigns the 2 to variable a. Execution proceeds to the return statement and the e sub-generator exits with a value of 4. Now f resumes on the left-hand side of its yield from expression, and assigns the received 4 to variable c. After the print call there're no further yield or yield from expressions, so f() terminates, causing g.send(2) raises a StopIteration error.

This syntax eliminates the need for a trampoline like inlineCallbacks to dispatch calls from one generator to another, because it allows generators to directly delegate execution to other generators. With yield from, Python generators behave like true coroutines.

Coroutines async and await

Unfortunately, yield from still suffers from the same ambiguity that yield did: generators that accept values and those that ignore them appear the same to calling code. Versions of Python after 3.5 address this ambiguity by introducing new syntactic features on top of yield from that distinguish coroutines: async and await.

When applied to a function or method definition, the async marker turns that function or method into a *coroutine*:

```
>>>  async def function(): pass
...
>>> c = function()
>>> c
<coroutine object function at 0x9876543210>
```

Coroutines, unlike generators, cannot be iterated over:

```
>>> list(function())
Traceback (most recent call last):
  File "<stdin>", line 1, in <module>
TypeError: 'coroutine' object is not iterable
>>> next(function())
Traceback (most recent call last):
  File "<stdin>", line 1, in <module>
TypeError: 'coroutine' object is not iterable
```

Like generators, coroutines have *send* and *throw* methods with which callers can resume them:

```
>>> function().send(None)
Traceback (most recent call last):
```

```
  File "<stdin>", line 1, in <module>
StopIteration
>>> function().throw(Exception)
Traceback (most recent call last):
  File "<stdin>", line 1, in <module>
  File "<stdin>", line 1, in function
Exception
```

Coroutines can *await* other coroutines, with the same semantics as generators that yield from other generators:

```
>>> async def returnsValue(value):
...        return 1
...
>>> async def awaitsCoroutine(c):
...        value = await c
...        print(value)
...
>>> awaitsCoroutine(returnsValue(1)).send(None)
1
Traceback (most recent call last):
  File "<stdin>", line 1, in <module>
StopIteration
```

This behavior demonstrates the prerequisites to coroutine composition, but awaiting something that immediately returns a value doesn't motivate their use in asynchronous programming. We need to be able to send an arbitrary value into a paused coroutine, but because the purpose of async and await is to present an API that's incompatible with plain generators, we can neither await a plain generator, as we with yield from, nor omit its operand, as with yield:

```
>>> def plainGenerator():
...        yield 1
...
>>> async def brokenCoroutineAwaitsGenerator():
...        await plainGenerator()
...
```

```
>>> brokenCoroutineAwaitsGenerator().send(None)
Traceback (most recent call last):
  File "<stdin>", line 1, in <module>
  File "<stdin>", line 2, in brokenCoroutineAwaitsGenerator
TypeError: object generator can't be used in 'await' expression
>>> async def brokenCoroutineAwaitsNothing():
...     await
  File "<stdin>", line 2
    await
        ^
SyntaxError: invalid syntax
```

To learn how to resume coroutines with values, we return to yield from. Our previous example provided yield from with another generator, so that calls to the wrapping generator's send and throw methods were proxied through to the inner generator. There might have been many generators that each delegated execution to a successor via yield from, but at the bottom there would have to be something that yields values upward. Consider, for example, a stack of five generators, visualized in Figure 2-4.

```
>>> def g1(): yield from g2
...
>>> def g2(): yield from g3
...
>>> def g3(): yield from g4
...
>>> def g4(): yield from g5
...
>>> def g5(): yield 1
```

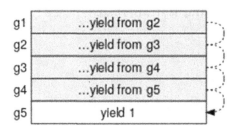

Figure 2-4. *A stack of generators. g1 through g4 have delegated execution downward to g5.*

g1, g2, g3, and g4 cannot make any progress until g5 yields a value that will propagate from g4 up to g1. g5 need not be a generator, however; as the following example demonstrates, yield from merely requires an *iterable object* to advance its generator:

```
>>> def yieldsToIterable(o):
...     print("Yielding from object of type", type(o))
...     yield from o
...
>>> list(yieldsToIterable(range(3)))
Yielding from object of type <class 'range'>
[0, 1, 2]
```

yieldsToIterable delegates execution to its argument, which in this case is a range object. Iterating over the yieldsToIterable generator by building a list out of it demonstrates that the range object takes over iteration just as a generator would.

Coroutines defined with async def share their implementation with yield from, and so with the proper steps, they too can await special kinds of iterables and generators.

Contrary to what previous examples appeared to demonstrate, generators *can* be awaited as long as they are marked as coroutines with the types.coroutine decorator. A coroutine that awaits such a decorated generator receives that generator's return value:

```
>>> import types
>>> @types.coroutine
... def makeBase():
...     return (yield "hello from a base object")
...
>>> async def awaitsBase(base):
...     value = await base
...     print("From awaitsBase:", value)
...
>>> awaiter = awaitsBase(makeBase())
>>> awaiter.send(None)
'hello from a base object'
>>> awaiter.send("the result")
From awaits base: the result
```

```
Traceback (most recent call last):
  File "<stdin>", line 1, in <module>
StopIteration
```

Starting the awaitsBase coroutine with send(None) jumps to the base generator's yield statement, and following the typical execution path for generators, returns "hello from base object." Now the coroutine has delegated execution to base, so send("the result") resumes base with that string. base immediately returns this value, which causes the coroutine's await to resolve to its value.

Iterable objects can also be awaited if they implement a special __await__ method that returns an iterator. The final value of this iterator – that is, whatever it yields last or wraps in a StopIteration exception – will become the result passed to await. An object that conforms to this interface said to be *future-like*. When we explore asyncio later, we'll see that its Futures provide this interface and so grant it their name.

A simple implementation of a future-like object demonstrates the control flow:

```python
class FutureLike(object):
    _MISSING="MISSING"
    def __init__(self):
        self.result = self._MISSING
    def __next__(self):
        if self.result is self._MISSING:
            return self
        raise StopIteration(self.result)
    def __iter__(self):
        return self
    def __await__(self):
        return iter(self)

async def awaitFutureLike(obj):
    result = await obj
    print(result)

obj = FutureLike()
coro = awaitFutureLike(obj)
assert coro.send(None) is obj
obj.result = "the result"
```

```
try:
    coro.send(None)
except StopIteration:
    pass
```

Instances of FutureLike are iterable because their __iter__ method returns an object that itself has a __next__ method. In this case, iterating over a FutureLike instance will produce that same instance over and over until its result attribute is set, at which point it will raise a StopIteration exception containing that value. This is equivalent to returning that value from a generator.

Instances of FutureLike are also future-like because their __await__ method returns an iterator, so awaitFutureLike can await an instance of FutureLike. As usual, the coroutine is started with send(None). This returns the FutureLike instance that the awaitFutureLike coroutine awaits, which is the same instance we passed to it. Setting the FutureLike object's result attribute allows us to resume the coroutine by resolving its await to a value, which receives the result, prints it, and then terminates with a StopIteration exception.

Note that the second coro.send call *also* passes None to the coroutine. Coroutines that await Future-like objects resolve to the last value provided by those object's iterators. They must still be resumed to make use of these values, but they necessarily ignore the argument to their send method.

Twisted provides an awaitable object and a coroutine adapter so that coroutines and existing APIs can interact seamlessly. As we've seen, coroutines are completely separate from asyncio, so the Twisted APIs we discuss in this section are insufficient to integrate the two. We'll learn about the necessary additional APIs in a subsequent chapter.

Awaiting Deferreds

As of Twisted 16.4.0, Deferreds are future-like objects providing conformant __next__, __iter__, and __await__ methods. This allows us to replace FutureLike in the preceding code with a Deferred:

```
from twisted.internet.defer import Deferred

async def awaitFutureLike(obj):
    result = await obj
    print(result)
```

```
obj = Deferred()
coro = awaitFutureLike(obj)
assert coro.send(None) is obj
obj.callback("the result")
try:
    coro.send(None)
except StopIteration:
    pass
```

awaiting a Deferred resolves to whatever the Deferred does after its normal callback and errback processing loop:

```
>>> from twisted.internet.defer import Deferred
>>> import operator
>>> d = Deferred()
>>> d.addCallback(print, "was received by a callback")
<Deferred at 0x7eff85886160>
>>> d.addCallback(operator.add, 2)
<Deferred at 0x7eff85886160>
>>> async def awaitDeferred():
...     await d
...
>>> g = awaitDeferred()
>>> g.send(None)
<Deferred at 0x7eff85886160>
>>> d.callback(1)
1 was received by a callback
>>> g.send(None)
Traceback (most recent call last):
  File "<stdin>", line 1, in <module>
  File "<stdin>", line 2, in awaitDeferred
  File "twisted/src/twisted/internet/defer.py", line 746, in send
    raise result.value
TypeError: unsupported operand type(s) for +: 'NoneType' and 'int'
```

Our Deferred's print callback runs but returns None, causing its second callback to fail with a TypeError when it attempts to add 2 to its first argument. The resumed coroutine consequently fails with the TypeError stored in the Deferred.

In this case the composition of coroutines and Deferreds exposed a bug, but the code paths exercised demonstrate that errors and data flow naturally between the two.

Awaitable Deferreds allow us to call Twisted APIs in our coroutines, but what if we want Twisted APIs to use one of our coroutines?

Coroutines to Deferreds with ensureDeferred

Twisted can wrap coroutines with Deferreds, allowing APIs that expect Deferreds to accept coroutines instead.

twisted.internet.defer.ensureDeferred accepts a coroutine object and returns a Deferred that will produce a result when the coroutine returns one:

```
>>> from twisted.internet.defer import Deferred, ensureDeferred
>>> async def asyncIncrement(d):
...     x = await d
...     return x + 1
...
>>> awaited = Deferred()
>>> addDeferred = ensureDeferred(asyncIncrement(awaited))
>>> addDeferred.addCallback(print)
<Deferred at0x12345>
>>> awaited.callback(1)
2
>>>
```

Our coroutine `asyncIncrement` `awaits` an object that resolves to a number, then returns the sum of that number and 1. We convert this to a `Deferred` with `ensureDeferred`, assign it to `addDeferred`, and then add a `print` callback to it. Calling back the `awaited` `Deferred` on which `asyncIncrement` waits in turn calls back the `addDeferred` `Deferred` returned by `ensureDeferred`, without our needing to call `send`. In other words, `addDeferred` behaves the same as a manually constructed `Deferred`. Exception propagation also works the same way:

```
>>>from twisted.internet.defer import Deferred, ensureDeferred
>>> async def asyncAdd(d):
...        x = await d
...        return x + 1
...
>>>awaited = Deferred()
>>>addDeferred = ensureDeferred(asyncAdd(awaited))
>>>addDeferred.addErrback(print)
Unhandled error in Deferred:

<Deferred at0x7eff857f0470>
>>>awaited.callback(None)
[Failure  instance:  Traceback:<  class 'TypeError'>:  ...
...
<stdin>:3:asyncAdd
]
```

Coroutines resemble synchronous code more closely than `Deferred`-managed callbacks do, and Twisted makes it easy enough to use coroutines that you might wonder if `Deferred`s are ever the trouble. One obvious answer is that they're already used; lots of Twisted code uses `Deferred`s, so even if you use them rarely, you'll still need to be familiar with them. Another reason that you might not use coroutines is that you must write code that works on Python 2. This is becoming less of an issue as Python 2's end of life approaches, and things like PyPy, an alternate Python runtime whose Just In Time (JIT) compiler can dramatically speed up pure Python code, expand their Python 3 support.

There are less obvious and more durable reasons, however, why Twisted's `Deferred`s remain valuable in a post-coroutine world.

Multiplexing Deferreds

What happens if we want the result of two asynchronous operations, either one of which might complete before the other? Suppose, for example, we write a program that issues two HTTP requests simultaneously:

```
def issueTwo(url1, url2):
    urlDeferreds = [retrieveURL(url1), retrieveURL(url2)]
    ...
```

A coroutine would let us wait for each one in turn:

```
async def issueTwo(url1, url2):
    urlDeferreds = [retrieveURL(url1),  retrieveURL(url2)]
    for d in urlDeferreds:
        result = await d
        doSomethingWith(result)
```

The reactor will progress in retrieving both url1 and url2 while issueTwo awaits the completion of either; waiting for url1's retrieval to complete does not prevent the reactor from retrieving url2. This concurrency is indeed the point of asynchronous and event-driven programming!

This efficiency becomes less important, however, as the operations become more complicated. Imagine that we only wanted the URL that's retrieved first. We cannot write a fastestOfTwo coroutine only using await because we don't know which to await first. Only the reactor knows when the underlying events occur that indicate a coroutine's value is ready, and if we only had coroutines, the event loop would have to expose a synchronization primitive that both simultaneously awaited multiple coroutines and checked if all had completed.

Fortunately, multiple Deferreds can easily be multiplexed into a single Deferred without a special reactor-level synchronization mechanism. At its simplest, a twisted.internet.defer.DeferredList is a Deferred that accepts a list of Deferreds and calls itself back when all those Deferreds have a value.

Consider the following code:

```
>>> from twisted.internet.defer import Deferred, DeferredList
>>>  url1 = Deferred()
>>>  url2 = Deferred()
```

```
>>> urlList = DeferredList([url1, url2])
>>> urlList.addCallback(print)
<Deferred at 0x123456>
>>> url2.callback("url2")
>>> url1.callback("url1")
[(True, "url1)", (True, "url2")]
```

The DeferredList urlList wraps the two url1 and url2 Deferreds and has as its own callback a print function. That callback only runs after both url1 and url2 have been called back, so urlList as written matches the all-or-nothing synchronization at play in the issueTwo coroutine above.

The first clue to DeferredList's greater feature set lies in the list it returns to its callback. Each element is a tuple of length 2; the second element is clearly the value of the Deferred at the same index in the passed-in list, so that index 0's second tuple member is "url1", corresponding to the url1 Deferred at index 0.

The first item in the tuple indicates whether or not the Deferred terminated successfully. Both url1 and url2 resolved to strings and not Failures, so the corresponding indices in the result list have True as their first element.

Causing at least one of a DeferredList's Deferreds to fail demonstrates how Failures are communicated:

```
>>> succeeds = Deferred()
>>> fails = Deferred()
>>> listOfDeferreds = DeferredList([succeeds, fails])
>>> listOfDeferreds.addCallback(print)
<Deferred at 0x1234567>
>>> fails.errback(Exception())
>>> succeeds.callback("OK")
[(True, 'OK'), (False, <twisted.python.failure.Failure builtins.Exception:
>)]
```

Now the second tuple in the returned list has False as its first element and a Failure representing the Exception that caused its Deferred to fail as its second item.

This special list of (success, value or Failure) pairs retains all possible information by using the traceback capturing facilities of Failures. As an example of the flexibility that this approach enables, users of DeferredList can easily filter aggregate results in a single callback.

With the basic behavior of DeferredList out of the way, we can investigate additional features that will allow us to implement fastestOfTwo: fireOnOneCallback.

The fireOnOneCallback option instructs the DeferredList to call itself back when any one of the Deferreds in its list has a value:

```
>>> noValue = Deferred()
>>> getsValue = Deferred()
>>> waitsForOne = DeferredList([noValue, getsValue], fireOnOneCallback=True)
>>> waitsForOne.addCallback(print)
<Deferred at 0x12345678>
>>> getsValue.callback("the value")
('the value', 1)
```

Now waitsForOne's print callback runs when only the getsValue Deferred resolves to a value. The value DeferredList passes to its callback is again a tuple of length 2, but this time, the first item is the value the corresponding Deferred resolved to, while the second item is its index in the list. getsValue was called back with "the value," and it was the second item in the list we passed DeferredList, so the callback receives ("the value," 1) as its result.

We can now implement fastestOfTwo:

```
def fastestOfTwo(url1, url2):
    def extractValue(valueAndIndex):
        value, index = valueAndIndex
        return value
    urlList = DeferredList([retrieveURL(url1), retrieveURL(url2)],
                           fireOnOneCallback=True,
                           fireOnOneErrback=True)
    return urlList.addCallback(extractValue)
```

DeferredList also allows analogous multiplexing of errors with fireOnOneErrback. Firing the DeferredList on the first error and and unwrapping its value is a common enough pattern that Twisted provides a convenient wrapper in twisted.internet. defer.gatherResults:

```
>>> from twisted.internet.defer import Deferred, gatherResults
>>> d1, d2 = Deferred(), Deferred()
>>> results = gatherResults([d1, d2])
```

```
>>> results.addCallback(print)
<Deferred at 0x123456789>
>>> d1.callback(1)
>>> d2.callback(2)
>>> [1, 2]
>>> d1, d2 = Deferred(), Deferred()
>>> fails = gatherResults([d1,   d2])
>>> fails.addErrback(print)
<Deferred at 0x1234567890>
>>> d1.errback(Exception())
[[Failure instance: Traceback ...: <class 'Exception'>: ]]
```

Recall that Failure's __str__ method returns a string that begins and ends in [], so the printed failure appears with two sets of brackets: one from its __str__ and another from its enclosing list.

Note also that gatherResults awaits *all* successful Deferreds, so it cannot be used for fastestOfTwo

DeferredList and gatherResults offer higher-level APIs that allow sophisticated behaviors but imply branching; the output of each depends on interaction between their own options and the output of the Deferreds they wrap. A change in any one might result in an unexpected output and thus an unpleasant bug.

This is beyond the general indirection that comes with Deferreds: because Deferred.callback is almost always called by the reactor and not by code user code that indirectly manipulates a socket, there can be a gap between the source of an exception and its ultimate cause.

Twisted addresses these difficulties inherent to asynchronous code by providing special support for testing Deferreds.

Testing Deferreds

In the previous chapter, we saw that Twisted's trial.unittest package provides a SynchronousTestCase whose API mimics unittest.TestCase's. In fact, SynchronousTestCase's API is a superset of unittest.TestCases, and an important part of its additional features involve assertions about Deferreds.

We can explore these features by writing tests for the fastestOfTwo function defined in the previous section. First, we'll generalize it to accept any two Deferreds instead of retrieving URLs itself:

```
def fastestOfTwo(d1, d2):
    def extractValue(valueAndIndex):
        value, index = valueAndIndex
        return value
    urlList = DeferredList([d1, d2],
                           fireOnOneCallback=True,
                           fireOnOneErrback=True)
    return urlList.addCallback(extractValue)
```

The first test we can write for this new version of fastestOfTwo asserts that the Deferred it returns does not resolve to a value when neither of its Deferreds have resolved to a value:

```
from twisted.internet import defer
from twisted.trial import unittest

class FastestOfTwoTests(unittest.SynchronousTestCase):
    def test_noResult(self):
        d1 = defer.Deferred()
        self.assertNoResult(d1)
        d2=defer.Deferred()
        self.assertNoResult(d2)
        self.assertNoResult(fastestOfTwo(d1, d2))
```

As its name suggests, SynchronousTestCase.assertNoResult asserts that the Deferred it's passed has no result, and is a valuable tool to ensure the matches your expections execution follows.

Deferreds, however, are most useful when they do have a result. In the case of fastestOfTwo, we expect the returned Deferred to take the value of the first of the two Deferreds that resolve:

```
def test_resultIsFirstDeferredsResult(self):
    getsResultFirst = defer.Deferred()
    neverGetsResult = defer.Deferred()
    fastestDeferred = fastestOfTwo(getsResultFirst, neverGetsResult)
```

```
        self.assertNoResult(fastestDeferred)
        result = "the result"
        getsResultFirst.callback(result)
        actualResult = self.successResultOf(fastestDeferred)
        self.assertIs(result, actualResult)
```

`SynchronousTestCase.successResultOf` either returns a `Deferred`'s current result or causes its test to fail. Our test uses this to extract `"the result"` from `fastestDeferred` after calling back `getsResultFirst` with it, so that the test can assert that `fastestOfTwo` did in fact return the first available result.

Note that we still assert that the `Deferred` returned by `fastestOfTwo` has no result before we callback `getsResultFirst`. This may seem redundant given that `test_noResult` already makes this assertion, but remember that `Deferreds` can be called back *before* your code adds callbacks or errbacks. In this case, `fastestOfTwo` could erroneously return a `Deferred` that was already called back with `'the result'`, disregarding the passed-in `Deferreds`, and yet our test would still pass. That's unlikely in such simple code, but implicit assumptions about *when* a `Deferred` gets a result can creep into code and cause tests to pass over bugs. It's good practice to assert that `Deferreds` are, in fact, in a given state and not assume so to avoid these bugs, and it is even better practice to test your code against a `Deferred` that already has a result as well as one that doesn't.

We can add a test that asserts `fastestOfTwo` works even when a `Deferred` has fired:

```
def test_firedDeferredIsFirstResult(self):
    result = "the result"
    fastestDeferred = fastestOfTwo(defer.Deferred(),
                                   defer.succeed(result))
    actualResult = self.successResultOf(fastestDeferred)
    self.assertIs(result, actualResult)
```

The `twisted.internet.defer.succeed` function accepts an argument and returns a `Deferred` that's immediately called back with that argument, so the second argument to `fastestOfTwo` is a `Deferred` that's been called back with `'the result'` before any of `fastestOfTwo` runs.

For completeness, we might also test what happens when fastestOfTwo receives two Deferreds that have already been called back:

```
def test_bothDeferredsFired(self):
    first = "first"
    second = "second"
    fastestDeferred = fastestOfTwo(defer.succeed(first),
                                   defer.succeed(second))
    actualResult = self.successResultOf(fastestDeferred)
    self.assertIs(first, actualResult)
```

The underlying DeferredList adds its internal processing callbacks to each Deferreds in its list in order. With fireOnOneCallback=True, the earliest Deferred in the list with a result calls back the Deferred representing the list. In our test, then, we expect first to be the value with which fastestDeferred is called back.

Error handling is a critical part of testing, so our tests for fastestDeferred should also test how it handles Failure. We'll show only the case when a Deferred has failed before being passed to fastestOfTwo to keep the test short:

```
def test_failDeferred(self):
    class ExceptionType(Exception):
        pass
fastestDeferred = fastestOfTwo(defer.fail(ExceptionType()),
                               defer.Deferred())
failure = self.failureResultOf(fastestDeferred)
failure.trap(defer.FirstError)
failure.value.subFailure.trap(ExceptionType)
```

Like SynchronousTestCase.successResultOf, SynchronousTestCase. failureResultOf returns the current Failure from a Deferred; if the Deferred hasn't been called back yet or has a non-Failure result, failureResultOf causes the test to fail.

Because the returned object is a Failure, all the methods and attributes we can use in errbacks are available in our tests. DeferredList with fireOnOneErrback=True wraps failures in twisted.internet.defer.FirstError exception, so we trap this type in our test; if the Failure wrapped any other exception, the trap would re-raise it. The underlying Failure that caused the FirstError is accessible on its subFailure attribute, and since we passed in an instance of ExceptionType, we trap that next to assert the first Deferred failed for the expected reason.

assertNoResult with successResultOf and failureResultOf encourage writing tests with explicit assumptions about the state of Deferreds. As fastestOfTwo demonstrates, even simple uses of Deferreds must be tested for implicit ordering dependencies and error handling. These are also concerns for coroutines, and any other concurrency primitive. Twisted's test suite naturally has the best tools for dealing with common concurrency issues in the context of Deferreds.

Summary

The chapter picked up event-driven programming where the previous left off by explaining that event handlers are a kind of _callback_. Programs of great complexity can be expressed with callbacks because of theoretical power of *continuation-passing style*. Callbacks pass values to other callbacks by invoking them directly instead of returning to their caller. We named this kind composition *internal composition* because it happens within the body of each callback.

Internal composition makes maintaining callback-driven programs hard: each callback must know the name and signature of its successor so that it can call it. Reordering a sequence of callbacks or eliminating one might involve modifying several. A solution lies in the paradigm of *asynchronous programming*, which allows programs to proceed before all inputs are ready. A *placeholder value* that represents an asynchronous result can collect callbacks and then run them when the real value becomes available. This placeholder allows callbacks to return values and thus compose *externally*, and in turn enables logical units to remain ignorant of how and where they're used. Event-driven code that uses these asynchronous placeholders can be factored in the ways that non-callback-driven code is.

Twisted's asynchronous placeholder value is the Deferred. We saw that Deferreds run their callbacks in a loop, passing the result of one to the next and invoking error handlers, or error backs, upon any exception. This processing loop inside Deferreds makes them a powerful *control-flow abstraction*.

An important part of that control-flow abstraction is responding to different errors in different ways. Twisted's Failure class captures traceback information along with the raised exception and exposes utility methods that allow errbacks to filter and re-raise exceptions. We saw how callbacks and errbacks can completely represent synchronous code that uses try and except.

Just as Deferreds allow callbacks to compose, they compose with themselves. When a callback or errback returns a Deferred's, that callback or errback's own Deferred pauses its execution until the new Deferred completes. This means that functions and methods that return Deferreds can be used as callbacks and errbacks without any special effort on developers' part.

As powerful as Deferreds are, they are not the only way to compose asynchronous actions. Python's *generators* can suspend their execution and resume it after receiving values from external sources. This control flow maps onto that provided by Deferreds, and callbacks and errbacks can be moved into a generator by using inlineCallbacks.

Generators, however, are ambiguous in that they may represent simple iterators or Deferred-like control flows. Python 3.5 added special support for *coroutines*, which are control-flow focused generators that can suspend themselves by delegating execution to other coroutines without the need for inlineCallbacks. Coroutines can await Twisted's Deferreds directly and can be turned into Deferreds with ensureDeferred. These APIs allow Twisted to use coroutines seamlessly.

Not all programs can be expressed directly with coroutines: our fastestOfTwo example requires waiting on two things at once. Fortunately, DeferredList, an abstraction built on top of Deferreds, allows Twisted to *multiplex* asynchronous results.

Twisted also has special support for testing Deferreds. SynchronousTestCase provides assertNoResult, successResultOf, and failureResultOf, which allows tests to make precise assertions about the state of Deferreds. Concurrency issues that affect all primitives – coroutines, generators, and Deferreds – can be tested with this suite of tools.

CHAPTER 3

Applications with treq and Klein

The previous chapters explained Twisted's fundamentals in depth. Familiarity with these core concepts is necessary but insufficient to write real applications. In this chapter, we'll explore modern, high-level APIs and whole program design by building a feed aggregator with two powerful Twisted web libraries: `treq` and Klein.

treq (`https://treq.readthedocs.io`) wraps `twisted.web.client.Agent` with an API inspired by the popular synchronous HTTP library `requests`. Its convenient and secure defaults make it easy to send asynchronous HTTP requests, while the fakes provided by `treq.testing` simplify and standardize writing tests.

Klein (`https://klein.readthedocs.io`) is a user-friendly wrapper around Twisted's venerable `twisted.web.server` web framework. It allows developing dynamic, asynchronous web applications with a familiar routing paradigm borrowed from Werkzeug (`https://werkzeug.readthedocs.io/`).

Why Libraries?

Twisted itself provides the core functionality of both Klein and `treq`. Why not just use those parts of Twisted directly, then? Both libraries' interfaces differ significantly from Twisted's own; `twisted.web`, for example, uses *object traversal* instead of *routing* to associate URL paths with Python code. A `twisted.web.server.Site` does not match a request's path and query string against a string template like "/some/"; instead, it matches path segments to nested `Resource` objects. This was the prevailing paradigm in Python web application frameworks at the time `twisted.web` was designed. Rather than add a new routing abstraction to Twisted itself, the authors of Klein opted to experiment

© Mark Williams, Cory Benfield, Brian Warner, Moshe Zadka, Dustin Mitchell, Kevin Samuel, Pierre Tardy 2019
M. Williams et al., *Expert Twisted*, https://doi.org/10.1007/978-1-4842-3742-7_3

with a different approach in a separate code base. Their result was successful, and Klein's independent existence has allowed it to grow and adapt without breaking applications that depend on `twisted.web.server`.

Similarly, `treq` encapsulates common `twisted.web.client.Agent` usage patterns in high-level APIs; for example, `Agent` requires expressing all request bodies, including payloads short enough to be expressed as byte strings, as `IBodyProducer` objects, while `treq`'s request methods accept byte string bodies directly. Using `treq` doesn't preclude you from using `Agent`, the full power of which remains accessible within Twisted.

`pip`, the tool used to install third-party Python packages, works well enough these days that additional requirements don't impose an undue burden on developers. We'll also see in a later chapter how Docker can be used to make development and deployment of Twisted applications that use third-party libraries robust and repeatable. Finally, both Klein and `treq` fall under the Twisted GitHub organization, and are developed and used by Twisted's core contributors. They're as low-risk as libraries can be.

Feed Aggregation

Web syndication dates back to a different, more open era of the internet's history. In its heyday, sites served *feed* files over HTTP that organized their content in a structured way so other sites could consume them for a variety of purposes. Open standards like *RSS* (Really Simple Syndication or Rich Document Format Site Summary) and *Atom* describe these structures and have allowed anyone to write consumers of these feeds. Services that *aggregated* many sites' feeds in a single place became a popular way for users to stay up-to-date on news and blogs. Extensions to these formats, such as RSS's enclosures, allowed feeds to reference external media, enabling the rise of things like podcasting.

The demise of Google Reader in 2013 coincided with a decline in the popularity of feeds. Sites removed their feeds and some consumer software lost the ability to consume them. Despite this decline, there is no single substitute for feed-based web syndication, and it remains an effective way to organize content from many different online sources.

Many standards define variations on RSS. Where it's necessary to work directly with the feed format, we'll only support the following subset of RSS 2.0 as defined by Harvard University's Berkman Center (http://cyber.harvard.edu/rss/rss.html):

1. A <channel> is the root element of an RSS 2.0 feed file and is described by its <title> and <link> elements;

2. Web pages within a <channel> are described by <item>s each with their own <title> and <link> elements.

We'll use test-driven development to write a feed aggregator with Klein and treq. Before we do that, however, we'll learn about them and the problem space that defines feed aggregation by writing exploratory programs. We'll then use what we learn to design, implement, and iteratively refine our application. Because we can't display feeds without first downloading them, we'll begin by exploring how to send HTTP requests with treq.

Introducing treq

A feed aggregator must download feeds before it can show them, so we'll begin by exploring treq. Note that the examples that follow should work on Python 2 and 3.

Create a new virtual environment with your preferred tool and install treq from PyPI into it. There are many tools to accomplish this; in the interest of generality, we recommend using virtualenv (https://virtualenv.pypa.io/en/stable/) and pip (https://pip.pypa.io/en/stable/) like so:

```
$ virtualenv treq-experiment-env
...
$ ./treq-experiment-env/bin/pip install treq
...
$ ./treq-experiment-env/bin/python experiment.py
```

where experiment.py contains the following code:

```
from argparse import ArgumentParser
from twisted.internet import defer, task
from twisted.web import http
import treq
```

```python
@defer.inlineCallbacks
def download(reactor):
    parser = ArgumentParser()
    parser.add_argument("url")
    arguments = parser.parse_args()
    response = yield treq.get(
        arguments.url, timeout=30.0, reactor=reactor)
    if response.code != http.OK:
        reason = http.RESPONSES[response.code]
    raise RuntimeError("Failed:{}{}".format(response.code,
                                            reason))
    content = yield response.content()
    print(content)

task.react(download)
```

The download function extracts a URL command-line argument with the standard library's argparse module and then uses treq.get to GET it. treq's client API accepts bytes or unicode URLs, encoding the latter according to the complicated rules that define text URLs. This makes our program easier to write, because ArgumentParser. parse_args returns str objects representing command-line arguments on both Python 2 and 3; on Python 2 these are byte strings, while on Python 3 they're unicode strings. We don't have to worry about encoding or decoding the URL str to the type appropriate to a particular version of Python because treq will do so correctly for us.

treq's client API accepts a timeout parameter that terminates requests that fail to *begin* within the specified timeout. The reactor argument specifies which reactor object to use for networking and internal bookkeeping. This is a form *dependency injection*: treq *depends* on the reactor, but rather than importing twisted.internet.reactor itself, treq can be provided this dependency. We'll see later how dependency injection makes testing and factoring our code easier.

treq.get returns a Deferred that resolves to a treq.response._Response object (the underscore in its name implies that we shouldn't construct instances on our own, not that we shouldn't interact with it). This implements the twisted.web.iweb.IRequest interface, so it contains the response's status code in its code attribute. Our example program checks the value of this to ensure that the server's response indicates our request was successful; if it wasn't, it raises a `RuntimeError` with the response's status code and its corresponding status phrase, courtesy of the `twisted.web.http.RESPONSES` dictionary that maps one to the other.

The `Deferred` can also resolve to a `Failure`. If, for example, the amount of time specified by the `timeout` parameter elapses before the `Response` object can be constructed, the `Deferred` will fail with a `CancelledError`.

`treq`'s responses also have additional methods that make interacting with them more convenient. One of these is `content`, which returns a `Deferred` that resolves to the entire body of the request as a single `bytes` object. `treq` handles all the details of collecting the response behind the scenes for us.

Finally, our example never calls `reactor.run` or `reactor.stop` directly. Instead, it uses a Twisted library function we haven't seen before: `twisted.internet.task.react`. `react` handles starting and stopping the reactor for us. It accepts as its only required argument a callable that it invokes with the running reactor; the callable itself must return a `Deferred` that causes the reactor to stop when it resolves to a value or `Failure`. The `download` function returns just such a `Deferred` courtesy of its `twisted.internet.defer.inlineCallbacks` decorator. Because `react` itself accepts a callable as its first argument, it too can be used as a decorator. We could have written our example like so:

```
..
from twisted.internet import defer, task
...

@task.react
@defer.inlineCallbacks
def main(reactor):
    ...
```

This is in fact a popular way to write short scripts with Twisted. Going forward, when we do use `react`, we'll use it as a decorator.

Running this `treq` example program against a web feed's URL retrieves that feed's content. We can modify our program to use the Python `feedparser` library to print a summary of a feed. First, install `feedparser` into your virtual environment with `pip`:

```
$ ./treq-experiment-env/bin/pip install feedparser
```

Then, save the following program to feedparser_experiment.py and run it against an RSS URL:

```
$ ./treq-experiment-env/bin/python feedparser_experiment.py
http://planet.twistedmatrix.com

from __future__ import print_function
from argparse import ArgumentParser
import feedparser
from twisted.internet import defer, task
from twisted.web import http
import treq

@task.react
@defer.inlineCallbacks
def download(reactor):
    parser = ArgumentParser()
    parser.add_argument("url")
    arguments = parser.parse_args()
    response = yield treq.get(arguments.url, reactor=reactor)
    if response.code != http.OK:
        reason = http.RESPONSES[response.code]
        raise RuntimeError("Failed:{}{}".format(response.code,
                                                reason))

    content = yield response.content()
    parsed = feedparser.parse(content)
    print(parsed['feed']['title'])
    print(parsed['feed']['description'])
    print("*** ENTRIES ***")
    for entry in parsed['entries']:
        print(entry['title'])
```

Running this should result in output like the following:

```
Planet Twisted
Planet Twisted - http://planet.twistedmatrix.com/
```

```
*** ENTRIES ***
Moshe Zadka: Exploration Driven Development
Hynek Schlawack: Python Application Deployment with Native Packages
Hynek Schlawack: Python Hashes and Equality
...
```

Introducing Klein

Now that we have an idea of how to retrieve and parse feeds with treq, we need to learn enough about Klein to render them within a website.

To keep our experiments organized, create a new virtual environment for Klein and install it with pip install Klein. Then, run the following example:

```
import klein

application = klein.Klein()

@application.route('/')
def hello(request):
    return b'Hello!'

application.run("localhost",8080)
```

Now visit http://localhost:8080/ in your favorite web browser. (You might have to change 8080 to another port if there's already a program bound to it.) You'll see the string Hello! returned from our program's hello route handler.

A Klein application begins with an instance of the Klein class. Callables are associated with routes by using Klein.route method as a decorator. The first argument to route is a Werkzeug-style URL pattern; the possible format directives match those in Werkzeug's routing documentation, available here: http://werkzeug.readthedocs.io/en/latest/routing/. Let's modify our program to use one such directive to extract an integer from the path:

```
import klein

application = klein.Klein()
```

```python
@application.route('/<int:amount>')
def increment(request, amount):
    newAmount = amount + 1
    message = 'Hello! Your new amount is:{} '.format(newAmount)
    return message.encode('ascii')

application.run("localhost",8080)
```

Running this program and visiting `http://localhost:8080/1` results in a web page that looks like Figure 3-1.

A URL pattern specifies a path component that Klein extracts, converts to the specified Python type, and passes to the handler function as a positional argument. The *amount* argument is the first path element, and it must be an integer; otherwise the request will fail with a 404. A list of *converters* is available from the Werkzeug documentation.

Figure 3-1. *increment.png*

Also note that handlers cannot return a unicode string; on Python 3; this means that native strings must be encoded to byte strings before they're returned from a Klein route's handler. We thus encode the `message` variable as `ascii` after we've performed string formatting. On Python 3.5 and later, we could have used byte string formatting, but at the time of this writing, Python 3.4 is still commonly used. Also, this code implicitly *decodes* `message` as `ascii` on Python 2. This unfortunate behavior results in a strange error message when used with anything other than the `ascii` encoding, but is a common pattern in Twisted code for dealing with native strings that only contain ASCII and that must work on both Python 2 and 3.

Klein and Deferreds

Klein is a Twisted project, so it naturally has special support for `Deferreds`. Handler functions that return `Deferreds` result in a response that waits for that Deferred to resolve to a value or `Failure`. We can see this in action by modifying our program to simulate a slow network operation by returning a `Deferred` that fires at least one second after the request is received:

```
from twisted.internet import task
from twisted.internet import reactor
import klein

application = klein.Klein()

@application.route('/<int:amount>')
def slowIncrement(request, amount):
    newAmount = amount + 1
    message = 'Hello! Your new amount is:{} '.format(newAmount)
    return task.deferLater(reactor,1.0, str.encode, message, 'ascii')

application.run("localhost",8080)
```

As expected, this program only responds to `http://localhost:8080/1` after a second has elapsed. It achieves this by using `twisted.internet.task.deferLater` which accepts a `twisted.internet.interfaces.IReactorTime` provider, a delay, and then a function and arguments that will be applied to the function after the delay has passed. Note that our choice of function and arguments makes use of the fact that instance methods are stored on their classes, and their first argument must be the instance to which they're bound; as a result, `str.encode(message, 'ascii')`, where `message` is a `str`, is equivalent to `message.encode('ascii')`. This is another pattern that occurs in Twisted code.

This last example demonstrates a limitation inherent to using decorators as a way to register routes: the arguments to the decorated function must be entirely provided by the routing framework. This makes it difficult to write handler functions that reference some state or depend on some existing object. In our example, our code depends on the reactor to satisfy `deferLater`'s API, but we cannot pass the reactor to our handler because only Klein can call it. Of the many ways this might be solved, Klein has special support for one: instance-specific Klein applications. We'll rewrite our `slowIncrement` example again to make use of this feature.

117

```
from twisted.internet import task
from twisted.internet import reactor
import klein

class SlowIncrementWebService(object):
    application = klein.Klein()
    def init (self, reactor):
        self._reactor = reactor
    @application.route('/<int:amount>')
    def slowIncrement(self, request, amount):
        newAmount = amount + 1
        message = 'Hello! Your new amount is:{} '.format(newAmount)
        return task.deferLater(self._reactor,1.0, str.encode, message,
        'ascii')

webService = SlowIncrementWebService(reactor) webService.application.
run("localhost",8080)
```

The SlowIncrementWebService class has a Klein application assigned to its application class-level variable. We can decorate methods on this class by with that variable's route method, in the same way we decorated the module-level slowIncrement function with the module-level Klein object's route method. Because we're now decorating instance methods, we can access instance variables, such as reactor. This allows us to *parameterize* our web applications without relying on module-level objects.

Klein objects themselves localize their internal state by implementing the descriptor protocol. webService.application returns a request-specific instance of Klein that contains all the routes and their handlers that we registered with SlowIncrementWebService's application. As a result, Klein maintains robust encapsulation and minimizes shared mutable state.

Klein Templates with Plating

The last thing we need before we're ready to build a simple version of our feed aggregator is a web page templating system. We could use Jinja2, or Mako, or any other Python templating system intended for generating web pages, but Klein comes with its own templating facility called *Plating*. Let's modify SlowIncrementWebService example to use klein.Plating to generate a more readable response:

```python
from twisted.internet import task, reactor
from twisted.web.template import tags, slot
from klein import Klein, Plating

class SlowIncrementWebService(object):
    application = Klein()
    commonPage = Plating(
        tags=tags.html( tags.head(
            tags.title(slot("title")),
            tags.style("#amount { font-weight: bold; }"
                       "#message { font-style: italic; }")),
            tags.body(
                tags.div(slot(Plating.CONTENT)))))
    def __init__ (self, reactor):
        self._reactor = reactor

    @commonPage.routed(
        application.route('/<int:amount>'),
        tags.div(
            tags.span("Hello! Your new amount is: ", id="message"),
            tags.span(slot("newAmount"), id="amount")),
    )
    def slowIncrement(self, request, amount):
        slots = {
            "title":"Slow Increment",
            "newAmount": amount + 1,
        }
        return task.deferLater(self._reactor,1.0, lambda: slots)

webService=SlowIncrementWebService(reactor)
webService.application.run("localhost",8080)
```

The new commonPage Plating object represents the fundamental change to our SlowIncrementWebService. Because Plating is built on top of Twisted's own venerable twisted.web.template system, we must learn its fundamentals before we can proceed.

`twisted.templates` are constructed of `twisted.web.template.Tag` and `twisted.web.template.slot` instances. `Tags` represent HTML tags like `html`, `body`, and `div`. They are created by accessing their names as methods on a tag factory instance available as `twisted.web.template.tags`. This, call, for example:

```
tags.div()
```

represents a `div` tag that will be rendered like this:

<div></div>

The positional arguments to these instance methods represent their tag's children, so we can add a `span` to our `div` by nesting their method calls:

```
tags.div(tags.span("A span."))
```

This simple tag tree will be rendered like this:

<div><span>A span.**</span></div>**

Note that the textual content of a tag is also represented as a child.

The keyword arguments to these methods represent their attributes, so we can include an image inside our div tree:

```
tags.div(tags.img(src="picture.png"), tags.span("A span."))
```

When rendered, this tree looks like this:

<div><img src="picture.png"**><span>**A span.**</span></div>**

`twisted.web.template` reserves one keyword argument for internal use: `render`. This is a string that names a special *render method* that will be used to render the tag to HTML. We'll see an example of a Klein-specific render method in a moment.

Sometimes it's more readable to write a tag's attributes before its children, but keyword arguments must always come before positional arguments. To provide this readability improvement without violating Python's syntax, `tags` can be *called* with their children. We can rewrite our tag tree so that its children are added that way:

```
tags.div()(tags.img(src="picture.png"), tags.span("A span."))
```

slots are placeholders that can be filled in by name during template rendering as we'll see later. They allow us to parameterize both tag contents and attributes. Given this tag tree, then:

```
tags.div(tags.img(src=slot('imageURL')), tags.span(slot("spanText")))
```

we can provide "anotherimage.png" as the value for the imageURL slot and "Different text." for the spanText slot, resulting in the following:

```
<div><img src="anotherimage.png"><span>Different text.</span></div>
```

When slots are filled in with strings that contain HTML literals, twisted. web.template escapes them to avoid misinterpreting user data as templating directives. This in turn mitigates common web application bugs, such as cross-site scripting (XSS) attacks. However, slots *can* be filled in with other tags, enabling sophisticated template reuse patterns. These rules mean that this tree:

```
tags.div(slot("child")).fillSlots(child="<div>")
```

Renders to:

```
<div>&lt;div&gt;</div>
```

While this tree:

```
tags.div(slot("child")).fillSlots(child=tags.div())
```

Renders to:

```
<div><div></div></div>
```

A First Draft of Feed Aggregation

Now that we're familiar with the fundamentals of twisted.web.template, we can return to our example application's klein.Plating object:

```
commonPage = Plating(
    tags=tags.html(
        tags.head(
            tags.title(slot("title")),
```

```
            tags.style("#amount { font-weight: bold; }"
                       "#message { font-style: italic; }")),
        tags.body(
            tags.div(slot(Plating.CONTENT)))))
```

The tag tree passed as the `tags` argument describes the structure of all HTML pages this `Plating` instance will render. It includes two slots: `title` and `Plating.CONTENT`. The `title` slot is just like any other; we will have to provide a value for this slot any time we want to render a page that's part of this tag tree. The `Plating.CONTENT` slot, however, represents the location in the tag tree into which `Plating` will insert page-specific content. Our example application renders only one page derived from `commonPage`:

```
@commonPage.routed(
    application.route('/<int:amount>'),
    tags.div(
        tags.span("Hello!    Your new amount is: ", id="message"),
        tags.span(slot("newAmount"), id="amount")),
)
def slowIncrement(self, request, amount):
    slots={
        "title":"Slow Increment",
        "newAmount": amount+1,
    }
    return task.deferLater(self._reactor,1.0, lambda: slots)
```

We represent a derived page by wrapping a Klein `route` with the base page's `routed` decorator. The second positional argument to the `routed` decorator represents the tag tree that will fill the base page's `Klein.CONTENT` slot. This `slowIncrement` page wraps the same route we defined before, and specifies as its content a tag tree that includes a slot for the incremented amount.

In Klein, slots are filled in by returning a dictionary that maps their names to values from the page's handler, or a `Deferred` that resolves to one. This handler remains slow by using `deferLater` to put off returning the slot dictionary until a second has passed.

The result is a web page with more personality as seen in Figure 3-2.

Klein's plating offers a unique feature: you can request that the slots dictionary be returned as serialized JSON by specifying the `json` query parameter. In Figure 3-3, We can see what our "Slow Increment" page looks like when this parameter is provided.

This allows Plating users to write handlers that render both to HTML and JSON, serving as simple pages in their own right or providing the back end for sophisticated Single Page Applications (SPA) or native mobile applications. Our feed aggregator's HTML front end won't become a SPA because this is a book on Twisted and not JavaScript, but we'll continue to support and explore JSON serialization as we develop our application.

We can now write a simple version of our feed aggregator to explore its design. We'll write a SimpleFeedAggregation class that accepts feed URLs and uses treq to retrieve them when a user visits the root URL. We'll render each feed as a table whose heading links to the feed and whose rows link to each feed item.

Begin by installing feedparser and treq into your Klein virtual environment the same way you did in your treq virtual environment.

Figure 3-2. *Increment in style*

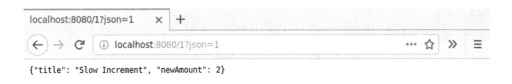

Figure 3-3. *Increment as JSON*

```
import feedparser

from twisted.internet import defer, reactor
from twisted.web.template import tags, slot
from twisted.web import http
from klein import Klein, Plating
import treq
```

```python
class SimpleFeedAggregation(object):
    application = Klein()
    commonPage = Plating(
        tags=tags.html(
            tags.head(
                tags.title("Feed Aggregator 1.0")),
            tags.body(
                tags.div(slot(Plating.CONTENT)))))

    def __init__(self, reactor, feedURLs):
        self._reactor = reactor
        self._feedURLs = feedURLs

    @defer.inlineCallbacks
    def retrieveFeed(self, url):
        response = yield treq.get(url, timeout=30.0, reactor=self._reactor)
        if response.code != http.OK:
            reason = http.RESPONSES[response.code]
            raise RuntimeError("Failed:{}{}".format(response.code,
                                                    reason))
        content = yield response.content()
        defer.returnValue(feedparser.parse(content))

@commonPage.routed(
    application.route('/'),
    tags.div(render="feeds:list")(slot("item")))
def feeds(self, request):

    def renderFeed(feed):
        feedTitle = feed[u"feed"][u"title"]
        feedLink = feed[u"feed"][u"link"]
        return tags.table(
            tags.tr(tags.th(tags.a(feedTitle, href=feedLink)))
        )([
            tags.tr(tags.td(tags.a(entry[u'title'], href=entry[u'link'])))
            for entry in feed[u'entries']
        ])
```

```
    return {
            u"feeds": [
                self.retrieveFeed(url).addCallback(renderFeed)
                for url in self._feedURLs
            ]
    }

webService = SimpleFeedAggregation(reactor,
                                   ["http://feeds.bbci.co.uk/news/technology/
                                   rss.xml",
                                   "http://planet.twistedmatrix.com/rss20.xml"])
webService.application.run("localhost",8080)
```

The retrieveFeed method resembles the download function from our first treq program, while the feeds method begins with a Plating decorator that resembles our slowIncrement Klein application. In the case of feeds, however, the route-specific template consists of a div tag with special *render method*. Klein interprets feeds:list as a direction to duplicate the div tag for each item in the list and place it in the item slot. If, for example, our feeds method were to return the following dictionary:

```
{"feeds": ["first","second","third"]}
```

Klein would render the following HTML for the feeds route:

```
<div>first</div><div>second</div>third</div>
```

Our feeds method not only returns a slot dictionary whose feeds key does return a list, but one that contains *Deferreds*. This leverages twisted.web.template's unique ability to render the results of Deferreds: when one is encountered, rendering pauses until it resolves to a value, which is then rendered, or a failure occurs.

Each Deferred in our feeds list originates with a retrieveURL call that creates a parsed feed for a URL courtesy of treq and feedparser. The renderFeed callback transforms a parsed feed into a tag tree that renders the feed into a table of links. This makes use of twisted.web.template's ability to embed tag elements within slots.

Visiting this page in a browser renders the BBC feed first, then the larger and slower Twisted Matrix feed, as seen in in Figures 3-4 and 3-5.

Our SimpleFeedAggregation class successfully retrieves and renders feeds. Its basic design reflects the flow of data through the service: given an iterable of feed URLs, retrieve them concurrently on every request to our service by applying treq.get to each. Data flow often informs the design of Twisted programs.

Our implementation, however, is lacking:

1. Its error reporting is poor. While the `RuntimeError` raised by
    `SimpleFeedAggregation.retrieveFeed` is informative, it's
    presented to users in way that's unactionable, especially to those
    that have requested JSON.

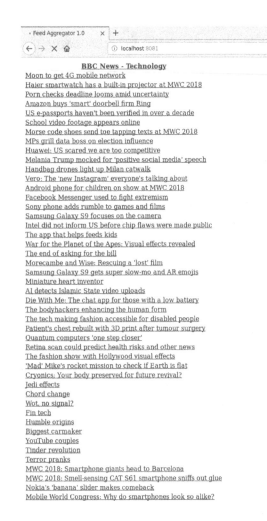

Figure 3-4. *An incomplete page with just the BBC feed*

Figure 3-5. *A complete page with both the BBC and Twisted Matrix feeds*

2. It has bugs. Users can't actually request JSON, because the tag trees representing each feed aren't JSON serializable.

Before we address these and other issues, we need a test suite. We'll ensure that the next implementation of our feed aggregator matches our expectations by using test-driven development to guide us.

Test-Driven Development with Klein and `treq`

Writing tests takes time and effort. Test-driven development eases this by making tests part of the development process. We begin with an *interface* that some unit of code should implement. Next, we write an empty implementation, such as a class with empty method bodies, and then tests that verify the desired outputs for that implementation given known inputs. Running these tests should fail at first, and development becomes a process of filling in the implementation so that the tests pass. As a result, we find out if one part of the implementation conflicts with other parts early on, and at the end we have a complete test suite.

Tests take time to write, so it's important to start at the most valuable interface. For a web application, that's the HTTP interface clients will use, so our firsts tests will involve using an in-memory HTTP client against our `FeedAggregation` Klein application.

Running Test on an Installable Project

Test-driven development requires running a project's tests repeatedly, so before we begin writing any, we need to set things up so that `trial`, Twisted's test runner, can find them.

The `trial` command accepts as its only mandatory argument the *fully qualified path name* of something that contains or represents runnable test cases. `trial`'s design follows the same xUnit-influenced pattern as Python's `unittest`, so its test cases are subclasses of `twisted.trial.unittest.TestCase` or `twisted.trial.unittest.SynchronousTestCase`. These names are themselves fully qualified path names, or FQPNs; beginning with the top-most package, they specify the attribute access path downward to a specific function, class, or method. The following command line, for example, runs the `test_sillyEmptyThing` method of the `ParsingTests` test case that resides in Twisted's own test suite for the Asynchronous Message Protocol (AMP):

```
trial twisted.test.test_amp.ParsingTests.test_sillyEmptyThing
```

Given a shorter and consequently more general FQPN, `trial` recurs into the module and package tree looking for tests, just like `python -m unittest discover`. For example, you can run all of Twisted's own tests with `trial twisted`.

Because tests are specified with FQPNs, they must be importable. `trial` goes beyond this by requiring that they also reside under one of the Python runtime's *module search paths*. This aligns with Twisted's convention of including tests within library code under special `test` subpackages.

Python allows programmers to influence its search paths in several ways. Setting the `PYTHONPATH` environment variable or directly manipulating `sys.path` both allow it to import code from project-specific locations. However, telling Python about new locations in which it can find code is brittle, because it depends on bespoke configuration and particular runtime entry points. A better approach is to rely on virtual environments to localize Python's search paths to a project-specific directory tree, and to then install the project and its dependencies into that. Managing our own applications the same way we manage its dependencies gives us greater consistency by leveraging the same tools and patterns.

A full discussion of virtual environments and Python packaging is beyond the scope of this book. Instead, we'll outline a minimal project layout and configuration, show how to link our project into a virtual environment, and then provide a sample `trial` invocation for an empty test suite.

The project's directory structure is as follows:

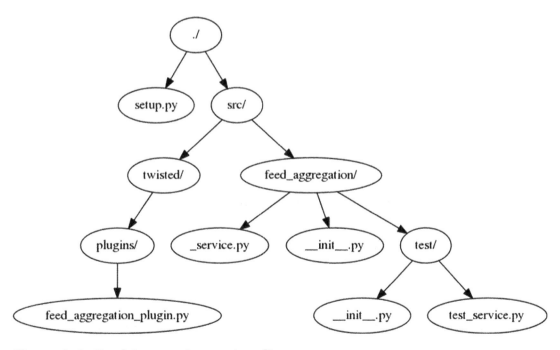

Figure 3-6. *Feed Aggregation project directory structure*

That is, under some directory taken as the present working one, there exists a
setup.py and src/ directory. The src/ directory in turn contains the top-level feed_
aggregation package and a _service submodule. feed_aggregation.test.test_
service will house the test cases for the code in _service.

src/twisted/plugins/feed_aggregation_plugin.py will contain a Twisted
application plugin that will make running our Klein application easier.

We'll put our FeedAggregation class in feed_aggregation._service:

```
class FeedAggregation(object):
    pass
```

This is a private module, so we'll make our class publicly accessible by exporting it in
feed_aggregation/__init__.py:

```
from feed_aggregation._service import FeedAggregation
__all__ =["FeedAggregation"]
```

Placing the implementation in a private submodule and then exposing it in the
top-level package's __init__.py is a common pattern in Twisted code. It ensures that
documentation tools, linters, and IDEs see the origin of public APIs as public packages,
limiting the exposure of private implementation details.

We'll leave feedaggregation/test/ __init__.py empty but put a trivial subclass
of SynchronousTestCase into feed_aggregation/test/test_service.py so that trial
has something to run after we've finished our setup:

```
from twisted.trial.unittest import SynchronousTestCase
```

```
class FeedAggregationTests(SynchronousTestCase):
    def test_nothing(self):
        pass
```

Leaving twisted/plugins/feed_aggregation_plugin.py empty as well, we're ready
to consider setup.py:

```
from setuptools import setup, find_packages
```

```
setup(
    name="feed_aggregation",
    install_requires=["feedparser", "Klein", "Twisted", "treq"],
```

```
    package_dir={"": "src"},
    packages=find_packages("src") + ["twisted.plugins"],
)
```

This declares our project's name to be feed_aggregation and its dependencies to be feedparser (for parsing feeds), Klein (for our web application), Twisted (for trial), and treq (for retrieving feeds). It also instructs setuptools to look for packages under src, and include feed_aggregation_plugin.py under twisted/plugins.

Supposing we have a fresh virtual environment activated for our project and we're in the project root, we can now run this:

```
pip install -e .
```

The -e flag instructs pip install to perform an *editable installation* of our project, which places a pointer from the virtual environment back into our project root's directory. As a result, edits will appear within the virtual environment as soon as we save them.

Finally, trial feed_aggregation should display the following:

```
feed_aggregation.test.test_service
  FeedAggregationTests
    test_nothing ...                                                     [OK]

-------------------------------------------------------------------------------
Ran 1 tests in 0.001s

PASSED (successes=1)
```

demonstrating that we have in fact made our project available to trial via our virtual environment.

Testing Klein with StubTreq

Now we that can run tests, we can replace FeedAggregationTests.test_nothing with methods that test something. That something, as discussed above, should be the HTTP interface our Klein application will present to clients.

One way to test HTTP services is to run a web server as it would be for a live service, perhaps bound to localhost on a predictable port, and use an HTTP client library to connect to it. This can be slow, and worse still, ports are an operating system resource whose scarcity can cause instability in tests that acquire them.

Fortunately, the power of Twisted's transports and protocols allows us to run an in-memory HTTP client and server pair within our tests. In particular, treq comes with a powerful testing utility in treq.testing.StubTreq. Instances of the StubTreq expose the same interface as the treq module, so that code that acquires treq through dependency injection can instead use this stub implementation in tests. It's up to the treq project to verify that StubTreq conforms to the same API as the treq module; we don't have to do this in our tests.

StubTreq takes as its first argument a twisted.web.resource.Resource whose responses determine the outcome of various treq calls. Because Klein instances expose a resource() method that generates a twisted.web.resource.Resource, we can bind a StubTreq to our web application to get an in-memory HTTP client suitable for our tests.

Let's replace test_nothing with a method that uses StubTreq to request our service's root URL:

```
# src/feed_aggregation/tests/test_service.py
from twisted.trial.unittest import SynchronousTestCase
from twisted.internet import defer
from treq.testing import StubTreq
from .. import FeedAggregation


class FeedAggregationTests(SynchronousTestCase):
    def setUp(self):
        self.client = StubTreq(FeedAggregation().resource())
    @defer.inlineCallbacks
    def test_requestRoot(self):
        response = yield self.client.get(u'http://test.invalid/')
        self.assertEqual(response.code,200)
```

The setUp method creates a StubTreq instance bound to the twisted.web.resource.Resource for our FeedAggregation's Klein application. test_requestRoot uses this client to issue a GET request against that Klein resource, verifying that it received a successful response.

Note that only the path portion of the URL passed to self.client.get matters for our test. treq, and thus StubTreq, can only issues requests against a complete web URL with a scheme and netloc, so we use a .invalid domain to satisfy this requirement. The .invalid top-level domain is defined to never resolve to an actual internet address, making it a perfect choice for our tests.

Running this new version of FeedAggregationTests with trial feed_aggregation fails with an AttributeError because instances of our FeedAggregation class don't have a resource method. Adding the correct implementation of this won't make the test pass, however; we also need to construct a Klein application that responds to a request for /. We'll modify the _service module to satisfy both of these requirements.

```python
# src/feed_aggregation/_service.py
from klein import Klein

class FeedAggregation(object):
    _app=Klein()
    def resource(self):
        return self._app.resource()
    @_app.route("/")
    def root(self, request):
        return b""
```

The new resource instance method delegates its calls to the Klein application associated with the class. This is an example of *the law of Demeter*, a principle in software development that argues against calling methods on instance attributes; instead, delegation methods like FeedAggregation.resource wrap these attributes' methods, so that code that uses FeedAggregation remains ignorant of its internal implementation. We've named our Klein application _app to make it clear that it's part of FeedAggregation's internal, private API.

The root method acts as a trivial handler for the root URL path /, and together with FeedAggregation.resource, makes FeedAggregation.test_requestRoot pass.

We've now completed a single test-driven development cycle. We began with by writing a minimal failing test and then made it pass with a minimal amount of application code.

Let's skip ahead and replace FeedAggregationTests with a more complete test suite that exercises both the HTML and JSON feed renderings.

```python
# src/feed_aggregation/test/test_service.py
import json
from lxml import html
from twisted.internet import defer
```

```
from twisted.trial.unittest import SynchronousTestCase
from treq.testing import StubTreq
from .. import FeedAggregation

class FeedAggregationTests(SynchronousTestCase):
    def setUp(self):
        self.client = StubTreq(FeedAggregation().resource())
    @defer.inlineCallbacks
    def get(self, url):
        response = yield self.client.get(url)
        self.assertEqual(response.code,200)
        content = yield response.content()
        defer.returnValue(content)
    def test_renderHTML(self):
        content = self.successResultOf(self.get(u"http://test.invalid/"))
        parsed = html.fromstring(content)
        self.assertEqual(parsed.xpath(u'/html/body/div/table/tr/th/a/text()'),
                    [u"First feed",u"Second feed"])
        self.assertEqual(parsed.xpath('/html/body/div/table/tr/th/a/@href'),
                    [u"http://feed-1/",u"http://feed-2/"])
        self.assertEqual(parsed.xpath('/html/body/div/table/tr/td/a/text()'),
                    [u"First item",u"Second item"])
        self.assertEqual(parsed.xpath('/html/body/div/table/tr/td/a/@href'),
                    [u"#first",u"#second"])
    def test_renderJSON(self):
        content = self.successResultOf(self.get(u"http://test.
                invalid/?json=true"))
        parsed = json.loads(content)
        self.assertEqual(
            parsed,
            {u"feeds": [{u"title": u"First feed", u"link": u"http://feed-1/",
             u"items": [{u"title": u"First item",u"link": u"#first"}]},
            {u"title": u"Second feed", u"link": u"http://feed-2/",
             u"items": [{u"title": u"Second item", u"link": u"#second"}]}]})
```

There's a lot going on in this test case. There are two tests, test_renderHTML and test_renderJSON, which verify the structure and content of the HTML and JSON we expect our FeedAggregation web service to return. test_requestRoot has been replaced with a get method that can be used by both test_renderHTML and test_renderJSON to retrieve a particular URL for our Klein application. Both test_renderHTML and test_renderJSON use SynchronousTestCase.successResultOf to assert that the Deferred returned by get has fired and extracted the value.

test_renderHTML uses the lxml library (https://lxml.de/) to parse and inspect the HTML returned by our Klein application. As a result, we must add lxml to the install_requires list in our setup.py. Note that you can synchronize your virtual environment with your project's dependencies by running pip install -e . again.

XPaths locate and extract the contents and attributes of specific elements within the DOM. The implied table structure matches what we developed in our prototype: feeds reside in tables whose headers are links to the feed's home page and whose rows link to each feed's items.

test_renderJSON requests the feeds rendered as JSON, parses it into a dictionary, and then asserts that it's equal to the expected output.

These new tests naturally fail because the existing FeedAggregation merely returns a response with an empty body. Let's make them pass by replacing FeedAggregation with the minimum necessary implementation.

```
# src/feed_aggregation/_service.py
from klein import Klein, Plating
from twisted.web.template import tags as t, slot

class FeedAggregation(object):
    _app = Klein()
    _plating = Plating(
        tags=t.html(
            t.head(t.title("Feed Aggregator 2.0")),
            t.body(slot(Plating.CONTENT))))
    def resource(self):
        return self._app.resource()
    @_plating.routed(
```

```
        _app.route("/"),
        t.div(render="feeds:list")(slot("item")),
    )
    def root(self, request):
        return {u"feeds": [
    t.table(t.tr(t.th(t.a(href=u"http://feed-1/")(u"First feed"))),
            t.tr(t.td(t.a(href=u"#first")(u"First item")))),
    t.table(t.tr(t.th(t.a(href=u"http://feed-2/")(u"Second feed"))),
            t.tr(t.td(t.a(href=u"#second")(u"Second item")))))
]}
```

Because we haven't written tests for feed retrieval, this implementation doesn't yet retrieve RSS feeds. Instead it satisfies our tests by returning hard-coded data that matches our assertions. Aside from this, it resembles our prototype: a root method handles the root URL path that uses Klein's :list renderer to turn a sequence of twisted.web.template.tags into HTML.

This version of FeedAggregation passes test_renderHTML but fails on test_renderJSON:

```
(feed_aggregation) $ trial feed_aggregation
feed_aggregation.test.test_service
  FeedAggregationTests
    test_renderHTML ...                                           [OK]
    test_renderJSON ...                                           [ERROR]
                                                                  [ERROR]


===========================================================================
[ERROR]
Traceback (most recent call last):
...
exceptions.TypeError: Tag('table', ...) not JSON serializable

feed_aggregation.test.test_service.FeedAggregationTests.test_renderJSON
===========================================================================
[ERROR]
Traceback (most recent call last):
...
```

136

```
twisted.trial.unittest.FailTest: 500 != 200
```

```
feed_aggregation.test.test_service.FeedAggregationTests.test_renderJSON
```

```
Ran 2 tests in 0.029s
```

```
FAILED (failures=1, errors=1, successes=1)
```

The second error corresponds to `self.assertEqual(response.code, 200)` in `FeedAggregationTests.get`, while the first indicates the real problem: Klein can't serialize the `tags` returned by `FeedAggregation.root` to JSON.

The simplest solution consists of detecting when a request should be serialized to JSON and returning a serializable dictionary instead. The current design would require copying the data necessary to satisfy the tests, so while we address the bug, let's also add container classes that store the feed data, and a top-level class that stores the feed's provenance and controls its presentation. These will allow us to define the data once but render it to both HTML and JSON. Indeed, we can arrange for `FeedAggregation` to accept instances of the top-level feed container class in its initializer, so that the tests can instead use their own fixture data. Let's rewrite _service.py following this approach. We'll use Hynek Schlawack's `attrs` (https://attrs.readthedocs.io) library to keep our code short and clear; be sure to add it to your `setup.py`'s `install_requires`.

```
# src/feed_aggregation/_service.py
import attr
from klein import Klein, Plating
from twisted.web.template import tags as t, slot

@attr.s(frozen=True)
class Channel(object):
    title = attr.ib()
    link = attr.ib()
    items = attr.ib()

@attr.s(frozen=True)
class Item(object):
    title = attr.ib()
    link = attr.ib()
```

```python
@attr.s(frozen=True)
class Feed(object):
    _source = attr.ib()
    _channel = attr.ib()

    def asJSON(self):
        return attr.asdict(self._channel)

    def asHTML(self):
        header = t.th(t.a(href=self._channel.link)
                    (self._channel.title))
        return t.table(t.tr(header))(
                [t.tr(t.td(t.a(href=item.link)(item.title)))
                for item in self._channel.items])

@attr.s
class FeedAggregation(object):
    _feeds = attr.ib()
    _app = Klein()
    _plating = Plating(
        tags=t.html(
        t.head(t.title("Feed Aggregator 2.0")),
        t.body(slot(Plating.CONTENT))))
def resource(self):
    return self._app.resource()
@_plating.routed(
    _app.route("/"),
t.div(render="feeds:list")(slot("item")),
)
def root(self, request):
    jsonRequested = request.args.get(b"json")
    def convert(feed):
        return feed.asJSON() if jsonRequested else feed.asHTML()
    return {"feeds": [convert(feed) for feed in self._feeds]}
```

Using attrs makes it easy to define container classes like Channel and Item. In its most basic operation, the attr.s class decorator generates an init method that sets instance variables corresponding to the class's attr.ib variables.

attrs also makes it easy to define classes whose instances are *immutable* via its decorator's frozen argument. Immutablity is a good match for our container classes because they represent external data; changing it after we've received it would certainly be a bug. attrs, lxml, must be added to the install_requires list inside setup.py.

The Feed class wraps a feed's source URL and the Channel instance representing its contents, and exposes two presentation methods. asJSON uses attrs.asdict to recursively convert the channel instance to a JSON-serializable dictionary, while asHTML returns a tree of twisted.web.template.tags to be rendered by Klein's Plating system.

FeedAggregation.root now checks the request's json query parameter, available in the args dictionary, to determine whether the response should be rendered as JSON or HTML, and invokes asJSON or asHTML as appropriate.

Finally, FeedAggregation is now itself an attrs decorated class whose initializer accepts an iterable of Feed objects to render.

As a result, FeedAggregationTests.setUp must be refactored to pass an iterable of Feed objects to its FeedAggregation instance:

```
# src/feed_aggregation/test/test_service.py
...
from .._service import Feed, Channel, Item

FEEDS = (
    Feed("http://feed-1.invalid/rss.xml",
        Channel(title="First feed", link="http://feed-1/",
                items=(Item(title="First item", link="#first"),))),
    Feed("http://feed-2.invald/rss.xml",
        Channel(title="Second feed", link="http://feed-2/",
                items=(Item(title="Second item", link="#second"),))),
)

class FeedAggregationTests(SynchronousTestCase):
    def setUp(self):
        self.client = StubTreq(FeedAggregation(FEEDS).resource())
...
```

This latest version has its benefits: most obviously, the test_renderJSON now passes, but additionally the fixture's data now resides in the same place as the tests, so that it will be easier to keep in sync with their assertions.

It also has its downsides. Not only is FeedAggregation useless as a feed aggregation service without the ability to retrieve RSS feeds, but the tests now import and depend on our container classes. Tests that depend on internal implementation details like these are brittle and hard to refactor.

We'll address both of these shortcomings by writing the feed retrieval logic.

Testing treq with Klein

We used StubTreq to test our Klein application in the previous section. Reversing the relationship allows us to succinctly test treq code.

Once again, we'll begin by writing tests. We'll add them to the test_service module, with new imports shown at the top, and our new test case at the bottom.

```
# src/feed_aggregation/test/test_service.py
import attr
...
from hyperlink import URL
from klein import Klein
from lxml.builder import E
from lxml.etree import tostring
...
from .. import FeedRetrieval

@attr.s
class StubFeed(object):
    _feeds = attr.ib()
    _app = Klein()
    def resource(self):
        return self._app.resource()
    @_app.route("/rss.xml")
    def returnXML(self, request):
        host = request.getHeader(b    'host')
        try:
            return self._feeds[host]
        except KeyError:
            request.setResponseCode(404)
            return b'Unknown host: ' +host
```

```
def makeXML(feed):
    channel = feed._channel
    return tostring(
    E.rss(E.channel(E.title(channel.title), E.link(channel.link),
                    *[E.item(E.title(item.title), E.link(item.link))
                        for item in channel.items],
        version = u"2.0")))

class FeedRetrievalTests(SynchronousTestCase):
    def setUp(self):
        service = StubFeed(
            {URL.from_text(feed._source).host.encode('ascii'): makeXML(feed)
             for feed in FEEDS})
        treq = StubTreq(service.resource())
        self.retriever = FeedRetrieval(treq=treq)
    def test_retrieve(self):
        for feed in FEEDS:
            parsed = self.successResultOf(
                self.retriever.retrieve(feed._source))
            self.assertEqual(parsed, feed)
```

The FeedRetrievalTests class, like FeedAggregationTests before it, depends on some new concepts. StubFeed is a Klein application whose /rss.xml route returns an XML document specific to the request's host. This allows it to return different responses for http://feed-1.invalid and http://feed-2.invalid. As a precaution, requests for an unknown host result in an informative 404 "Not Found" response.

The makeXML function transforms a Feed and its associated Items into an RSS 2.0-compliant XML document. We use lxml.builder's E tag factory, whose API resembles twisted.web.template.tags, as an XML templating system, and serialize its tag tree to bytes with lxml.etree.tostring (despite its name, it *does* return bytes on Python 3).

The FeedRetrievalTests.setUp fixture method creates a list of Feeds and passes them to a StubFeed instance, which it them associates with a StubTreq instance. This in turn is passed to a FeedRetrieval instance, which will contain our feed retrieval code. Parameterizing this class on a treq implementation is an example dependency injection easing the process of writing tests.

Note that we derive the host for each feed from the URL in its `link` element by using `hyperlink.URL`. Hyperlink (`https://hyperlink.readthedocs.io`) URLs are immutable objects that represent parsed URLs. The Hyperlink library was abstracted out from Twisted's own `twisted.python.url` module and provides a superset of that original API. As a result, Twisted now depends on it, so it's implicitly available to any project that depends on Twisted. The best practice with any dependency, however, is to make it explicit, so we must add the `hyperlink` package to our `setup.py`'s `install_requires` list. Here's what our `setup.py` should look like now:

```
# setup.py
from setuptools import setup, find_packages

setup(
    name="feed_aggregation",
    install_requires=["attrs","feedparser","hyperlink","Klein",
                      "lxml","Twisted","treq"],
    package_dir={"":"src"},
    packages=find_packages("src")+["twisted.plugins"],
)
```

(Remember that we we added `attrs` and lxml above.)

The one test in our `FeedAggregationTests` test case, `test_retrieve`, asserts that `FeedRetrieval.retrieve` parses a feed retrieved from its `_source` URL into a Feed object that matches its XML representation.

Now that we have a test for a feed retriever, we can implement one. First, we'll add `FeedRetrieval` to src/feed_aggregation/__init__.py so that it can be imported without interacting with private APIs:

```
# src/feed_aggregation/ init .py
from ._service import FeedAggregation, FeedRetrieval

__all__ = ["FeedAggregation","FeedRetrieval"]
```

Now we can implement the minimum code necessary to make the tests pass:

```
# src/feed_aggregation/_service.py

...
import treq
import feedparser
```

```
@attr.s
class FeedRetrieval(object):
    _treq = attr.ib()
    def retrieve(self, url):
        feedDeferred = self._treq.get(url)
        feedDeferred.addCallback(treq.content)
        feedDeferred.addCallback(feedparser.parse)
    def toFeed(parsed):
        feed = parsed[u'feed']
        entries = parsed[u'entries']
        channel = Channel(feed[u'title'], feed[u'link'],
                          tuple(Item(e[u'title'], e[u'link'])
                                for e in entries))
        return Feed(url, channel)

        feedDeferred.addCallback(toFeed)
        return feedDeferred
```

As expected, FeedRetrieval accepts a treq implementation as its only argument via the attr.s class decorator and a _treq attr.ib. Its retrieve method follows the same pattern as our exploratory program's: first it uses treq to retrieve the provided URL and collect its body, then it uses feedparser to parse the collected XML into a Python dictionary.

Next, toFeed extracts the feed's title, link, and its items' titles and links, and then assembles them into a Channel, Items, and a Feed.

This version of FeedRetrieval makes our test pass, but it lacks error handling. What if a feed has been removed or the returned XML is invalid? As it stands, the Deferred returned by FeedRetrieval.retrieve will fail with an exception, which will be FeedAggregation's problem.

Neither a website nor a JSON service should display tracebacks. At the same time, something should record any tracebacks to aid debugging. Fortunately, Twisted has a sophisticated logging system that we can use to track our application's behavior.

Logging with **twisted.logger**

Twisted has provided its own logging system for many releases. As of Twisted 15.2.0, twisted.logger has become the preferred method for recording events in Twisted programs.

Like the standard library's `logging` module, applications emit log messages at
various *levels* by calling the appropriate methods on a `twisted.logger.Logger` instance.
The following code emits a message at the `info` level.

```
from twisted.logger import Logger
Logger().info("A message with{key}", key="value")
```

Like `logging`, emission methods like `Logger.info` accept a format string and values
to interpolate; unlike `logging`, this is a *new style* formatting string, and it's sent along
in the underlying log event. Also unlike Python's standard `logging` system, `twisted.`
`logger.Logger`s are not hierarchical, but instead route their messages through
observers. The fact that the format string is preserved enables one of `twisted.logger`'s
most powerful features: it can emit log messages in the traditional format intended
for human consumption, and it can emit them as JSON-serialized objects. The latter
allows sophisticated filtering and collection in systems like Kibana. We'll see how to
switch between these formats when we write a Twisted application plugin for our feed
aggregation application.

`Logger`s also use the descriptor protocol to capture information about an associated
class, so we'll create a `Logger` for our `FeedRetrieval` class. We'll then arrange
for messages to be emitted before a feed is requested and when it's either parsed
successfully or fails with an exception. Before we can do so, however, we must decide
what `FeedRetrieval.retrieve`'s `Deferred` should resolve to when an exception occurs.
It cannot be a `Feed` instance, because there won't be any XML to parse into a `Channel`
instance; but `FeedAggregation` expects an object that provides `asJSON` and `asHTML`
methods, the only implementations of which exist on `Feed`.

We can solve this problem with polymorphism. We can define a new class,
`FailedFeed`, that represents `FeedRetrieval`'s failure to retrieve a feed. It will satisfy
the same interface as `Feed` by implementing its own `asJSON` and `asHTML` methods that
present the error in the appropriate format.

As usual, we'll begin by writing tests. The exception conditions `FeedRetrieval.`
`retrieve` might encounter can be divided into two categories: a response with any
status code other than 200, and any other exception. We'll model the first with a
custom exception type, `ResponseNotOK`, that retrieve will raise and handle internally
and which we can solicit in our tests by requesting a feed from a host `StubFeed` doesn't
know about. The latter can be solicited by providing `StubFeed` with a host that returns
the empty string, which `feedparser` will fail to parse. Let's add some tests to our
`FeedRetrievalTests` class.

```python
# src/feed_aggregation/test/test_service.py
from .. import FeedRetrieval
from .._service import Feed, Channel, Item, ResponseNotOK
from xml.sax import SAXParseException

...

class FeedRetrievalTests(SynchronousTestCase):
    ...
    def assertTag(self, tag, name, attributes, text):
        self.assertEqual(tag.tagName, name)
        self.assertEqual(tag.attributes, attributes)
        self.assertEqual(tag.children, [text])
    def test_responseNotOK(self):
        noFeed = StubFeed({})
        retriever = FeedRetrieval(StubTreq(noFeed.resource()))
        failedFeed = self.successResultOf(
            retriever.retrieve("http://missing.invalid/rss.xml"))
        self.assertEqual(
            failedFeed.asJSON(),
            {"error":"Failed to load http://missing.invalid/rss.xml: 404"}
        )
        self.assertTag(failedFeed.asHTML(),
            "a", {"href":"http://missing.invalid/rss.xml"},
            "Failed to load feed: 404")
    def test_unexpectedFailure(self):
        empty = StubFeed({b"empty.invalid": b""})
        retriever = FeedRetrieval(StubTreq(empty.resource()))
        failedFeed = self.successResultOf(
            retriever.retrieve("http://empty.invalid/rss.xml"))
        msg = "SAXParseException('no element found',)"
        self.assertEqual(
            failedFeed.asJSON(),
            {"error":"Failed to load http://empty.invalid/rss.xml: " + msg}
        )
```

```
        self.assertTag(failedFeed.asHTML(),
           "a", {"href": "http://empty.invalid/rss.xml"},
           "Failed to load feed: " + msg)
        self.assertTrue(self.flushLoggedErrors(SAXParseException))
```

The `assertTag` method ensures that a `twisted.web.template` tag tree of depth one has the given name, attributes, and children, simplifying the `test_responseNotOK` and `test_unexpectedFailure` methods.

The `test_responseNotOK` method creates an empty `StubFeed` application, which will respond with a 404 to any request the test makes. It then asserts that retrieving a URL results in a fired `Deferred`, and renders the resulting `FailedFeed` to both JSON and a tag tree. The JSON should contain the URL and the HTTP status code, while the HTML should link to the feed that failed and also contain the status code.

The `test_unexpectedFailure` method creates a `StubFeed` that responds to requests for `empty.invalid` with an empty string. The HTML and JSON renders of the resulting `FailedFeed` instance checked for the source URL as well as the `repr` of the exception that caused to the failure. We choose the `repr` because many exceptions' messages, like `KeyError`'s, are incomprehensible without their class name.

The last line of `test_unexpectedFailure` is worth special attention. `trial`, unlike Python's `unittest`, fails any test that doesn't recover exceptions logged by the code it calls. Note that this does not include errors raised by the test itself.

`SynchronousTestCase.flushLoggedErrors` returns a list of `twisted.python. failure.Failures` that have been logged up until that point; if exception types are passed as arguments, only `Failures` matching those types are returned. The "flush" in `flushLoggedErrors` means that it's a destructive call, so that a given `Failure` cannot appear in the lists returned by two consecutive calls. A test fails when it completes with a non-empty list of logged errors. Our tests' assertion that at least one `SAXParseException` was raised by `feedparser` has the side effect of clearing the logged error list, which should allow the test to pass.

Let's write the code necessary to make these new tests pass. We'll show the new version of the `FeedRetrieval` in its entirety so its error handling can be seen in context.

```python
# src/feed_aggregation/_service.py
...
import treq import feedparser
from twisted.logger import Logger
from functools import partial
...

@attr.s(frozen=True)
class FailedFeed(object):
    _source = attr.ib()
    _reason = attr.ib()

    def asJSON(self):
        return {"error":"Failed to load{}:{}".format(
            self._source,self._reason)}

    def asHTML(self):
        return t.a(href=self._source)(
            "Failed to load feed:{}.".format(self._reason))

class ResponseNotOK(Exception):
    """A response returned a non-200 status code."""

@attr.s
class FeedRetrieval(object):
    _treq = attr.ib()
    _logger = Logger()
    def retrieve(self, url):
        self._logger.info("Downloading feed{url}", url=url)
        feedDeferred = self._treq.get(url)

        def checkCode(response):
            if response.code != 200:
                raise ResponseNotOK(response.code)
            return response

        feedDeferred.addCallback(checkCode)
        feedDeferred.addCallback(treq.content)
        feedDeferred.addCallback(feedparser.parse)
```

```python
def toFeed(parsed):
    if parsed[u'bozo']:
        raise parsed[u'bozo_exception']
    feed=parsed[u'feed']
    entries = parsed[u'entries']
    channel = Channel(feed[u'title'], feed[u'link'],
                    tuple(Item(e[u'title'], e[u'link'])
                        for e in entries))
    return Feed(url, channel)

feedDeferred.addCallback(toFeed)

def failedFeedWhenNotOK(reason):
    reason.trap(ResponseNotOK)
    self._logger.error("Could not download feed{url}:{code}",
                    url=url, code=str(reason.value))
    return FailedFeed(url, str(reason.value))

def failedFeedOnUnknown(failure):
    self._logger.failure("Unexpected failure downloading{url}",
                    failure=failure, url=url)
    return FailedFeed(url, repr(failure.value))

feedDeferred.addErrback(failedFeedWhenNotOK)
feedDeferred.addErrback(failedFeedOnUnknown)
return feedDeferred
```

The FailedFeed class implements asJSON and asHTML in accordance with Feed's interface. Because the initializer is private, we can define a new reason argument that explains why the feed failed to download.

The ResponseNotOK exception represents the category of errors arising from a non-200 status code. This is also the first change to the retrieve itself: a checkCode callback raises ResponseNotOK when the status code of the response returned by treq.get indicates a failure, passing the code to the exception.

toFeed has also changed to accommodate feedparser's awkward error reporting API. feedparser's approach to lenient parsing means that feedparser.parse never raise an exception directly; instead, it set the bozo key in the returned dictionary to True and the bozo_exception key to the actual exception.

This second raise falls into the second category of unexpected errors. Of course, there are many more possible unexpected errors, and it's important that we ensure our code handles these, too.

The `failedFeedWhenNotOK` errback handles the first category by trapping `ResponseNotOK` and logging an `error` message with the feed's URL and the failing response code, while the `failedFeedOnUnknown` errback handles the second by logging a `critical` message that includes the failure's traceback via the `Logger.failure` helper method. Both return a `FailedFeed` instance that renders their respective failures according to the expectations of the tests we added.

Both when we add the errbacks to `feedDeferred` and the order we add them are significant. Recall that when a callback raises an exception, the next registered errback handles it. By adding the errbacks after all callbacks, we make it clear that these handle any exception raised. Also, since an errback that raises its own exception effectively passes it to the next registered errback, we add the more specific `failedFeedWhenNotOK` *before* the catch-all `failedFeedOnUnknown`. The net effect of these errbacks is equivalent to the following synchronous code:

```
try:
...
except ResponseNotOK:
    self._logger.error(...)
    return FailedFeed(...)
except:
    self._logger.failure(...)
    return FailedFeed(...)
```

Running Twisted Applications with `twist`

We've divided the project into two independent functional halves: `FeedAggregation`, which handles incoming web requests; and `FeedRetrieval`, which retrieves and parses RSS feeds. `Feed` and `FailedFeed` bind the two together by a common interface, but it's not possible to compose the application into a working whole without one last change.

Just like our exploratory `SimpleFeedAggregation` program, `FeedAggregation` should drive `FeedRetrieval` when an incoming HTTP request arrives. This flow of control implies that a `FeedAggregation` instance should wrap a `FeedRetrieval` instance,

149

which we can achieve via dependency injection; instead of passing a list of Feed items to FeedAggregation, we can instead pass the retrieve method of a FeedRetrieval instance and a list of feed URLs to request. Let's modify FeedAggregationTests to do that:

```
# src/feed_aggregation/test/test_service.py
...
class FeedAggregationTests(SynchronousTestCase):
    def setUp(self):
        service = StubFeed(
            {URL.from_text(feed._source).host.encode('ascii'): makeXML(feed)
             for feed in FEEDS})
        treq = StubTreq(service.resource())
        urls = [feed._source for feed in FEEDS]
        retriever = FeedRetrieval(treq)
        self.client = StubTreq(
            FeedAggregation(retriever.retrieve, urls).resource())

        ...
```

Now we can make FeedAggregation adhere to this new API:

```
# src/feed_aggregation/_service.py
@attr.s
class FeedAggregation(object):
    _retrieve = attr.ib()
    _urls = attr.ib()
    _app = Klein()
    _plating = Plating(
        tags=t.html(
            t.head(t.title("Feed Aggregator 2.0")),
            t.body(slot(Plating.CONTENT))))
    def resource(self):
        return self._app.resource()
    @_plating.routed(
        _app.route("/"),
        t.div(render="feeds:list")(slot("item")),
    )
```

```
def root(self, request):
    def convert(feed):
        return feed.asJSON() if request.args.get(b"json") else feed.
        asHTML()
    return {"feeds": [self._retrieve(url).addCallback(convert)
                      for url in self._urls]}
```

The FeedAggregation initializer accepts two new arguments: a retrieve callable that accepts a URL and returns a Deferred that resolves to a Feed or FailedFeed instance, and a urls iterable representing the RSS feed URLs to retrieve. The root handler combines these two by applying the _retrieve callable to each of the provided _urls and then arranging to render the result via the convert callback.

Now that we can compose the service half of application with the retrieval half, we can write a Twisted application plugin in the file src/twisted/plugins/feed_aggregation_plugin.py that loads and runs our feed aggregation service.

Twisted's twist command-line program allows users to run a variety of Twisted services out of the box, like a static web server with twist web --path=/path/to/serve. It's also extensible via Twisted's plugin mechanism. Let's write a plugin that runs our feed aggregation web service.

```
# src/twisted/plugins/feed_aggregation_plugin.py
from twisted import plugin
from twisted.application import service, strports
from twisted.python.usage import Options
from twisted.web.server import Site
import treq
from feed_aggregation import FeedAggregation, FeedRetrieval
from zope.interface import implementer

class FeedAggregationOptions(Options):
    optParameters = [["listen", "l", "tcp:8080", "How to listen for requests"]]

@implementer(plugin.IPlugin, service.IServiceMaker)
class FeedAggregationServiceMaker(service.Service):
    tapname = "feed"
    description = "Aggregate RSS feeds."
    options = FeedAggregationOptions
```

```
    def makeService(self, config):
        urls = ["http://feeds.bbci.co.uk/news/technology/rss.xml",
                "http://planet.twistedmatrix.com/rss20.xml"]
        aggregator = FeedAggregation(FeedRetrieval(treq).retrieve, urls)
        factory = Site(aggregator.resource())
        return strports.service(config['listen'], factory)

makeFeedService = FeedAggregationServiceMaker()
```

A `twisted.application.service.IService` is the unit of code run by `twist`, while a `twisted.application.service.IServiceMaker` allows `twist` to discover `IService` providers, and a `twisted.plugin.IPlugin` allows `twisted.plugin` to discover plugins. The `FeedAggregationServiceMaker` class implements both of these interfaces, so that instances of it within `twisted/plugins` are picked up by `twist`.

The `tapname` attribute represents the name of the `twist` subcommand under which our service will be available, while the `description` attribute is the documentation that `twist` will present command users. The `options` attribute contains an instance of `twisted.python.usage.Options` that parses command-line options into a dictionary that's passed to the `makeService` method. Our `FeedAggregationOptions` subclass contains one command-line option, `--listen` or `-l`, which represents an *endpoint string description* that defaults to `tcp:8080`. We'll explain what these are and how they work shortly.

`FeedAggregationServiceMaker.makeService` accepts the parsed configuration return by our Options class and returns an `IService` provider that runs our `FeedAggregation` web service. We construct a `FeedAggregation` instance here the same way we did in our tests, except this time, we provide the actual `treq` implementation to `FeedRetrieval`.

The `twisted.web.server.Site` class is actually a factory that knows how to respond to HTTP requests. It accepts as its first argument a `twisted.web.resource.Resource` that will respond to incoming requests, just like `StubTreq` did in our tests, and so we again use `FeedAggregation.resource` to create one from the underlying Klein application.

The `strports.service` function parses the endpoint string description into an `IService` provider that manages the specified port. Endpoint string descriptions afford Twisted applications great flexibility in how they listen for clients by leveraging protocols and transports.

The default of `tcp:8080` causes Twisted to bind TCP port 8080 on all available interfaces and will associate a TCP transport with protocol instances created by the Site factory. It could be switched, however, to `ssl:port=8443;privateKey=server.pem`, which set up an TLS listener on port 8443 that used the `server.pem` certificate to establish connections. Protocols created by the Site factory would then be bound to TLS-wrapped transports that automatically encrypted and decrypted connections with clients. The `strports` parsers are extendable by third-party plugins, as well; `txtorcon` (`https://txtorcon.readthedocs.io/en/latest/`), for instance, allows starting a TOR server via the `onion:` endpoint string description.

We can now invoke our feed aggregation service with the `twist` program within our virtual environment:

```
$ twist feed
2018-02-01T12:12:12-0800 [-] Site starting on 8080
2018-02-01T12:12:12-0800 [twisted.web.server.Site#info] Starting factory
<twisted.web.serve
2018-02-01T12:12:12-0800 [twisted.application.runner._runner.Runner#info]
Starting reactor.
2018-02-01T12:13:13-0800 [feed_aggregation._service.FeedRetrieval#info]
Downloading feed
2018-02-01T12:13:13-0800 [feed_aggregation._service.FeedRetrieval#info]
Downloading feed
...
```

twist sets up `twisted.logger` to format and print log messages to standard out. The FeedRetrieval messages correspond to the `info` message emitted in `FeedRetrieval.retrieve` and imply that a client accessed our application.

twist can also emit log messages as JSON objects with the `--log-format=json` command line option:

```
$ twist --log-format=json feed
...
{"log_namespace": "...FeedRetrieval", "url": "http://feeds.bbci.co.uk/news/technology/rss.x
{"log_namespace": "...FeedRetrieval", "url": "http://planet.twistedmatrix.com/rss20.xml", .
...
```

We've omitted many details to make the output more readable. Notice, however, that the `url` parameter to `FeedRetrieval._retrieve`'s `info` call is a property on the returned JSON objects. This allows a log aggregation service to extract data from log messages without heuristics like regular expressions. Like `strports`, this change in behavior did not require us to alter our application code at all.

Summary

This chapter introduced Klein and `treq`. These two libraries provide high-level wrappers around Twisted's web APIs that ease common development patterns.

We wrote an RSS 2.0 feed aggregation service using the venerable `feedparser` library, beginning with a simple prototype and then using test-driven development to build a fully functional Twisted application runnable with the `twist` command-line program. We used `treq.testing.StubTreq` to test our web service without any actual network requests and `SynchronousTestCase` to verify that our concurrent operations complete deterministically given various inputs. Along the way we saw how Klein's Plating feature enables us to build web services that can respond with both JSON and HTML, and how we can log structured data with `twisted.logger`.

The use of third-party libraries that have no assumptions about concurrency, like `feedparser`, `lxml`, and `attrs`, demonstrates how Twisted programs integrate with the modern Python ecosystem. At the same time, our program used classic Twisted concepts like `Deferred`s; our feed aggregation service shows the the power combining Python's vast libraries with Twisted's own concepts and code.

PART 2

Projects

## CHAPTER 4

Twisted in Docker

Docker is often used in micro-services architectures. Those are based on different components communicating over a network. Twisted, with its native support for several networking paradigms, is often a good fit for Docker-based architectures.

Docker, and containers in general, are new. Both the tooling and the consensus on how to use the tooling are evolving fast. We are giving here the foundations on how to use Docker, so we can build the understanding of how to use Twisted in Docker on top of it.

Note that Docker is a Linux-based technology. Though other operating systems have similar facilities, Docker is built on taking advantage of specific Linux-kernel facilities. Docker for Windows does have the ability to run "Windows Containers," but this is beyond the scope of this chapter.

Docker for Mac and Docker for Windows use a Virtual Machine running Linux, and have just enough integration with the host OS (OS X and Windows, respectively) to make the interaction seamless. However, it is important to remember that a Docker container is always running on a Linux kernel, even when running it on a Mac or Windows laptop.

Intro to Docker

Because Docker is both new and popular, several distinct things are called "Docker." Understanding exactly what Docker *is* itself is nontrivial. We try to break "Docker" here into distinct concepts. Note that each of these is often referred to as "Docker," as well as the whole comprising them.

Containers

Containers are processes that are run with more isolation than is possible in traditional UNIX processes.

© Mark Williams, Cory Benfield, Brian Warner, Moshe Zadka, Dustin Mitchell, Kevin Samuel, Pierre Tardy 2019
M. Williams et al., *Expert Twisted*, https://doi.org/10.1007/978-1-4842-3742-7_4

In a container, the only processes visible are those started by the root process of the container that appears as process ID 1 inside the container. Note that this is optional: a container can share the host's process IDs. Using the Docker command line, this is done with the argument `--pid host`.

Likewise, containers will have their own network address. This means processes inside the container can listen on a given port, without coordinating with the host or other running containers. Again, a container can be run with a special argument, `--net host`, in order to share the host network namespace.

Finally, each container has its own filesystem. For example, this means we can install different Pythons in different containers without any concerns – or even conflicting Python packages. Sharing the host filesystem directly is tricky.

However, we can use Docker's "volume mount" option. The volume mount option asks to make a directory from the host accessible ("mount") inside the container. The syntax for the option is to separate the directory from the host (on the left) and the directory it will be "mounted into" in the container (on the right) with a colon.

Thus, running Docker with `--volume /:/from-host` will make all the host's files accessible. Note that they will be accessible, inside the container, not in their usual location, but in the `/from-host` directory.

Containers are isolated exactly to the extent they are desired to be isolated. This is similar to the clone system call's flags indicating what is shared between parent and child processes: for example, the `CLONE_FILES` flag indicating a shared file descriptor table.

Container Images

While *containers* are running, isolated, sets of processes, *container images* allow us to instantiate a container – they are the equivalent of an executable image.

Internally, a container image is made of *layers*, each of which represents a file system. The final file system the container will see (often referred to as a union filesystem) is the combination of all layers, with higher ones overriding lower ones. An upper layer can modify, add, or even "delete" files from a previous layer. While the lower layer will not be affected, the final file system visible inside the container will be affected.

This is important, since it means deleting files in an upper layer *does not* save space. For example, if the first layer has a tarball, and then it is expanded, the tarball is often redundant. An upper layer will often have `rm/path/to/file.tar.gz` or a similar command. This is good insofar as that filename will not be visible – however, in the final size of the entire container image – for example, how many bytes need to be downloaded to run it – the tarball will still be included.

Container images are *named* (or more precisely tagged) after their ultimate location. The usual naming scheme is `[optional host/][optional user/]name[:optional tag]`. Images that are never meant to leave the host they are built on will usually omit the `host` and `user` parts, though there are exceptions.

If the tag is left off, the default is `:latest`. If the host is left off, the default is `docker.io`. Note that the same container image can have multiple tags.

Container images move between *registries* and *hosts*: they can be "pushed" to registries and "pulled" to hosts.

Runc and Containerd

In order to run a container from an image, a special program called `runc` ("run container") is used. This program is in charge of setting up the proper isolation mechanisms: it uses Linux kernel facilities, such as cgroups and namespaces, in order to properly isolate the filesystem, process namespace, and network addresses.

Usually, container users do not interact with `runc` directly. It is used under the covers, however, by both the Docker stack as well as almost all alternative container stacks, such as Rocket.

In order to manage running containers, it is necessary to know which containers are running, and what their states are. For this reason, one "daemon" program, called `containerd`, spawns all containers from images by calling `runc`.

Note that in previous versions of Docker, runc was embedded into `containerd` – and so a lot of materials still refer to the "Docker daemon" as running containers.

Client

The command-line `docker run`, contrary to what might be expected, does not run containers. Instead, it communicates with the `containerd` daemon, and asks it to run containers with `runc`.

By default, it uses a UNIX domain socket to communicate with the server. UNIX domain sockets are a special interprocess communication facility on UNIX-based operating systems. Their API resembles that of TCP sockets, but they are only used for communication inside the same machine, allowing the kernel to make some shortcuts. Instead of IP addresses and ports, UNIX domain sockets use file paths as their addresses. This allows the usual UNIX file permission model to apply.

By default, the UNIX domain socket to which `docker` connects is `/var/run/docker.sock`. Depending on the exact details of the Docker installation, it might be accessible by the `docker` group or the `root` group. The Docker client can also connect to the server using TLS over TCP, mutually authenticating using TLS certificates.

This is also true for all other subcommands of `docker`, such as `build`, `images`, etc. (Note that `docker login` is an exception, but the explanation of how remote registry login works is beyond our current scope.)

Because the command-line `docker` is mostly used to send Remote Procedure Calls to the daemon, we call it "the client."

Registry

Docker saves images in a (usually remote) *registry*. The registry stores each image as some metadata, plus a set of *layers*. The metadata notes the layer order, as well as some details about the container image.

Note that because of this storage method, the same layer will only be stored once. The usual case where several images share layers will be by having common ancestry – meaning, multiple images built from a common base image will not require their own copy of that image.

Also note that the default registry `docker.io` is built into the software – if no registry is specified, the default registry is assumed – usually referred to as "DockerHub."

This is a slightly distinct usage of the word "Docker," which again should be noted as potentially confusing terminology.

Build

The usual way to build images is to use the `docker build` command line. This uses a configuration file referred to as a `Dockerfile`. The `Dockerfile` begins with a `FROM` line. The `FROM` identifies the ancestor image. If an empty image is desired, `FROM scratch` will use the `scratch` image, which has no layers. However, this is rare.

Usually, builds will start with a common Linux distribution, which are all available from the default Docker registry, DockerHub. For example, Debian, Ubuntu, and CentOS are all available.

Every following line in the Dockerfile is a "build stage." Every build stage creates a layer, and layers are cached. This means that when modifying a Dockerfile, only changed lines (and ones following them) will be executed.

The following example is such a Dockerfile that will run the Twisted web demo server.

```
FROM debian:latest
RUN python3 -m pip install --user Twisted
ENTRYPOINT ["python3", "-m", "twisted", "web"]
```

This does not demonstrate best practices, which we will cover as we look at more sophisticated features, but it does show three important parts that will almost always be present in a Dockerfile:

- The FROM line. Here, we ask for the latest version of debian. Note that because we are not using a name with slashes, this is from the "library" on DockerHub – a set of semi-official base images.

- The RUN line runs a command inside the container being built, with the usual effect to mutate it in some way. In this case, we install Twisted into a user installation.

- The ENTRYPOINT line sets the program that will run when the container launches.

Multi-stage Build

The explanation above is missing an important new feature, added in mid-2017, in docker build. These are the multi-stage builds. A multi-stage build happens when there is more than one FROM line in the Dockerfile.

When this happens, the build process starts to build a new image – and at the end of the build, all nonfinal images will be discarded. However, *while the build is running*, the other images are accessible to one Dockerfile command – COPY.

When using COPY --from=<image>, it will copy file not from the context, but from a previous image. Although in theory, multi-stage builds can have any number of stages, it is very rare to need more than two. The sequencing of images uses 0-based numbering. Most "multistage" builds are really "two-stage" builds. The first stage will build all the artifacts, using a "thick" image full of compilers and build tools. The second stage picks up all the artifacts from the first stage and produces the final image to distribute. Because of this, the usual form a COPY instruction between stages takes is COPY --from=0.

This comes in useful when needing a sophisticated build environment to generate some of the products that will be deployed – and it is better not to ship a sophisticated build environment in the final runtime container: this reduces the size, number of layers, and potential security risks.

The following is an example of a multistage build. Note that in this case, the final output is not intended to be used directly, but to be built upon in other builds. This is a common pattern: building standard bases that have common elements has several advantages – for example, this saves space in both the registry and in the running server (if multiple different images are running on one server, as they often are). Another advantage is that there is one place to upgrade base packages when bugs are fixed in those.

```
FROM python:3
RUN mkdir /wheels
RUN pip wheel --wheel-dir /wheels pyrsistent

FROM python:3-slim
COPY --from=0 /wheels /wheels
RUN pip install --no-index --find-links /wheel pyrsistent
```

Again, we'll go line by line to explain what is going on here:

```
FROM python:3
```

The python:3 base is another example of a standard "DockerHub library" base. It includes Python 3, but it also includes enough tools to build native-code wheels – at least simple ones, without further dependencies.

```
RUN mkdir /wheels
```

We create the directory to store the wheels in. Note that because this stage is not going to be in the final output, we are not sensitive to creating extra layers. In fact, extra layers are good – they create more caching points. This is less interesting in this case, but often the build base includes installing many more build dependencies.

```
RUN pip wheel --wheel-dir /wheels pyrsistent
```

The `pip wheel` subcommand is useful in multi-stage builds. It builds a wheel for the specified requirements, and all of their dependencies. It will use a binary wheel from PyPI built for `manylinux`, if the platform is compatible – but this behavior can be turned off, if desired, with `pip wheel --no-binary :all`.

```
FROM python:3-slim
```

The `python:3-slim` base is similar to python:3 but does not include the complicated set of build-time dependencies. Note that many :code:`setup.py` in Python distributions auto-detect lack of compilers or dependencies, and will silently turn off native-code modules build. `pyrsistent`, for example, has a C-optimized persistent vector implementation, which we want in our image. Therefore, we do not want to install `pyrsistent` from sources in this stage.

```
COPY --from=0 /wheels /wheels
```

We copy the `pyrsistent` wheel we just built, and any dependencies from the first stage (stage 0) to the current stage. The second `FROM` line indicates this is a multi-stage build – but this `COPY` line is the one that makes the multi-stage build useful.

```
RUN pip install --no-index --find-links /wheel pyrsistent
```

Finally, we install the library into the local Python environment. We are careful to specify the `--no-index` and `--find-links` options to `pip` so that it will use the wheels from the first stage, instead of getting fresh distributions from PyPI.

Python on Docker

There is a huge variety of ways to deploy Python applications on Docker – like there is on any UNIX platform. They are not all equivalent – some are better than others. We will survey the options that tend to work well.

Deployment Options

Full env

A "full environment" deployment means that there is a custom Python interpreter installed exactly for the use of the application. This Python can be either custom built from source, as part of the Docker build process or before it –or it can come from a meta-distribution –such as `conda` or `nix`.

Installing a custom Python interpreter is often useful: we can customize the build options on it, pin the interpreter version and even, in especially extreme cases, apply custom patches. However, this means we have taken on the task of keeping the interpreter up to date.

However we install this interpreter, it will be used exactly for our application. We use `pip install` to install packages in it – or, if it comes from a meta-distribution (such as `conda` or `nix`), we can also install packages from the meta-distribution. This is especially useful with conda, since many data science-related Python packages are available to be installed.

Here is an example `Dockerfile` that builds a custom Python interpreter, loaded with the necessary packages.

```
FROM buildpack-deps:stretch

ENV PYTHON_VERSION 3.6.4
ENV PREFIX https://www.python.org/ftp/python

ENV LANG C.UTF-8

ENV GPG_KEY 0D96DF4D4110E5C43FBFB17F2D347EA6AA65421D

RUN apt-get update
RUN apt-get install -y --no-install-recommends \
        tcl \
        tk \
        dpkg-dev \
        tcl-dev \
        tk-dev

RUN wget -O python.tar.xz \
    "$PREFIX/${PYTHON_VERSION%%[a-z]*}/Python-$PYTHON_VERSION.tar.xz"
RUN wget -O python.tar.xz.asc \
    "$PREFIX/${PYTHON_VERSION%%[a-z]*}/Python-$PYTHON_VERSION.tar.xz.asc"
RUN export GNUPGHOME="$(mktemp -d)" && \
    gpg --keyserver ha.pool.sks-keyservers.net --recv-keys "$GPG_KEY" && \
    gpg --batch --verify python.tar.xz.asc python.tar.xz
RUN mkdir -p /usr/src/python
RUN tar -xJC /usr/src/python --strip-components=1 -f python.tar.xz
```

```
WORKDIR /usr/src/python

RUN gnuArch="$(dpkg-architecture --query DEB_BUILD_GNU_TYPE)"
RUN ./configure \
    --build="$gnuArch" \
    --enable-loadable-sqlite-extensions \
    --enable-shared \
        --prefix=/opt/custom-python/
RUN make -j
RUN make install
RUN ldconfig /opt/custom-python/lib
RUN /opt/custom-python/bin/python3 -m pip install twisted

FROM debian:stretch

COPY --from=0 /opt/custom-python /opt/custom-python
RUN apt-get update && \
    apt-get install libffi6 libssl1.1 && \
    ldconfig /opt/custom-python/lib
ENTRYPOINT ["/opt/custom-python/bin/python3", "-m", "twisted", "web"]
```

Building custom Python interpreters, though useful, is not trivial. We go through this file line by line:

```
FROM buildpack-deps:stretch
```

The buildpack-deps is a useful base image for building. Since we are going to be using Debian "stretch" as our deployment version, being the latest stable Debian version at time of writing, we get the stretch-compatible buildpack.

```
ENV PYTHON_VERSION 3.6.4
ENV PREFIX https://www.python.org/ftp/python
```

Setting those allows us to easily modify which Python version we use – this is essential to getting new security fixes and bug fixes from upstream. The easier we make it to upgrade Python, the better off we are.

```
ENV LANG C.UTF-8
```

Setting the language to explicitly UTF-8 is necessary to avoid an obscure bug in the Python build process. While not illuminating pedagogically, this is useful as a place to put these work-arounds. Putting those details in the Dockerfile is a convenient place to make sure builds succeed – whether on a continuous integration system or locally.

```
ENV GPG_KEY 0D96DF4D4110E5C43FBFB17F2D347EA6AA65421D
```

This is the GnuPG public key that corresponds to the private key that signs the Python tarball uploads. Gnu Privacy Guard is a tool that uses cryptography to achieve security guarantees. In this case, the key allows us to know that the source has not been tampered with. It is a good idea to add defense-in-depth and to use multiple ways to verify that our sources are authentic. This `Dockerfile`, or ones similar to it, are often used in Continuous Integration environments, where they are run repeatedly and automatically. It only takes a one-time breach to severely compromise infrastructure. Ensuring the build fails if the source is not guaranteed can eliminate a costly production breach.

Keeping the key fingerprint in the Dockerfile, which is probably checked into source control, is a way to root the trust in checked-in code.

```
RUN apt-get update
RUN apt-get install -y --no-install-recommends \
        tcl \
        tk \
        dpkg-dev \
        tcl-dev \
        tk-dev
```

Above and beyond the buildpack, we need some extra libraries. We install those here.

```
RUN wget -O python.tar.xz \
    "$PREFIX/${PYTHON_VERSION%%[a-z]*}/Python-$PYTHON_VERSION.tar.xz"
```

Next, we download the Python source tarball. Defining the variables above allows us to keep this line short and succinct. In addition, even though not necessary for stable releases, this command line will work line for versions like `3.6.1rc2` – necessary if we want to use this Dockerfile, with only minor changes, to test compatibility with release candidate releases.

```
RUN wget -O python.tar.xz.asc \
    "$PREFIX/${PYTHON_VERSION%%[a-z]*}/Python-$PYTHON_VERSION.tar.xz.asc"
```

We download the detached public key signature. Though we download both from TLS-enabled website, one that is prefixed with https and not http, checking the signature is a good defense-in-depth measure.

```
RUN export GNUPGHOME="$(mktemp -d)" && \
    gpg --keyserver ha.pool.sks-keyservers.net --recv-keys "$GPG_KEY" && \
    gpg --batch --verify python.tar.xz.asc python.tar.xz
```

This command line verifies the public key. Note that this is an example of a command that does *not* change the local state. However, since any failing command will stop the docker build process, a key verification error will lead to a halted build.

```
RUN mkdir -p /usr/src/python
```

We create a directory for the unpacked source code. Note that since this is a multi-stage build, we are not concerned about the eventual cleanup of this directory – the entire container will be cleaned up!

```
RUN tar -xJC /usr/src/python --strip-components=1 -f python.tar.xz
```

We unpack the Python tarball into the newly created directory.

```
WORKDIR /usr/src/python
```

We set the current working directory to the source code directory. This makes the subsequent build instructions, which need to be run from inside of it, shorter and easier to understand.

```
RUN gnuArch="$(dpkg-architecture --query DEB_BUILD_GNU_TYPE)" && \
  ./configure \
    --build="$gnuArch" \
    --enable-loadable-sqlite-extensions \
    --enable-shared \
        --prefix=/opt/custom-python/
```

We run the ./configure script, with a custom prefix. The custom prefix, /opt/custom-python, is what ensures us that we will be in a pristine directory. We also give a few options to make sure our Python build is correct:

- The architecture is calculated using dpkg-architecture and passed to the configure script explicitly. This is more reliable than having the configure script auto-detect it.

- We enable the `sqlite` module. Since it is a built-in, many third-party modules will depend on it without declaring a dependency, so it is important to make sure it is part of the installation.

- We enable the shared library. This is not strictly necessary in our example, but it allows cases of embedding Python.

```
RUN make -j
```

Calculating the exact number of CPUs is nontrivial. In this example, we just run make with maximum parallelism. This is what the `-j` flag does. Note that in general, it is recommended to set the parallelism to a reasonable level, by giving `-j` a number parameter, for example, `-j 4`.

```
RUN make install
```

This stage will copy the files, with correct permissions, into the installation directory.

```
RUN ldconfig /opt/custom-python/lib
```

We add the directory to our library search path – otherwise Python (which is dynamically linked) cannot run.

```
RUN /opt/custom-python/bin/python3 -m pip install twisted
```

We install Twisted. Among many other benefits of Twisted, it contains a convenient default web server, which is useful for demos.

```
FROM debian:stretch
```

For the production build, we start with a suitably minimal Debian distribution – keeping it as a matching version to the buildpack.

```
COPY --from=0 /opt/custom-python /opt/custom-python
```

We copy the entire environment – including the installed third-party libraries: in this case, Twisted and its dependencies.

```
RUN apt-get update && \
    apt-get install libffi6 libssl1.1 && \
    ldconfig /opt/custom-python/lib
```

We install necessary libraries and run `ldconfig` in the production image.

```
ENTRYPOINT ["/opt/custom-python/bin/python3", "-m", "twisted", "web"]
```

We set the entry point to run the demo web server built into Twisted. If we build and run this docker image, the web server will be running – and if we export the port, we can even check it with our browser.

Virtualenv

The alternative to a full environment is a "lightweight" environment – or as they have come to be known, a virtual environment. When using Python 2.7, we create a virtual environment using the `virtualenv` package. It is possible to install `virtualenv` using `pip`, but this has issues: after all, if the reason to create a virtual environment is to avoid changing the real environment, this undoes the benefit. One way is to get `virtualenv` the same way we got Python. Another one is to install it using

```
pip install --user virtualenv
```

This will put it under the *user* directory (on Docker, usually under /root). It often means `virtualenv` is not on the default shell path – but since it is on the Python path,

```
python -m virtualenv <directory>
```

will still work and create a virtual environment.

When using Python 3.x, these concerns are moot: `python -m venv` is the best way to create a virtual environment for Python 3.x. Note that some documentation has not been updated, and virtualenv *does* work on Python 3.x – which makes it harder to make sure all of these are up to date. However, the existence of a `venv` built-in module highly simplifies bootstrapping virtual environments.

One of the benefits of installing code in a virtual environment is that we know that the virtual environment's directory contains no more than what is necessary to run it – except for the interpreter. This feature will come in handy when we build Docker images.

Putting all these ideas together, we might end up with a `Dockerfile` like this:

```
FROM python:3
```

Since we are going to build a virtual environment, we need to have a full environment already installed. One of the easiest ways to do it is to start with the python container.

```
RUN python -m venv /opt/venv-python
```

We create a virtual environment in /opt/venv-python.

```
RUN /opt/venv-python/bin/pip install Twisted
```

We install Twisted in it. Note that installing Twisted means installing a few packages with C extensions – this stage requires a C compiler. The python:3 container image has all the tooling needed for building C extensions.

```
FROM python:3-slim
```

The python:3-slim container image has no build tools. Since this is the image we will ship, this means we do not ship a C compiler to production.

```
COPY --from=0 /opt/venv-python /opt/venv-python
```

We copy the virtual environment. Note that virtual environments have several hard-coded paths in them. This is why we make sure to create it with the same path where it will be deployed.

```
ENTRYPOINT ["/opt/venv-python/bin/python", "-m", "twisted", "web"]
```

The entry point is nearly identical to the one before. The only difference is the path – this time pointing to a virtual environment, not a full one.

Pex

The most self-contained option is that of Pex – a Python executable format pioneered by Twitter. Pex uses a combination of features of UNIX, Python, and Zip archives to have a one-file format that contains all application code and third-party dependencies.

A Pex file is supposed to be marked executable at the file system level, using chmod +x, for example, and is produced with a shebang line (!#) that calls a Python interpreter. Since Zip archives have the unique property that they are detected, and parsed, by their final bytes – and not their first bytes – the rest of the file is a Zip file.

When the Python interpreter accepts a Zip file, or a Zip file with arbitrary content prepended, it treats it as a sys.path addition, and will additionally execute the __main __.py file in the archive. Pex files generate a custom __main__ .py that calls either an entry point or executes a Python module, depending on the parameters passed to the Pex builder.

Pex can be built either by using the pex command line (installed with pip install pex), by using pex as a Python library and using its creation API, or by most modern metabuilders –Pants, Bazel, and Buck all have the ability to generate Pex output.

```
FROM python:3
RUN python -m venv /opt/venv-python
```

We create a virtual environment. While we are not going to *ship* this environment, it will help us build the Pex file.

```
RUN /opt/venv-python/bin/pip install pex
```

We install the pex utility.

```
RUN mkdir /opt/wheels /opt/pex
```

We create two directories to contain different kind of products.

```
RUN /opt/venv-python/bin/pip wheel --wheel-dir /opt/wheels Twisted
```

We use pip to build the wheels. This means we are going to use the pip dependency resolution algorithm. While not objectively better than the pex algorithm, it is the one used everywhere else. This means that if packages run into problems with the pip dependency resolution process, they will add whatever hints they need to install correctly. There is no such guarantee about pex, which is less frequently used.

```
RUN /opt/venv-python/bin/pex --find-links /opt/wheels --no-index \
                     Twisted -m twisted -o /opt/pex/twisted.pex
```

We build the Pex file. Note that we tell pex to ignore the PyPI index, and only collect packages from a specific directory – the one where pip put all the wheels it built. We configure the Pex file to behave as though we run Python with -m twisted, and we put the output in /opt/pex. While the suffix is not strictly necessary, it is useful when inspecting Docker container images to help understand how things are running.

```
FROM python:3-slim
```

Once again, we avoid shipping build tools to production using a second-stage slim image.

```
COPY --from=0 /opt/pex /opt/pex
```

We copy the directory – which, this time, only has one file. Also note that this time, the file is relocatable: it is possible (though we do not do this here) to copy to a different path.

```
ENTRYPOINT ["/opt/pex/twisted.pex", "web"]
```

Some of the logic that in the previous examples resides in the ENTRYPOINT (that we want to run python -m twisted) is now built into the Pex file. Our ENTRYPOINT is now shorter.

Build Options

Regardless of the way Python is *run*, the way the Docker container is *built* also has a lot of options.

One Big Bag

One way is to eschew a multi-stage build altogether and build a container with whatever tools we need to build the environment. This often means containers that are big and have many layers.

While this approach is certainly simple, straightforward, and easy to debug, it does have downsides. The container size can easily start being a problem in production. The number of layers, similarly, slows down container deployment. Finally, putting a lot of packages in a container that is exposed to potentially hostile user input can lead to more attack vectors than are necessary.

Copying Wheels Between Stages

Another way is to build all wheels in the build stage, including any binary wheels, and then copy them over to the production stage. The production stage still needs, in this case, enough tooling to create a virtual environment and install those wheels in it – although since venv is a Python built-in module in Python 3, this is no longer usually a hardship.

There are two other issues: the wheels stay around after being installed, since it is impossible to really remove a file after switching layers; and it often creates extra layers (though with clever reordering and backslash-continued lines, this can sometimes be avoided).

Copying Environment Between Stages

Another deployment option is to copy an environment (which could be full or virtual) from the build stage to the production stage. This has the advantage of being fast and straightforward, but the disadvantage that there is no compatibility checking, dependency checking, or location checking. Still, if there are decent tests for the resulting container, those will usually find basic incompatibility issues.

Copying the Pex Executable Between Stages

Finally, if a Pex executable file is produced in the build stage, copying it is straightforward. The Pex file, of course, will look for dependencies at runtime. However, it will do a reliable check, so even starting the container is enough to test for that.

It is also relocatable, so it does not matter where it is copied from – or where to. Pex and Docker are often a good pairing. However, the inherent limitations of Pex (for example, poor pre-build binary wheels support or poor PyPy support) sometimes make it a nonstarter.

Automation with Dockerpy

A package called `dockerpy` allows automation of Docker steps with Python. While usually for running containers in production, we will use an orchestration framework, this is often useful to build and test containers. The `dockerpy` library allows us to carefully fine-tune the context we send to the Docker daemon – using the `tarfile` Python module, it is possible to craft exactly the context needed.

Twisted on Docker
ENTRYPOINT and PID 1

The process in Docker's ENTRYPOINT Dockerfile instruction will have, inside the container, process ID 1. Process ID 1 has a special responsibility on Linux. When a process's parent dies before it dies, PID 1 "adopts" it – becomes its parent. This means that when the child process dies, PID 1 needs to "reap it" – wait on its exit status in order to clear out the process entry from the process table.

This responsibility is a little weird, and many programs are not set up for it. When running a program that does not reap adopted children, the process table will fill up. In the best case, this will crash the container. In the worst case, when process limits have not been carefully set up, this can crash the entire machine (virtual or physical) the container is running on.

Luckily, *any* Twisted program is set up to be PID 1. This is because Twisted's process infrastructure will automatically reap both expected and unexpected children.

This means when building a container, if we are using it to run WSGI applications, or Klein applications, or a Buildbot master, it is fine to have it be the entry point.

In fact, for this reason, if there is any custom start-up code to do, consider implementing it a tap plugin. This way, Twisted can still be the entry point.

Custom Plugins

When writing a Twisted application to run in Docker, we almost always want to deliver it as a custom tap plugin. This allows the ENTRYPOINT to be simply

```
["/path/to/python", "-m", "twisted", "custom_plugin"]
```

This means the plugin can get any arguments passed to the docker run command – since those arguments are directly added to the ENTRYPOINT arguments. It also means the plugin can directly read any environment variables passed to the docker run via --env.

In a plugin, the makeService function is the one that returns the running service. Note that the plugin can do any initialization it wants in that function – the event loop is not yet running at that point.

NColony

Sometimes, it is necessary to run more than one process inside a Docker container. Perhaps some side process to do file cleanup, or maybe a multi-process setup in order to use more than one CPU. In those cases, a process supervisor is useful – to run several processes, monitor them, and restart them if necessary.

NColony is a Twisted-based process supervisor. It is a small shim around `twisted.runner.procmon`, which allows several flexible configuration options. NColony consumes configuration as a directory of JSON-formatted files describing processes.

Of course, it is possible to create those files directly by opening a file and writing JSON into it. However, NColony also comes with a command-line utility – `python -m ncolony ctl` – to create such files as well as a Python library – `ncolony.ctllib`.

One advantage of the directory model is that it means it interacts well with the layer model of Docker container. A local base container can have an `ENTRYPOINT` of `["python", "-m", "twisted", "ncolony", ...]`, and even several base processes in the configuration directory – typically `/var/run/ncolony/config/`. Then, specific containerd can dump their own files, created in the build stage of the container using, for example, `python -m ncolony ctl`, in this directory. The resulting container would run both the side process and the main one.

Here is an example putting much of what has been talked about this chapter into concrete detail:

```
FROM python:3
RUN python3 -m venv /application/env
RUN /application/env/bin/pip install ncolony
RUN mkdir /application/config /application/messages
RUN /application/env/bin/python -m ncolony \
    --config /application/config \
    --messages /application/messages \
    ctl \
    --cmd /application/env/bin/python \
    --arg=-m \
    --arg=twisted \
    --arg=web
```

```
FROM python:3-slim
COPY --from=0 /application/ /application/
ENTRYPOINT ["/application/env/bin/python", \
            "-m", \
            "twisted", \
            "ncolony", \
            "--config", "/application/config", \
            "--messages", "/application/messages"]
```

We go over this line by line – there is a lot packed here.

```
FROM python:3
```

One way to get our Python environment is to use the official Docker ("library") image. This is based on the Debian distribution, and has Python – as well as all tools needed to build Python, and Python extension modules, in it.

```
RUN python3 -m venv /application/env
```

We create a virtual environment in /application/env. As mentioned before, Python 3 makes virtual environments a built-in notion, and we take full advantage of it.

```
RUN /application/env/bin/pip install ncolony
```

For better reproducible builds, it would be better to copy a requirements file in – ideally one that also has hashes – and pip install that. However, it is easier to see what is going on when we directly use a package name.

```
RUN mkdir /application/config /application/messages
```

NColony needs two directories to function properly: one for configuration and one for messages. We create both of them under /application. Configuration is the set of processes that need to be run, and their parameters. Messages are transient requests – usually ones to restart one or more processes.

```
RUN /application/env/bin/python -m ncolony \
```

We run a subcommand from the NColony we have installed inside the / application/env virtual environment.

```
--config /application/config \
--messages /application/messages \
```

176

We pass the parameters of NColony. Though in this case the messages directory is not used, it is good to pass them both to all commands.

```
ctl \
```

Control (`ctl`) is the NColony subcommand that controls configuration.

```
--cmd /application/env/bin/python \
```

We run the same Python we were run with. Note that in general, this is not necessary for NColony. However, it would be confusing to write code that uses radically different interpreters for different uses.

```
--arg=-m \
--arg=twisted \
```

The process NColony is monitoring does not have to be a Twisted process, but in our case, it is going to be a Twisted process – in fact, another `tap` plugin.

```
--arg=web
```

When no arguments are given, the web `tap` plugin displays a demo web application. It is surprisingly useful for quick demos and checks – as in this case.

```
FROM python:3-slim
```

The second `FROM` line begins the production Docker image. Note – everything built up to this point will be *thrown away* when the build is done. The only reason the earlier steps exist is to copy from that ephemeral stage. This source image is a minimal Debian, plus an installed Python 3.

```
COPY --from=0 /application/ /application/
```

We copy the entire application directory. Since this directory has both the virtual environment and the NColony configuration, there is nothing else we need. The simplicity of this line explains the value of all the careful work we did to set this directory up.

```
ENTRYPOINT ["/application/env/bin/python", \ "-m", \
            "twisted", \ "ncolony", \
            "--config", "/application/config", \
            "--messages", "/application/messages"]
```

Finally, we configure the entry point. Since NColony itself is a tap plugin, once again the command we run is `python -m twisted <plugin>`.

In this example we could have run the web server directly as the entry point. However, a more realistic example that really needs several processes would obscure the basic mechanics of getting NColony to run in Docker.

Summary

Docker, Python, and Twisted are complementary technologies. Docker, with multi-stage builds and registries, gives Python a standardized way to specify build process and packaging. Twisted, with its process management primitives, gives Docker a useful PID 1 that either does useful work by itself – for example, a web server – or a powerful base layer – with NColony being a good fit for the Docker layer model.

Docker is a practical way to build, package, and run Twisted applications, and Twisted is a useful thing to run inside Docker.

CHAPTER 5

Using Twisted as a WSGI Server

Introduction to WSGI

WSGI – the Web Standard Gateway Interface – is a Python standard. It is loosely based on the CGI – common gateway interface – standard, which web servers used to interact with scripts. With higher loads came the need to have a persistent Python process, inside the web server. Originally, each server had its own unique way of running Python applications. That meant each application had to decide on a web server and could not move away. WSGI was designed as a low-level standard for web applications written in Python to interact with web servers that can run Python internally (either by being written in Python themselves, or by embedding the Python interpreter).

The WSGI standard defines an interface between two things: the WSGI web *application* and the WSGI web *server.*

Twisted has a web server that, while implementing its own unique web-based APIs, also implements the WSGI standard. Because it implements the WSGI standard, it can run any Python web application that supports WSGI.

Usually, Python web applications will not interact with WSGI directly. Instead, it is the responsibility of web frameworks – such as Django, Flask, or Pyramid – to interface to WSGI as applications, and present a higher-level interface to the web application. These interfaces are specific to the web framework – it is not expected that an application will be easy to port from, say Django to Pyramid.

As an analogy, think of the choice of the web framework as similar to the choice of a programming language, and the choice of a web server as similar to choosing an operating system. We expect that moving between operating systems will allow us to keep most code intact (portability) but we do not expect the same when switching programming language.

© Mark Williams, Cory Benfield, Brian Warner, Moshe Zadka, Dustin Mitchell, Kevin Samuel, Pierre Tardy 2019
M. Williams et al., *Expert Twisted*, https://doi.org/10.1007/978-1-4842-3742-7_5

From the point of view of web servers, supporting WSGI means that they are agnostic to the web framework used – running a Pyramid application is the same as running Flask. From the point of view of web frameworks, supporting WSGI means that they are agnostic to the web server used – running on top of Apache is the same as running on top of uwsgi.

WSGI was not born in a vacuum. At the time it was designed, there were already many servers and many Python web frameworks. Because of this, WSGI was designed to be easy to implement – both on the side of the servers, and on the side of the web frameworks. Indeed, its similarity to CGI is the result. Many of these frameworks already supported CGI, and adding WSGI support included little work.

WSGI was designed in 2003. The names of many of the frameworks it mentions – Quixote and Webware, for example – are now relics of early experimentation with web frameworks. Though it does not explicitly mention it by name, the only server that mattered back then was Apache – which has fallen dramatically in popularity since.

However, despite the fact that both the popular frameworks and popular servers are more recent, the WSGI standard has endured remarkably well.

The definition of the WSGI API is subtle. The standard it is trying to abstract, HTTP, is complex. Modern web applications need access to much of that complexity. The definition spans two documents and can sometimes appear overwhelming.

This section will break down WSGI and explain the parts that make it up.

PEP

All major enhancements to Python go through a PEP (Python Enhancement Proposal) process. WSGI, as a major feature, was originally described in PEP 0333. PEP 0333 was originally created in December of 2003 and finalized in August of 2004.

While this PEP is still correct for Python 2.x, PEP 3333 describes how to implement WSGI for both Python 2.x and Python 3.x. PEP 3333 was created in September of 2010 and finalized in October of 2010.

It was a fairly minor change to PEP 0333, dealing with proper implementation of WSGI across Python 2.x and Python 3.x. In order to understand why it was necessary, it is important to understand what changed between Python 2.x and Python 3.x.

One of the major changes between Python 2.x and Python 3.x was the handling of unicode – and specifically, the bytes, string, and unicode types saw major changes. WSGI, as a standard dealing with (ultimately) transmitting bytes over TCP connections, needed to be refined to clarify which types belong where in Python 3.x.

While a detailed explanation of those changes is beyond our current scope, some explanation is important to clarify those issues. Both Python 2.7+ and Python 3.x have a bytes type, which is a sequence of bytes, and a unicode type, which is a sequence of unicode code points. The string type, however, is equivalent to the bytes type in Python 2.7+ and to unicode in Python 3.x.

An encoding is a (possibly partial) map between bytes and unicode. ASCII is one such encoding – mapping bytes under 128 to unicode points of the same value, and declaring all other bytes to be invalid. Latin-1 (or ISO-8859-1) is an encoding that maps all bytes to unicode points of the same value – and if no unicode point of that value exists, declares the byte to be invalid.

In HTTP, the protocol that governs the web, it is divided into headers, followed by a body; and if the body is textual, the headers will indicate what encoding it is in.

The issue of encoding the headers themselves is subtle: PEP 3333 treats them as Latin-1 (also known as ISO-8859-1), while Twisted encodes them as UTF-8. The safest thing to do is to make sure that all headers stick to the common subset of UTF-8 and Latin-1: ASCII. This makes sure that no matter what encoding/decoding our headers go through, they will remain intact.

In PEP 3333, the headers are expected to be the native string type – bytes for Python 2.x and unicode for Python 3.x – while the content is always expected to be bytes.

PEP 3333, as well as PEP 0333, also describes the idea of WSGI middleware – something that looks like a server to the application, and like the application to the server. While some WSGI middleware exists, note that some popular frameworks – Django and Pyramid, notably – have their own native notions of middleware. Flask, however, relies on WSGI middleware.

Raw Example

The simplest WSGI application is simple indeed:

```
def application(
            environment,
            start_response):
    start_response('200 OK', [('Content-Type', 'text/html')])
    return [b'hello world']
```

We will go line by line and explain the three main parts that every WSGI application should have:

```
def application(
```

In Python, function definitions accomplish two things:

- Create a *function object*.

- Assign it to a name.

This function definition, in particular, *creates* a function object and assigns it to the name `application`.

This means that `application` now points to a callable object. That is what WSGI applications are, a per PEP 3333: callable objects.

```
environment,
```

The first parameter is the so-called "environment." This name hearkens back to WSGI's origins as a quick adaptation of the CGI standard.

The CGI standard deals with how web servers execute scripts. A part of this standard defines the environment variables that those scripts have access to. Indeed, most of the data about the web request is available from environment variables under CGI. The WSGI standard took the same variable names, and the notion of an environment, and called it the first parameter to the WSGI application.

The `environment` parameter is a Python dictionary, mapping specified names to data about the web request. In the example application above, this parameter was ignored, since we always use a constant value. If this was all we needed to do, we would just have a static HTML page – most real applications depend, in some way, on user input.

```
start_response):
```

The second parameter, conventionally known as `start_response`, is a subtle – and often misunderstood – parameter. It is a callable accepting two arguments: the HTTP response code and the HTTP headers.

```
start_response('200 OK', [('Content-Type', 'text/html')])
```

The first thing we do is call the `start_response` callable. The first argument is 200 OK, indicating a regular successful HTTP response. The second argument is a list of headers. In this case, the only header we send is the `Content-Type` header. This indicates that our response should be interpreted by the browser as HTML text.

```
return [b'hello world']
```

The next line returns a list of byte strings. Since we did not include an explicit encoding in our `Content-Type`, the browser will use its default encoding. This is reasonably safe in this case – modern browsers' encoding detection will always work correctly with bytes in the ASCII range.

In general, depending on browsers to be smart is not a good idea: the best approach is to usually to use UTF-8, and indicate it clearly in the `Content-Type`.

This is important, since HTML is *always* defined in terms of unicode. The browser will translate this to the unicode string u`'hello world'`, which will display the greeting message to the user.

We will assume, for the rest of this chapter, that this code is in a file called

`wsgi_hello.py`.

Reference Implementation

Although PEP 333 (and 3333) has suggested that there is no need to implement WSGI in core Python, experience proved differently. The module `wsgiref` implements a simple web server, which can support WSGI applications.

The following command line will work in any bash-like shell, where quoting allows lines to be broken. This is done for readability – substituting semicolons for the first two line breaks, and removing the rest, would result in a completely portable command – that is, however, harder to read and explain line by line.

```
python -c '
from wsgiref import simple_server
import wsgi_hello
simple_server.make_server(
    "127.0.0.1",
    8000,
    wsgi_hello.application
).serve_forever()
'
```

We will go through this line by line:

```
python -c '
```

Python has an option -c, which treats the next argument as Python code and executes it. This is a convenient way to execute short programs without having to put the code in a separate file.

```
from wsgiref import simple_server
```

Import the wsgiref.simple_server module. This module implements a single-threaded single-process synchronous web server. While this server is not up to production, it is sometimes convenient for simple demonstrations.

```
import wsgi_hello
```

The assumption that the code above was in a file called wsgi_hello.py is important here. It is also important that:

- The file is in the current working directory.

- The current working directory is on the Python module path when using -c.

This will become important later, in the discussion about the subtleties of finding the WSGI application code.

```
simple_server.make_server(
```

This is the main function in the simple_server module – the one that creates a simple server.

```
"127.0.0.1",
```

Many examples (including the one in the official documentation) will use "" here. This will cause the WSGI server to bind to 0.0.0.0, the so-called "any" interface. Note that wsgiref is not a production server – but even if it was, we are using it here to run test and example code. Binding it to the any interface means that potentially, depending on firewall settings, outsiders can connect to the code.

Instead, in this example we bind to "127.0.0.1," the local interface. Only programs running on the same machine can connect now. This is useful – we can easily test the running server with a browser, but only one running on the same machine as the server.

```
8000,
```

The standard web port is 80, as defined by the IANA standard. However, on UNIX systems, ports below 1024 are reserved for the administrator (`root`) user account. This prevents unprivileged users from "hijacking" system ports. While the specific thread model that leads this need is receding in importance, now that it is uncommon to have many unprivileged users to directly log in to the system running the web server, it is still a component of threat mitigation and, most importantly, still enforced on modern UNIX-like systems such as Linux.

It became a tradition in development to bind to a port that "looks similar," such as 80, 8888, or 8080.

```
wsgi_hello.application
```

This is the actual WSGI application. As we mentioned, a WSGI application is a *callable Python object*.

```
).serve_forever()
```

Having created the server, we run it in an infinite loop.

This is an easy way to quickly run WSGI applications, for testing, with no dependencies other than Python's standard library.

WebOb Example

The WebOb package is an example of a low-level web framework. It is usually not used directly, although it is certainly possible to do so.

```python
import webob
def application(environment, start_response):
    request = webob.Request(environment)
    response = webob.Response(
                    text='Hello world!')
    return response(environment, start_response)
```

Here is the line-by-line explanation:

```
import webob
```

The WebOb library is small enough so that everything we need is at the top level.

```
def application(environment, start_response):
```

The WSGI application itself, in this case, is just a regular function – as though we were not using any framework.

```
request = webob.Request(environment)
```

The request object is built from the WSGI environment dictionary. Though this application does not inspect the request object, it has a parsed view of many parameters: URLs and query parameters, as well as cookies and more.

```
response = webob.Response(
```

We create the response object. Creating the response object frees us from dealing with some lower-level details.

```
text='Hello world!')
```

For example, here we set the text property, without having to care about transforming it to a list of byte strings.

```
return response(environment, start_response)
```

The response object knows how to call start_response and write out its body.

Pyramid Example

Pyramid is a framework intended to impose minimal overhead but scale well to large projects.

```
from pyramid import config, response
def hello_world(request):
    return response.Response('Hello World!')
with config.Configurator() as conf:
    conf.add_route('hello',  '/')
    conf.add_view(hello_world, route_name='hello')
    application = conf.make_wsgi_app()
```

We go through the application line by line.

```
from pyramid import config, response
```

Pyramid has quite a few moving parts. For this example, we only need these two modules.

```
def hello_world(request):
```

Note how `hello_world` is a regular Python function. It is not wrapped in any way. This makes it easier to reuse it: for example, we can write tests for it, or use it in a different function.

```
return response.Response('Hello World!')
```

We create a response object, similar to using `WebOb` or `werkzeug`.

```
with config.Configurator() as conf:
```

Using the configurator as a context manager means that at the end of the block, assuming no exceptions were raised, it will automatically commit the configuration and end it.

```
conf.add_route('hello', '/')
```

Routing in Pyramid is a two-step process. Mapping a URL to a "logical name" is the first one.

```
conf.add_view(hello_world, route_name='hello')
```

The second step is to map the logical name to a `view`.

```
application = conf.make_wsgi_app()
```

Finally, we ask the configuration to represent itself as a WSGI application.

Getting Started

While the documentation for running WSGI applications through Twisted is all correct, it is distributed through a handful of documents. Here we will show a complete working example for running a WSGI application, building it one block at a time.

WSGI Server

The Twisted WSGI server is an option on the web tap plugin. In the demonstrations here, we will use uniquely the python -m twisted way of invoking the plugin. Though it is a little more long winded, it ends up being a useful thing to use in production.

Though it is not using WSGI, it is useful to see how to run the web plugin in general – many of the options will end up being relevant to operating a WSGI server, and it is useful to be able to operate the "listening side" on its own for troubleshooting.

Assuming Twisted is installed in the environment, it is possible to run:

```
$ python -m twisted web --port tcp:8000
```

and get a web server running the so-called "demo." The demo web application just greets with a hello message – in this case, on port 8000.

Running a WSGI application is easy – we have six of them above!

```
$ python -m twisted web --port tcp:8000 --wsgi wsgi_hello.application
$ python -m twisted web --port tcp:8000 --wsgi werkzeug_hello.application
$ python -m twisted web --port tcp:8000 --wsgi flask_hello.application
$ python -m twisted web --port tcp:8000 --wsgi webob_hello.application
$ python -m twisted web --port tcp:8000 --wsgi pyramid_hello.application
$ python -m twisted web --port tcp:8000 --wsgi django_hello.application
```

It is important to note that this was actually *easier* than using the reference implementation. For the reference implementation, we had to write a little shell script that included a 4-statement Python blob as a -c argument. While it is nice that the Python command line and the UNIX shell cooperate to give those useful facilities, it is nice to be able to do without them.

The --port option is actually more powerful than it seems.

```
$ python -m twisted web --port tcp:8000:interface=127.0.0.1 \
                    --wsgi wsgi_hello.application
```

This will run the web server only on the local host interface, and make it unreachable from the outside. Probably something good when developing your next-gen web application using a coffee shop's network!

The full power of endpoints is available in the --port command-line option, including plugins. Some endpoint plugins will be important enough to merit a special mention later.

Note that unlike other full-featured WSGI servers, Twisted does not have a configuration file. There are a handful of options on the command line for small tweaks, but a lot of things just assume the defaults – for example, the size of the WSGI thread pool.

Customizing those is done via a custom plugin.

```
# put in twisted/plugins/twisted_book_wsgi.py
from zope import interface
from twisted.python import usage, threadpool
from twisted import plugin
from twisted.application import service, strports
from twisted.web import wsgi, server
from twisted.internet import reactor
import wsgi_hello
@interface.implementer(service.IServiceMaker, plugin.IPlugin)
class ServiceMaker(object):
    tapname = "twisted_book_wsgi"
    description = "WSGI for book"
    class options(usage.Options): pass
    def makeService(self, options):
        pool = threadpool.ThreadPool(minthreads=1, maxthreads=100)
        reactor.callWhenRunning(pool.start)
        reactor.addSystemEventTrigger('after', 'shutdown', pool.stop)
        root = wsgi.WSGIResource(reactor, pool, wsgi_hello.application)
        site = server.Site(root)
        return strports.service('tcp:8000', site)
        serviceMaker = ServiceMaker()
```

We go through the non-import lines one by one:

```
@interface.implementer(service.IServiceMaker, plugin.IPlugin)
```

This is in general how to write a Twisted tap plugin. It marks a class as

- Something that is a plugin (plugin.IPlugin);

- Something that knows how to transform a command line to a service (service.IServiceMaker).

It does so by using the `zope.interface` framework, which allows explicit marking of interfaces and their implementations – as well as programmatic access to that information. This programmatic interface is what allows the Twisted plugin system to work.

```
class ServiceMaker(object):
```

The name of the class is actually not important. The only important thing is that the name of the instance is `serviceMaker`.

```
tapname = "twisted_book_wsgi"
```

This is the name of the plugin to be used as the first argument to `python -m twisted`.

```
description = "WSGI for book"
```

Usually the description should be more informative, since this appears in the help text when running `python -m twisted` without an argument.

```
class options(usage.Options): pass
```

Since this is a minimal plugin, we "hard code" everything. It is not really hard coding – at some point, the decision of which port, and which app, has to be made. Making it at plugin writing time often makes sense, especially if using something like twelve-factors and querying all configurations from environment variables.

However, it is often useful to at least make the port option available from the command line.

```
def makeService(self, options):
```

This function accepts the options instance after it has parsed the command line.

```
pool = threadpool.ThreadPool(minthreads=1, maxthreads=100)
```

This is *not* an example of a good configuration. In fact, this is almost certain to be a bad thread pool configuration. However, often some fine-tuning of the number of threads does make sense. This obviously depends on the application, machines, and usage characteristics.

```
reactor.callWhenRunning(pool.start)
```

Start the pool when the reactor starts.

```
reactor.addSystemEventTrigger('after', 'shutdown', pool.stop)
```

Shut down the pool when the reactor finishes.

```
root = wsgi.WSGIResource(reactor, pool, wsgi_hello.application)
```

Build the root resource. Here is where we combine a specific thread pool with a specific WSGI application.

```
site = server.Site(root)
```

Build the `Site` object, which actually understands HTTP, from the resource object.

```
return strports.service('tcp:8000', site)
```

Build an endpoint and listen for HTTP protocol.

```
serviceMaker = ServiceMaker()
```

As mentioned, the actual plugin depends on an instance – not a class. We create an instance of the class we defined.

This allows us to run the same hello world application with a better (or, in this case, worse) tuned thread pool. It is also possible to build a plugin for many other reasons – some of them we will cover in the rest of the chapter.

Finding Code

The single most important thing the Twisted WSGI server needs to be able to do is to find the WSGI application it needs to run. However, this has been traditionally a tricky thing.

Default Path

When starting up Python using `-c` or `-m`, the current directory, `.` is on the import path. Above, when using the reference implementation, we used `-c`, and when using the Twisted WSGI server, we used `-m`.

However, when running a Python directly with a script, the `script's` directory, not the current directory, is added to the path instead. Since this is how console scripts entry points work, if we use `twist`, instead of `python -m twisted`, the current directory is no longer on the import path.

Relying on the current directory being in the path works – right up to when it does not, for seemingly small reasons. While it is fine for demonstration purposes, for production uses, we need something stronger.

PYTHONPATH

One way is to set the environment variable PYTHONPATH to a value. The first question is which value: some do PYTHONPATH=., whereas others PYTHONPATH=$(pwd). The first option has the advantage that it can follow around on the shell – but that strength is equally its weakness, because something as simple as cd can break it.

The next one has the advantage of being concrete – but again, has the problem of action at a distance, where running Python at some later time can suddenly import an old WSGI app. This is especially a problem for projects that look for things on the Python path – like Twisted's plugin implementation. Having an extra plugin show up can be quite surprising.

setup.py

The best solution is to write a setup.py file and turn the code into a proper package. A name will have to be chosen, true, but usually the name of the topmost module will be good enough. A version has to be chosen, but if no intent to distribute it exists, 0.0.0dev1 is an easy, safe choice.

For development purposes, it is often easiest to install it into a virtual environment with pip install -e .. This will track changes as these are made to source files, allowing minimal hassle while integrating with the virtual environment system – or any other virtualenv-like system, such as Nix or Conda.

Why Twisted

Twisted is certainly not the only option for running WSGI applications. Gunicorn, uwsgi, and Apache's mod_wsgi can all do that. However, Twisted has a few specific benefits.

Production vs. Development

Most web frameworks come with their own built-in server, often based on the wsgiref implementation. Without fail, those web servers will have warnings on them like "DO NOT USE THIS SERVER IN A PRODUCTION SETTING. It has not gone through security audits or performance tests." (This is a quotation from Django's documentation.) In the worst cases, these warnings are not heeded – for ignorance or expediency –and websites go live on top of development servers.

In the best cases, these warnings are addressed, and developers use the development server, while production uses a production-grade server. This leads to environment drift – some subtle differences in the implementation of WSGI, for example, means some behavior in production does not reproduce in development. On top of that, developers will not be familiar with the regular operations of the production-grade web server. The logs, the error messages, and the failure modes will all be unique – often leading to disconnect between developers and operations.

Last, but not least, when using two web servers, there needs to be some logic deciding when to run where. Often tooling can get confused and accidentally run the development server in production. Since the development server is not completely broken, this often does not result in immediate breakage, but a weird pattern of problems – perhaps some obscure performance issue.

Twisted, in contrast, is usable for both development and production usage. It is possible to use Twisted directly from the command line, as we have done above, passing just the name of the application. If, later on, it turns out to be useful to write a custom plugin, it is usually the case that this plugin can be used in development as well. This allows eliminating much potential production/development drift.

Some of the more advanced development servers do support a useful feature – automatic reloading of the code. However, with a little bit of configuration, this is possible with Twisted too. The first step is to install our code with `pip install -e`, so that merely restarting the server will be enough. Then, instead of running the server directly, we run

```
$ watchmedo shell-command \
    --patterns="*.py" \
    --recursive \
    --command='python -m twisted web --wsgi=wsgi_hello.application' \
    .
```

This will automatically restart the server whenever a file changes. It takes advantage of the `watchdog` PyPI package.

TLS

TLS (Transport Layer Security) is the latest version of what used to be called SSL (Secure Socket Layer). TLS is an encryption and key-exchange protocol that works on top of TCP.

TLS does two things:

- Encryption: communication using TLS is resistant to wire-taps.

- Endpoint authentication: when using TLS, it is possible to verify we are talking to the endpoint we expect.

While the first one often is popular in explanation of the importance of TLS, the second one is even more important. It is possible that some WSGI applications hold little sensitive data: however, since they send HTML, JavaScript, and CSS to potentially vulnerable browsers, making sure that no malware is delivered over the lines is always important.

The way TLS authenticates endpoints is by checking certificates, signed by certificate authorities. In general, the two ways to get a certificate authority to sign a certificate are either to convince it that you are the legitimate endpoint, or to create your own certificate authority. While creating a real certificate authority is nigh impossible, this if often the preferred solution inside data centers, where the same person, or group, is responsible for both ends of the connection.

Assuming the key is in key.pem and the certificate is in cert.pem,

```
$ python -m twisted web \
          --port ssl:port=8443:privateKey=key.pem:certKey=cert.pem \
          --wsgi wsgi_hello.application
```

will run a TLS server with the application. Note that in this case, the environment dictionary will set wsgi.url_scheme to "https." WSGI applications can check that to see if they are behind TLS.

This is one advantage of directly implementing TLS in the WSGI server. Otherwise, obscure and nonstandard HTTP headers need to be consulted to know if the request is secure or not.

Server Name Indication

WSGI applications have access to the headers, which include the `Host` header. This means a WSGI application can use the host the client accessed it on as one of its parameters – say, serve different content on `example.com` and `m.example.com`, as a way to support mobile browsers.

Assuming we want the application to still have TLS, which verifies the host- name, this means we need to have certificates for both `m.example.com` and `example.com`, and know which one to serve. TLS supports an extension called "Server Name Indication," which allows the client to indicate which name the server should prove it owns.

In order to support SNI in WSGI, we need to do several things:

- Get the relevant certificates and keys.

- For each host name, *concatenate* the certificate and key into one file (often using the UNIX command `cat`). This file should be named `<host>.pem`, e.g., `m.example.com.pem`.

- Put all those files in one directory, say `/var/lib/keys`.

- Install the `txsni` package from PyPI.

- Run.

```
$ python -m twisted web \
          --port txsni:/var/lib/keys:tcp:8443 \
          --wsgi wsgi_hello.application
```

This example would work well for the case where we want to serve the same content (securely) from two different domain names – for example, `example.com` and `www.example.com`.

If we want to serve different content for different subdomains, for example, `app.example.com` for the dynamic application and `static.example.com` for the static files, we could use the same `port` argument with a custom plugin that creates a `twisted.web.vhost.NameVirtualHost` resource.

Here is an example plugin that does exactly that:

```
from zope import interface
```

```
from twisted.python import usage, threadpool
from twisted import plugin
from twisted.application import service, strports
from twisted.web import wsgi, server, static, vhost
from twisted.internet import reactor

import wsgi_hello


@interface.implementer(service.IServiceMaker, plugin.IPlugin)
class ServiceMaker(object):
    tapname = "twisted_book_vhost"
    description = "Virtual hosting for book"
    class options(usage.Options):
        optParameters = [["port", "p", None,
                          "strports description of the port to "
                          "start the server on."]]
    def makeService(self, options):
        application = wsgi_hello.application
        pool = threadpool.ThreadPool(minthreads=1, maxthreads=100)
        reactor.callWhenRunning(pool.start)
        reactor.addSystemEventTrigger('after', 'shutdown', pool.stop)
        dynamic = wsgi.WSGIResource(reactor, pool, application)
        files = static.File('static')
        root = vhost.NameVirtualHost()
        root.addHost(b'app.example.org', dynamic)
        root.addHost(b'static.example.org', files)
        site = server.Site(root)
        return strports.service(options['port'], site)
serviceMaker = ServiceMaker()
```

The interesting lines are

```
root = vhost.NameVirtualHost()
root.addHost(b'app.example.org', dynamic)
root.addHost(b'static.example.org', files)
```

This creates a root resource that redirects all requests for `app.example.org` to the dynamic resource, and all requests for `static.example.org` to the static one. Note that because we chose `example.org`, it is safe to point those names, for testing purposes, to `127.0.0.1` in your hosts file.

Note that in this case, we did not choose a default. Going to a site via a different name (e.g., `localhost`) would cause a 404 error. It is possible to set the `default` property on a `NameVirtualHost` to set a default root for all other names.

Static Files

One thing that using Twisted as a WSGI server allows us to do is to serve static assets, as well as dynamic applications, from the same web server. This includes images, JavaScript files, and CSS files, as well as any other files.

Twisted is was originally built to be a high-performance networking application, and the Twisted web server, when serving static files, can keep up with all but the most taxing needs. When serving those needs, however, most applications will be served behind a Content Distribution Network (CDN).

The CDN will mean any differences in how fast static files are served are irrelevant. However, in those cases, being able to set the Cache-Control headers from Python code is convenient. Teams that write WSGI applications in Python are usually proficient in Python and prefer using it to learn another highly-specific domain language such as most servers' built-in configuration language.

However, to understand how to do that, it is important to delve deeper into how the Twisted web server API – and, as a side effect, understand a little more some of the things that were laid out earlier with little explanation.

Resource Model

Most modern web application servers, if they have a routing model at all, have a *pattern match* routing model. Flask, Django, and Pyramid, as we have seen earlier, all map URL patterns to code in some way.

Twisted web predates all of those. Before URL pattern matching became popular, treating the web resources as a `tree` was also an alternative – and this is the alternative that Twisted web took. As a result, it has a model of resources that have children.

This is not too important as long as we only used WSGI: the WSGI resource marks itself with isLeaf = True. This means it does not have children, and tree traversal is stopped when it is reached. This allows the WSGI resource to pass the path to the web application framework, for its own routing. Since we used a WSGI resource as the root resource – the one passed directly to the Site constructor – it meant that the resource tree model was only theoretical.

However, when combining different resources together, the details of this model are crucially important.

Pure Static

In order to understand how to do static file serving with Twisted web, it is worthwhile to first write a plugin to do just that – with no dynamic resources.

```
from zope import interface

from twisted.python import usage, threadpool
from twisted import plugin
from twisted.application import service, strports
from twisted.web import static, server
from twisted.internet import reactor

@interface.implementer(service.IServiceMaker, plugin.IPlugin)
class ServiceMaker(object):
    tapname = "twisted_book_static"
    description = "Static for book"
    class options(usage.Options):
        pass
    def makeService(self, options):
        root = static.File('static')
        site = server.Site(root)
        return strports.service('tcp:8000', site)
serviceMaker = ServiceMaker()
```

The only line that is new here is

```
root = static.File('static')
```

This defines a File resource. The File resource is also a leaf resource, which will map the rest of the URL to a path on the disk. This uses a relative path, static, to the current working directory. This works wonderfully for illustration purposes, but production applications usually will use a full path.

One way to get a full path is to package the files directly with the Python code. It takes a little setup hacking to package it, as well as to find it at runtime.

Here is an example setup.py, and the plugin that uses it:

```python
import setuptools
setuptools.setup(
    name='static_server',
    license='MIT',
    description="Server: Static",
    long_description="Static, the web server",
    version="0.0.1",
    author="Moshe Zadka",
    author_email="zadka.moshe@gmail.com",
    packages=setuptools.find_packages(where='src') + ['twisted/plugins'],
    package_dir={"": "src"},
    include_package_data=True,
    install_requires=['twisted', 'setuptools'],
)
```

The most interesting line is include_package_data=True. In order to actually have some interesting data, we need a manifest: in MANIFEST.in, we put

```
include src/static_server/a_file.html
```

The plugin to serve this file (in this case, on /) looks like this:

```python
import pkg_resources

from zope import interface

from twisted.python import usage, threadpool
from twisted import plugin
from twisted.application import service, strports
from twisted.web import static, server, resource
from twisted.internet import reactor
```

```
@interface.implementer(service.IServiceMaker, plugin.IPlugin)
class ServiceMaker(object):
    tapname = "twisted_book_pkg_resources"
    description = "Static for book"
    class options(usage.Options):
        pass
    def makeService(self, options):
        root = resource.Resource()
        fname = pkg_resources.resource_filename("static_server",
                                                "a_file.html")

        static_resource = static.File(fname)
        root.putChild(", static_resource)
        site = server.Site(root)
        return strports.service('tcp:8000', site)
serviceMaker = ServiceMaker()
```

The interesting new line here is:

```
fname = pkg_resources.resource_filename("static_server",
                                        "a_file.html")
static_resource = static.File(fname)
```

This uses the pkg_resources package, a part of setuptools, to find the filename at runtime.

Note that this will work even if, say, our package is deployed directly as a zip using a tool like pex (or the built-in zipapp): pkg_resources is smart enough to transparently unpack the file before giving the filename.

This technique is also useful for including template files when using a system like Jinja2 or Chameleon.

Combining Static Files with WSGI

We can also serve static resources for a WSGI application through Twisted's own web server.

```
import os
from zope import interface
from twisted.python import usage, threadpool
from twisted import plugin
```

```
from twisted.application import service, strports
from twisted.web import wsgi, server, static, resource
from twisted.internet import reactor
import wsgi_hello
class DelegatingResource(resource.Resource):
    def __init__ (self, wsgi_resource):
        resource.Resource. __init__ (self)
        self._wsgi_resource = wsgi_resource
    def getChild(self, name, request):
        request.prepath = []
        request.postpath.insert(0, name)
        return self._wsgi_resource
@interface.implementer(service.IServiceMaker, plugin.IPlugin)
class ServiceMaker(object):
    tapname = "twisted_book_combined"
    description = "twisted_book_combined"
    class options(usage.Options): pass
    def makeService(self, options):
        application = wsgi_hello.application
        pool = threadpool.ThreadPool()
        reactor.callWhenRunning(pool.start)
        reactor.addSystemEventTrigger('after', 'shutdown', pool.stop)
        wsgi_resource = wsgi.WSGIResource(reactor, pool, application)
        static_resource = static.File('.')
        root = DelegatingResource(wsgi_resource)
        root.putChild('static', static_resource)
        site = server.Site(root)
        return strports.service('tcp:8000', site)
serviceMaker = ServiceMaker()
```

We go line by line over the new code:

```
class DelegatingResource(resource.Resource):
```

We define a class called DelegatingResource. This is going to be our root. It inherits from resource.Resource. Note that it is *not* a leaf resource – and so the site will traverse it.

```
def __init__ (self, wsgi_resource):
```

We initialize the delegator with a WSGI resource.

```
resource.Resource. __init__ (self)
```

As appropriate, we call the superclass constructor. This is crucially important – Resource would not function correctly without its constructor.

```
self.wsgi_resource = wsgi_resource
```

We save the WSGI resource in an attribute.

```
def getChild(self, name, request):
```

The name of getChild is a bit confusing. The semantics are of getting a *dynamic* child. A static child, that is, one which has been manually added to a Resource, will prevent this method from being called. The root will never be called to render: even a URL like / will result in a child traversal with an empty string as name.

```
request.prepath = []
request.postpath.insert(0, name)
```

We move the name from the prepath to the postpath, thus tricking the delegated – to resource that is the root. Note that this trick works only if this resource is at root.

```
return self.wsgi_resource
```

After tricking the path to pretend one less traversal has been done, we return the WSGI resource.

```
static_resource = static.File('.')
```

We create the static resource. This is no different from the pure static resource case.

```
root = DelegatingResource(wsgi_resource)
```

We create the delegating resource as our root resource.

```
root.putChild('static', static_resource)
```

As indicated earlier, the manually introduced child will override the getChild method. So for any path that starts with /static/, a static resource will be served.

Built-In Scheduled Tasks

For the following example, we want a WSGI app that depends on a parameter we can change.

```
class _Application(object):
    def __init__ (self, greeting='hello world'):
        self.greeting = greeting
    def __call__ (self, environment, start_response):
        start_response('200 OK', [('Content-Type',
                                   'text/html; charset=utf-8')])
        return [self.greeting.encode('utf-8')]
application = _Application()
```

We will go through the code line by line:

```
class _Application(object):
```

As mentioned earlier, the only assumption about WSGI applications is that they are callable objects. In this case, we create a callable object by defining a class with a __call__ method.

```
def __init__ (self, greeting='hello world'):
```

We initialize with a greeting, with the standard default.

```
self.greeting = greeting
```

In the constructor, we do not do anything more interesting than setting attributes.

```
def __call__ (self, environment, start_response):
```

Since this is a WSGI application, it is called with the standard parameter.

```
start_response('200 OK', [('Content-Type',
                           'text/html; charset=utf-8')])
```

This is the same start_response call as before, with the exception of the addition of an explicit character set. Since it is possible for the creator to pass arbitrary unicode strings, and we encode them to utf-8, we need to let the browser know this is what we do.

```
return [self.greeting.encode('utf-8')]
```

We want to be able to set greetings as strings. Therefore, this must encode them to bytes.

```
application = _Application()
```

We do not care about the class – what we want is an instance of it as the application.

```
import time
from zope import interface
from twisted.python import usage, reflect, threadpool, filepath
from twisted import plugin
from twisted.application import service, strports, internet
from twisted.web import wsgi, server, static
from twisted.internet import reactor
import wsgi_param

def update(application, reactor):
    stamp = time.ctime(reactor.seconds())
    application.greeting = "hello world, it's {}".format(stamp)

@interface.implementer(service.IServiceMaker, plugin.IPlugin)
class ServiceMaker(object):
    tapname = "twisted_book_scheduled"
    description = "Changing application"
    class options(usage.Options): pass
    def makeService(self, options):
        s = service.MultiService()
        pool = threadpool.ThreadPool()
        reactor.callWhenRunning(pool.start)
        reactor.addSystemEventTrigger('after', 'shutdown', pool.stop)
        root = wsgi.WSGIResource(reactor, pool, wsgi_param.application)
        site = server.Site(root)
        strports.service('tcp:8000', site).setServiceParent(s)
        ts = internet.TimerService(1, update, wsgi_param.application, reactor)
        ts.setServiceParent(s)
        return s
serviceMaker = ServiceMaker()

def update(application, reactor):
```

This function will be called periodically to update the application.

```
stamp = time.ctime(reactor.seconds())
```

We use `reactor.seconds()` here, rather than `time.time()`. If this code were to grow bigger, this would aid in testability.

```
application.greeting = "hello world, it's {}".format(stamp)
```

This sets the application greeting attribute. Since it is public, it is considered part of the class's API.

Note: this is taking advantage of mutable global state, which in general is a dangerous pattern – doubly so in the case of threads. While the main loop of Twisted features no threads, WSGI works all run inside of Twisted's thread pool.

However, in this specific case, the change is safe – a thread will either see the old greeting or a new one. This is because of Python's global interpreter lock, which ensures Python threads see a consistent state – and because this is just replacing one string with another.

```
s = service.MultiService()
```

This creates a service that starts multiple services. It allows us to do both the web serving, and the updating, from the same service.

```
strports.service('tcp:8000', site).setServiceParent(s)
```

This time, instead of returning the `strports.service` result, we set its parent to the `MultiService`. This will attach it to the `MultiService` as a child.

```
ts = internet.TimerService(1, update, wsgi_param.application, reactor)
```

Here we create a timer that fires every 1 second and calls the function `update` with the parameters `wsgi_param.application` and `reactor`.

```
ts.setServiceParent(s)
```

Attach the timer to the return value.

```
return s
```

And return the `MultiService`.

While this is definitely not the best way to display a clock, there are many cases where this separation between retrieval of a value and displaying it make sense. Imagine a stock ticker application: it is better to retrieve the stock price once a second, and display a value from memory when a web request happens, rather make every web request wait for a (potentially slow) back-end service.

This shows the benefits of the scheduled service running in process. Of course, even things that do not *have* to be in process can be scheduled this way – log cleanup, for example. This allows application configuration to be kept in one place, rather than having to add a dependency on a service like `cron`.

Control Channels

Often it is useful to modify the configuration of web applications at runtime, without restarting or rebuilding. Some examples of this are:

- Modifying debugging levels when troubleshooting a problem.

- Modifying control/test percentage in an A/B test.

- Switching a "feature flag" off if customers are reporting issues.

This means that besides the "application channel," over which the application end user is interacting with the application, we want a side channel, a "control channel," that will modify the behavior. Having this channel available via a different port, and potentially a different protocol, is much safer – the attack vector of an unauthorized user getting access to the control channel can be mitigated with conventional firewalls and network configuration, rather than only through application-level access control.

Since Twisted is, at heart, a networking event framework, it is ideally suited for adding control channels to WSGI applications. Since such control channels, by nature, cross thread boundaries, it is necessary to take care and think about thread safety.

However, it does allow interesting behaviors to be added to WSGI applications.

The following plugin shows a way to control the greeting using the network.

```
from zope import interface

from twisted.python import usage, reflect, threadpool, filepath
from twisted import plugin
from twisted.application import service, strports, internet
```

```
from twisted.web import wsgi, server, static
from twisted.internet import reactor, protocol
from twisted.protocols import basic

import wsgi_param

class UpdateMessage(basic.LineReceiver):

    def lineReceived(self, line):
        self.factory.application.greeting = line.decode('utf-8')
        self.transport.writeSequence([b"greeting is now: ", line, b"\r\n"])
        self.transport.loseConnection()

@interface.implementer(service.IServiceMaker, plugin.IPlugin)
class ServiceMaker(object):
    tapname = "twisted_book_control"
    description = "Changing application"
    class options(usage.Options): pass
    def makeService(self, options):
        s = service.MultiService()
        pool = threadpool.ThreadPool()
        reactor.callWhenRunning(pool.start)
        reactor.addSystemEventTrigger('after', 'shutdown', pool.stop)
        root = wsgi.WSGIResource(reactor, pool, wsgi_param.application)
        site = server.Site(root)
        strports.service('tcp:8000', site).setServiceParent(s)
        factory = protocol.Factory.forProtocol(UpdateMessage)
        factory.application = wsgi_param.application
        strports.service('tcp:8001',factory).setServiceParent(s)
        return s
serviceMaker = ServiceMaker()
```

We go through the new code line by line:

```
class UpdateMessage(basic.LineReceiver):
```

This defines a subclass of the protocol basic.LineReceiver. It chunks messages into lines, allowing us to easily delimit messages.

```
def lineReceived(self, line):
```

207

This will be called when a line is received – note that the line will *not* contain the termination character (by default, carriage return followed by a newline, \r\n).

```
self.factory.application.greeting = line
```

We set the greeting to the incoming line.

```
factory = protocol.Factory.forProtocol(UpdateMessage)
```

We create the factory that will produce instances of UpdateMessage upon client connection.

```
factory.application = wsgi_param.application
```

We set the application on the factory to the WSGI application. This allows the protocol object to have access to the application, in order to change the greeting.

```
strports.service('tcp:8001',factory).setServiceParent(s)
```

We bind this protocol to one port higher.

Strategies for Using Multiple Cores

The one limitation Twisted as a WSGI server has is that it runs one process. Since Python has the global interpreter lock, this means that on a multi-core machine, only one core will be used for WSGI. Frequently, this is not a problem: in some environments, a lower layer will present a one-core "machine" to applications. For example, this is the case when using a virtualization platform or a container orchestration framework.

However, for many reasons, sometimes the correct multi-process solution needs to be solved at the application layer. Here we showcase some of these approaches.

Load Balancer

The simplest way is to start multiple Twisted WSGI processes, and put a load balancer in front of them. One popular load balancer is HAProxy. Having a complete HAProxy tutorial is beyond our scope, but the following is an example HAProxy configuration. In order to simplify the configuration, the configuration is for plain-text HTTP – although HAProxy is often used to terminate SSL.

```
defaults
    log       global
    mode      http
frontend localnodes
    bind *:8080
    mode http
    default_backend nodes
backend nodes
    mode http
    balance roundrobin
    option forwardfor
    http-request set-header X-Forwarded-Port %[dst_port]
    http-request add-header X-Forwarded-Proto https if { ssl_fc }
    option httpchk HEAD / HTTP/1.1\r\nHost:localhost
    server web01 127.0.0.1:9000 check
    server web02 127.0.0.1:9001 check
    server web03 127.0.0.1:9002 check
```

The last three lines are the most important: they forward to three different local web servers.

Now, we need something to run all four processes – HAProxy and the three web servers. In this example, we will use ncolony.

```
$ alias add="python -m ncolony --messages /var/run/messages \
                                --config /var/run config add"
$ add --cmd haproxy --arg=-f --arg=/my/haproxy.cfg haproxy
$ add --cmd python --arg=-m --arg=twisted \
                   --arg=web --arg=--wsgi \
                   --arg=wsgi_hello.application \
                   --arg=--port --arg=tcp:9001 web1
$ add --cmd python --arg=-m --arg=twisted \
                   --arg=web --arg=--wsgi \
                   --arg=wsgi_hello.application \
                   --arg=--port --arg=tcp:9002 web2
$ add --cmd python --arg=-m --arg=twisted \
                   --arg=web --arg=--wsgi \
```

```
                    --arg=wsgi_hello.application \
                    --arg=--port --arg=tcp:9003 web3
$ python -m twisted ncolony --messages /var/run/messages \
                    --config /var/run config add
```

Opening Socket in Shared Mode

A fairly recent feature of Linux kernels is the SO_REUSEPORT socket option. This allows several servers to listen on the same port. However, since the feature is fairly recent, Twisted does not support it out of the box.

In order to take advantage of it, we will need to plug into the lower layers of Twisted.

```python
import socket

import attr

from zope import interface

from twisted.python import usage, threadpool
from twisted import plugin
from twisted.application import service, internet as tainternet
from twisted.web import wsgi, server
from twisted.internet import reactor, tcp, interfaces as tiinterfaces,
defer

import wsgi_hello

@interface.implementer(tiinterfaces.IStreamServerEndpoint)
@attr.s
class ListenerWithReuseEndPoint(object):
    port = attr.ib()
    reactor = attr.ib(default=None)
    backlog = attr.ib(default=50)
    interface = attr.ib(default=")

    def listen(self, protocolFactory):
        p = tcp.Port(self.port, protocolFactory, self.backlog, self.interface,
                     self.reactor)
        self._sock = sock = p.createInternetSocket()
```

```
        sock.setsockopt(socket.SOL_SOCKET, socket.SO_REUSEPORT, 1)
        sock.bind((self.interface, self.port))
        sock.listen(self.backlog)
        return defer.succeed(reactor.adoptStreamPort(sock.fileno(),
                                                     p.addressFamily,
                                                     protocolFactory))

@interface.implementer(service.IServiceMaker, plugin.IPlugin)
class ServiceMaker(object):
    tapname = "twisted_book_reuseport"
    description = "Reuse port"
    class options(usage.Options): pass
    def makeService(self, options):
        application = wsgi_hello.application
        pool = threadpool.ThreadPool(minthreads=1, maxthreads=100)
        reactor.callWhenRunning(pool.start)
        reactor.addSystemEventTrigger('after', 'shutdown', pool.stop)
        root = wsgi.WSGIResource(reactor, pool, application)
        site = server.Site(root)
        endpoint = ListenerWithReuseEndPoint(8000)
        service = tainternet.StreamServerEndpointService(endpoint, site)
        return service
serviceMaker = ServiceMaker()
```

This has certainly been the most complicated plugin we have written so far. In production code, this would be too big for a plugin – certainly most of the logic should be broken out.

However, for illustration purposes, showing all the code close together serves to make it clearer.

```
@interface.implementer(tiinterfaces.IStreamServerEndpoint)
```

The module name seems strange. Twisted's deep module hierarchy means some names are repeated at different points in the hierarchy. A useful convention is to import the module with some letters of the hierarchy still there, in order to make the purpose clearer. In this case, tiinterfaces stands for twisted.internet.interfaces.

We implement the `IStreamServerEndpoint` interface, as we need to implement a new kind of endpoint – one that opens sockets in REUSEPORT mode.

`@attr.s`

Since this class has a lot of data members, we use the `attrs` package to make the code simpler.

```
class ListenerWithReuseEndPoint(object):
    port = attr.ib()
    reactor = attr.ib(default=None)
    backlog = attr.ib(default=50)
    interface = attr.ib(default=")
```

We accept exactly the same arguments as the `reactor.listenTCP` call. This is intentional.

```
def listen(self, protocolFactory):
```

This is the sole method in the `IStreamServerEndpoint` interface.

```
p = tcp.Port(self.port, protocolFactory, self.backlog, self.interface,
             self.reactor)
self._sock = sock = p.createInternetSocket()
```

Twisted's lower-level TCP facilities, in `tcp.Port`, make sure that the right options for non-blocking will be set on the socket. We keep a reference to the socket object, in order to keep it from being collected. This is important, since we will be creating a new Python-level socket object from the same file descriptor.

```
sock.setsockopt(socket.SOL_SOCKET, socket.SO_REUSEPORT, 1)
```

This is the real reason for all this rigamarole – to set the SO_REUSEPORT option.

```
sock.bind((self.interface, self.port))
```

We bind to the interface.

```
sock.listen(self.backlog)
```

We start listening.

```
return defer.succeed(reactor.adoptStreamPort(sock.fileno(),
                                             p.addressFamily,
                                             protocolFactory))
```

We take the file descriptor from the socket object and allow Twisted to "adopt" it. This returns an IListeningPort. Since the contract for listen is to return a deferred, we wrap it in defer.succeed.

In order to put this in production, we can use ncolony again.

```
$ alias add="python -m ncolony --messages /var/run/messages \
                               --config /var/run config add"
$ add --cmd python --arg=-m --arg=twisteded \
                   --arg=twisted_book_reuseport web1
$ add --cmd python --arg=-m --arg=twisteded \
                   --arg=twisted_book_reuseport web2
$ add --cmd python --arg=-m --arg=twisteded \
                   --arg=twisted_book_reuseport web3
$ python -m twist ncolony --messages /var/run/messages \
                          --config /var/run config add
```

As in the last example, we run three web workers. Note that this time, the command-line for all three is identical – and the need for a load balancer is gone.

Other Options

There are, in general, a few other options for multi-processing in Twisted. It is possible to create a socket, and then spawn processes that will listen on it. This means tying in the process management and the listening code in somewhat awkward ways. For example, using ncolony is no longer possible – nor is using twisted.runner.procmon – to monitor the processes. If the "parent" process dies, we are left with the dilemma of whether to restart it, and kill all existing children, or wait for all children to die first.

Another option is to listen in one process, but then pass the file descriptors over a UNIX domain socket. This is nontrivial to do portably and requires quite a bit of delving into a socket system call esoterica.

In general, the options for port reuse or for load balancing are superior. Note that, like any performance improvement, the effect of a specific choice (such as port reuse vs. load balancing) should be measured in an environment that, as much as possible, approximates the production environment.

Dynamic Configuration

As noted earlier, using Twisted as a WSGI server allows adding control channels to your applications, allowing reconfiguration at runtime. Here we show a full-fledged example of such control, using the Asynchronous Messaging Protocol (AMP) as our control protocol. The example includes both the application and the control application.

A/B Testable Pyramid App

A/B testing means showing one version of a web application to some users and a different version to others – and checking the effect on various metrics. For example, an e-commerce application might experiment with the placement of the "Checkout" button, and test its effect on how many customers check out.

There are many full-featured A/B testing options for Python web frameworks. Here we do not have the scope to write a full-featured alternative, but we will show one of the basic pieces: varying the output. In general, the output should be constant when shown to a given user, but that requires a coherent session construct, again beyond our scope.

Our "test" will just be per request, deciding which version to show. We will do this based on a random choice. However, we will adopt an important feature of A/B test frameworks – biased choice. If we think the test might have a detrimental effect on users, we often run it on a small percentage.

Our default is to run the tests on 0% of users. We will depend on an external mechanism to increase those percentages.

```
import random

from pyramid import config, response

FEATURES = dict(capitalize=0.0, exclaim=0.0)
```

```python
def hello_world(request):
    if random.random() < FEATURES['capitalize']:
        message = 'Hello world'
    else:
        message = 'hello world'
    if random.random() < FEATURES['exclaim']:
        message += '!'
    return response.Response(message)

with config.Configurator() as conf:
    conf.add_route('hello', '/')
    conf.add_view(hello_world, route_name='hello')
    application = conf.make_wsgi_app()
```

We go over the new code line by line:

```python
FEATURES = dict(capitalize=0.0, exclaim=0.0)
```

We allow two "features" – `capitalize`, whether to capitalize our greeting; and exclaim, whether to add an exclamation mark. Note that these features, in the example, are independent: users can be exposed to four different greetings.

This is, in the small, a good simulation of actual environments that do A/B testing – in which users can often be, in theory, exposed to any of the 2**n possible options when running n experiments.

```python
if random.random() < FEATURES['capitalize']:
```

This is the basic logic of a so-called "biased coin toss" in Python. It will result in True about FEATURES['capitalize'] on average.

```python
message = 'Hello world'
```

Capitalized message.

```python
else:
    message = 'hello world'
```

Lowercase message.

```python
if random.random() < FEATURES['exclaim']:
    message += '!'
```

If exclamation is on, add an exclamation mark.

Custom Plugin with AMP

In order to be able to adjust the percentages, we use the AMP protocol. There are many alternative options, but this one balances flexibility and demonstrability. One nice thing is that support for AMP is built into Twisted, so no third-party packages are needed.

```python
from zope import interface

from twisted.python import usage, threadpool
from twisted import plugin
from twisted.application import service, strports
from twisted.web import wsgi, server
from twisted.internet import reactor, protocol
from twisted.protocols import amp

import pyramid_dynamic

class GetCapitalize(amp.Command):
    arguments = []
    response = [(b'value', amp.Float())]

class GetExclaim(amp.Command):
    arguments = []
    response = [(b'value',  amp.Float())]

class SetCapitalize(amp.Command):
    arguments = [(b'value', amp.Float())]
    response = []

class SetExclaim(amp.Command):
    arguments = [(b'value',  amp.Float())]
    response = []

class AppConfiguration(amp.CommandLocator):

    @GetCapitalize.responder
    def get_capitalize(self):
        return {'value':  pyramid_dynamic.FEATURES['capitalize']}
```

```python
    @GetExclaim.responder
    def get_exclaim(self):
        return {'value':  pyramid_dynamic.FEATURES['exclaim']}

    @SetCapitalize.responder
    def set_capitalize(self, value):
        pyramid_dynamic.FEATURES['capitalize'] = value
        return {}

    @SetExclaim.responder
    def set_exclaim(self, value):
        pyramid_dynamic.FEATURES['exclaim'] = value
        return {}

@interface.implementer(service.IServiceMaker, plugin.IPlugin)
class ServiceMaker(object):
    tapname = "twisted_book_configure"
    description = "WSGI for book"
    class options(usage.Options):
        pass
    def makeService(self, options):
        application = pyramid_dynamic.application
        pool = threadpool.ThreadPool(minthreads=1, maxthreads=100)
        reactor.callWhenRunning(pool.start)
        reactor.addSystemEventTrigger('after', 'shutdown', pool.stop)
        root = wsgi.WSGIResource(reactor, pool, application)
        site = server.Site(root)
        control = protocol.Factory()
        control.protocol = lambda: amp.AMP(locator=AppConfiguration())
        ret = service.MultiService()
        strports.service('tcp:8000', site).setServiceParent(ret)
        strports.service('tcp:8001', control).setServiceParent(ret)
        return ret
serviceMaker = ServiceMaker()
```

We will go over the new code:

```
class GetCapitalize(amp.Command):
    arguments = []
    response = [(b'value', amp.Float())]

class GetExclaim(amp.Command):
    arguments = []
    response = [(b'value', amp.Float())]

class SetCapitalize(amp.Command):
    arguments = [(b'value', amp.Float())]
    response = []

class SetExclaim(amp.Command):
    arguments = [(b'value', amp.Float())]
    response = []
```

These define AMP *commands*. Commands are the basic messages in AMP. While in theory, commands can be sent both ways, in most cases, they will be sent from the client to the server.

We intentionally made the commands for get/set allow only one field at a time, in order to be clear that no atomicity is guaranteed. Indeed, since it is hard to guarantee atomicity on the dictionary access without much more machinery, it is useful to indicate in the API that it is impossible to, say, set capitalize to 1 and *guarantee* that at the same time, exclaim is 0.

We could have made an API with claims to atomicity: for example, setting both attributes at once. We could even implement it in a way that would look atomic: for example, replacing the FEATURES dictionary wholesale, so that the access would be to either the old dictionary or a new one, and there was no intermediate step. However, a thread switch could happen between the line

```
if random.random() < FEATURES['capitalize']:
```

and the line

```
if random.random() < FEATURES['exclaim']:
```

which would render the atomicity pretense a lie. Instead, we choose to make it explicit that updates are not atomic,

```
class AppConfiguration(amp.CommandLocator):
```

```
@GetCapitalize.responder
def get_capitalize(self):
    return {'value': pyramid_dynamic.FEATURES['capitalize']}

@GetExclaim.responder
def get_exclaim(self):
    return {'value': pyramid_dynamic.FEATURES['exclaim']}

@SetCapitalize.responder
def set_capitalize(self, value):
    pyramid_dynamic.FEATURES['capitalize'] = value
    return {}

@SetExclaim.responder
def set_exclaim(self, value):
    pyramid_dynamic.FEATURES['exclaim'] = value
    return {}
```

We write a simple class that bridges the command to the pyramid_dynamic.
FEATURES dictionary, setting and getting the fields appropriately.

```
control = protocol.Factory()
control.protocol = lambda: amp.AMP(locator=AppConfiguration())
```

The control factory sets protocol to a function that creates a new amp.AMP with a
custom locator. There are other ways to bind an AMP protocol to the specific locator, but
this puts as much power at the hands of the integrator – the programmer who is writing
the plugin, as opposed to the one who is writing the command handling itself.

Control Program

Perhaps in other places, the control code itself would be using a synchronous style and
blocking network calls. However, in this book, this is an opportunity to show how to write
clients using Twisted. We chose to write this code in a way that is compatible with both
Python 2 and Python 3.

```
from twisted.internet import task, defer, endpoints, protocol
from twisted.protocols import amp

from twisted.plugins import twisted_book_configure
```

```
@task.react
@defer.inlineCallbacks
def main(reactor):
    endpoint = endpoints.TCP4ClientEndpoint(reactor, "127.0.0.1", 8001)
    prot = yield endpoint.connect(protocol.Factory.forProtocol(amp.AMP))
    res1 = yield prot.callRemote(twisted_book_configure.GetCapitalize)
    res2 = yield prot.callRemote(twisted_book_configure.GetExclaim)
    print(res1['value'],  res2['value'])
    yield prot.callRemote(twisted_book_configure.SetCapitalize, value=0.5)
    yield prot.callRemote(twisted_book_configure.SetExclaim, value=0.5)
    res1 = yield prot.callRemote(twisted_book_configure.GetCapitalize)
    res2 = yield prot.callRemote(twisted_book_configure.GetExclaim)
    print(res1['value'],  res2['value'])
@task.react
```

The react decorator will run the main function, immediately, with a reactor argument.

```
@defer.inlineCallbacks
```

We use an inlineCallbacks decorator to allow the code to flow better.

```
def main(reactor):
```

Note that here we accept the reactor as an argument, rather than importing it.

```
endpoint = endpoints.TCP4ClientEndpoint(reactor, "127.0.0.1", 8001)
```

Create client endpoint.

```
prot = yield endpoint.connect(protocol.Factory.forProtocol(amp.AMP))
```

Create client factory, and connect.

```
res1 = yield prot.callRemote(twisted_book_configure.GetCapitalize)
res2 = yield prot.callRemote(twisted_book_configure.GetExclaim)
```

Retrieve the values. Note that we are using the previously-defined command classes.

```
print(res1['value'], res2['value'])
```

Show value before the change

```
yield prot.callRemote(twisted_book_configure.SetCapitalize, value=0.5)
yield prot.callRemote(twisted_book_configure.SetExclaim, value=0.5)
```

Set the values

```
res1 = yield prot.callRemote(twisted_book_configure.GetCapitalize)
res2 = yield prot.callRemote(twisted_book_configure.GetExclaim)
print(res1['value'],  res2['value'])
```

Get them again. This verifies they have changed.

Those three parts together – the application, the plugin, and the control program – give us a web server whose internal parameters we can configure dynamically.

Summary

The Twisted WSGI server is easy to install and use in development – in fact, even easier than the reference implementation. Despite this ease of use, it is perfectly suitable to be used in production. This makes it handy in order to avoid differences between the development environment and the production one – differences that often make it hard to reproduce production issues.

Since it is based on the Twisted Web server, it inherits features like production-grade TLS implementations –which support features like SNI and Let's Encrypt, as well as HTTP/2 protocol support. It can also be configured as a static file web server, allowing it to serve the static assets, like images, JavaScript, and CSS files, from the same process as the dynamic application – thus avoiding a mismatch between the static assets and what the application accepts.

It does not define any configuration file format. Instead, for any configuration deeper than setting the listening port or naming the WSGI application, it is possible to write a Twisted plugin – which allows ultimate configuration in a language that, regardless of the web framework, all engineers who work on the application know and use.

The biggest perceived downside of Twisted as a WSGI container is taking advantage of multiple core machines. For this, it is possible – via several different configurations – to set up multiple WSGI processes. In general, separating the concerns of "how to listen on a socket" from "how to manage multiple processes" allows finding good solutions for each one – instead of having to bind together process management and socket code.

CHAPTER 6

Tahoe-LAFS: The Least-Authority File System

Tahoe-LAFS is a distributed storage system, started in 2006 as a robust back end for a personal-backup company named AllMyData (long since defunct). Before shutting down, the company open sourced the code, and now a community of hackers improves and maintains the project.

The system allows you to upload data from your computer into a network of servers called a "grid," and then retrieve your data from the grid later. In addition to providing a backup (e.g., in case your laptop hard drive fails), it offers flexible ways to share specific files or directories with other users on the same grid. In this way, it behaves somewhat like a "network drive" (SMB or NFS), or a file-transfer protocol (FTP or HTTP).

Tahoe's special feature is "provider-independent security." All files are encrypted and cryptographically hashed locally, before leaving your computer. The storage servers never get to see the plaintext (because of the encryption), nor can they make undetected changes (because of the hashes). In addition, the ciphertext is erasure coded into redundant shares, and uploaded to multiple independent servers. This means your data can survive the loss of a few servers, to improve durability and availability.

As a result, you can pick storage servers purely on the basis of their performance, cost, and uptime, without also needing to rely upon them for security. Most other network drives are entirely vulnerable to the servers: an attacker who compromises the hosting provider gets to see or modify your data, or delete it entirely. Tahoe's confidentiality and integrity are entirely independent of the storage providers, and the availability is improved too.

© Mark Williams, Cory Benfield, Brian Warner, Moshe Zadka, Dustin Mitchell, Kevin Samuel, Pierre Tardy 2019
M. Williams et al., *Expert Twisted*, https://doi.org/10.1007/978-1-4842-3742-7_6

How Tahoe-LAFS Works

A Tahoe "grid" consists of one or more Introducers, some Servers, and some Clients.

- Clients know how to upload and download data.

- Servers hold the encrypted shares.

- Introducers help Clients and Servers find and connect to each other.

The three node types communicate using a special protocol named "Foolscap," which is descended from Twisted's "Perspective Broker," but with added security and flexibility.

Tahoe uses "capability strings" to identify and access all files and directories. These are random-looking chunks of base32 data that contain the encryption key, integrity-protecting hashes, and share-location information. We abbreviate these as "filecaps" when they refer to a file, or "dircaps" for directories.

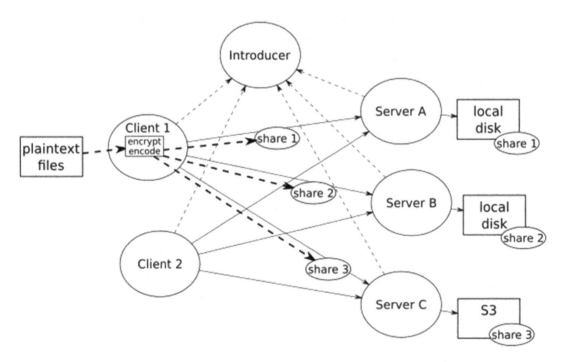

Figure 6-1. *Tahoe-LAFS Grid Diagram*

(The examples in this chapter are shortened for readability, but filecaps are normally about 100 characters long.)

They sometimes come in multiple flavors: a "writecap" gives whoever knows it the ability to change a file, whereas a "readcap" only lets them read the contents. There's even a "verifycap," which allows the holder to verify the encrypted server-side shares (and generate new ones if some have been lost), but not to read or modify the plaintext. You can safely give these to a delegated repair agent to maintain your files while your own computer is offline.

Tahoe's simplest API call is a command-line PUT that accepts plaintext data, uploads it into a brand-new immutable file, and returns the generated filecap:

```
$ tahoe put kittens.jpg
200 OK
URI:CHK:bz3lwnno6stuspjq5a:mwmb5vaecnd3jz3qc:2:3:3545
```

This filecap is the only way in the world to retrieve the file. You could write it down, or store it in another file, or store it in a Tahoe directory, but this string is both necessary and sufficient to recover the file. Downloads look like this (the tahoe get command writes the downloaded data to stdout, so we use the ">" shell syntax to redirect this into a file):

```
$ tahoe get URI:CHK:bz3lwnno6stuspjq5a:mwmb5vaecnd3jz3qc:2:3:3545
>downloaded.jpg
```

We frequently (and perhaps erroneously) refer to filecaps as URIs in many places, including the filecap strings themselves. "CHK" stands for "Content-Hash Key," which describes the specific kind of immutable file encoding we use: other kinds of caps have different identifiers. Immutable filecaps are always readcaps: nobody in the world can modify the file once it's been uploaded, even the original uploader.

Tahoe also offers *mutable* files, which means we can change the contents later. These have three API calls: create generates a mutable slot, publish writes new data into the slot (overwriting whatever was there before), and retrieve returns the current contents of the slot.

Mutable slots have both writecaps and readcaps. create gives you the writecap, but anyone who knows the writecap can "attenuate" it down into a readcap. This lets you share the readcap with others, but reserves the write authority for yourself.

In Tahoe, directories are just files that contain a specially encoded table, which maps a child name to a filecap or dircap of the child. Think of these directories as intermediate nodes in a directed graph.

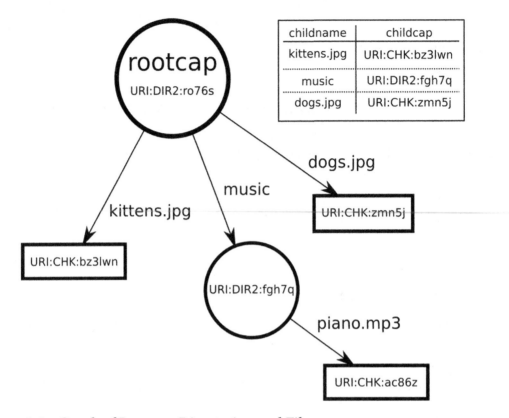

Figure 6-2. *Graph of Rootcap, Directories, and Files*

We can create one with the `mkdir` command. This defaults to creating a mutable directory (but we could also create fully-populated immutable directories, if we wanted to). Tahoe has `cp` and `ls` commands to copy files and list directories, and these know how to handle slash-delimited file paths as usual.

The CLI also tool offers "aliases," which simply store a "rootcap" directory in a local file (`~/.tahoe/private/aliases`), allowing other commands to abbreviate the dircap with a prefix that looks a lot like a network drive indicator (e.g., the Windows `E:` drive). This reduces typing and makes commands much easier to use:

```
$ tahoe mkdir
URI:DIR2:ro76sdlt25ywixu25:lgxvueurtm3
$ tahoe add-alias mydrive URI:DIR2:ro76sdlt25ywixu25:lgxvueurtm3
Alias 'mydrive' added
$ tahoe cp kittens.jpg dogs.jpg mydrive:
Success: files copied
```

```
$ tahoe ls URI:DIR2:ro76sdlt25ywixu25:lgxvueurtm3
kittens.jpg
dogs.jpg
$ tahoe mkdir mydrive:music
$ tahoe cp piano.mp3 mydrive:music
$ tahoe ls mydrive:
kittens.jpg
music
dogs.jpg
$ tahoe ls mydrive:music
piano.mp3
$ tahoe cp mydrive:dogs.jpg /tmp/newdogs.jpg
$ ls /tmp
newdogs.jpg
```

The command-line tools are built on top of the HTTP API, which we'll explore later.

System Architecture

The Client node is a long-lived gateway daemon, which accepts upload and download requests from a "front-end" protocol. The most basic front end is an HTTP server that listens on the loopback interface (127.0.0.1).

An HTTP GET is used to retrieve data, which involves multiple steps:

- parse the filecap to extract the decryption key and storage index;

- identify which pieces of each share we need to satisfy the client request, including both the share data and the intermediate hash tree nodes;

- use the storage index to identify which servers might have shares for this file;

- send download requests to those servers;

- track requests we've sent and requests that have completed, to avoid duplicate requests unless necessary;

- track server response time, to prefer faster servers;

- verify shares and reject corrupt ones;

- switch to faster servers when available or when connections are lost;

- reassemble shares into ciphertext;

- decrypt ciphertext and deliver plaintext to the front-end client.

This is managed by an event loop that is constantly ready to accept new `read()` requests from the front-end managers, or responses from servers, or timer expirations that indicate it's time to give up on a server and try a different one. This loop will juggle dozens or even hundreds of simultaneous connections and timers, and activity on any one them will cause things to happen on the others. Twisted's event loop is ideal for this design.

In the other direction, the HTTP PUT and POST actions cause data to be uploaded, which does many of the same steps, but backward:

- the client node accepts data from the front-end protocol and buffers it in a temporary file;

- the file is hashed to build the "convergent encryption key," which also serves to deduplicate files;

- the encryption key is hashed to form the storage index;

- the storage index identifies which servers we should try to use (the server list is sorted a different way for each storage index, and this list provides a priority ordering);

- send upload requests to those servers;

- if the file was uploaded earlier, the server will tell us they already have a share, in which case we don't need to store that one again;

- if a server rejects our request (not enough disk space), or doesn't answer fast enough, try a different server;

- gather responses until each share is mapped to a server;

- encrypt and encode each segment of plaintext, which takes a lot of CPU (at least compared to the network activity), so we push it off to a separate thread to take advantage of multiple cores;

- after encoding is done, upload the shares to the previously mapped servers;

- when all servers acknowledge receipt, build the final hash trees;

- build the filecap from the root of the hash tree and the encryption key;

- return the filecap in the HTTP response body.

Clients also implement other (non-HTTP) front-end protocols:

- FTP: by supplying a config file of usernames, passwords, and rootcaps, the Tahoe client node can pretend to be an FTP server with a separate virtual directory for each user;

- SFTP: like FTP, but layered on top of SSH;

- Magic-Folder: a Dropbox-like two-way directory synchronization tool.

Clients speak Foolscap to the Introducer, to learn about servers. They also speak Foolscap to the servers themselves.

The Tahoe-LAFS storage server can store the shares on local disk, or it can send them to a remote commodity storage service like S3 or Azure. The server speaks Foolscap on the front side, and, for example, HTTP-based S3 commands on the back.

On the storage server, the node must accept connections from an arbitrary number of clients, each of which will send overlapping share upload/download requests. For remote back ends like S3, each client-side request can provoke multiple S3-side API calls, each of which might fail or timeout (and need to be retried).

All node types also run an HTTP service for status and management. This currently renders using Nevow, but we intend to switch to Twisted's built-in HTTP templating facilities (`twisted.web.template`).

How It Uses Twisted

Tahoe-LAFS uses Twisted extensively: it's hard for us to imagine how we could have written it any other way.

The application is structured around a Twisted `MultiService` hierarchy, which controls startup and shutdown of the Uploader, the Downloader, the IntroducerClient, etc. This lets us start individual services during unit tests, without needing to launch an entire node each time.

The largest Service is the `Node`, which represents an entire Client, Server, or Introducer. This is the parent `MultiService` for everything else. Shutting down the service (and waiting for all network activity to come to a halt) is as easy as calling `stopService()` and waiting for the Deferred to fire. Nodes listen on ephemerally allocated ports by default, and announce their location to the Introducer. All state is restricted to the node's "base directory." This makes it easy to launch multiple clients/servers in a single process, for testing an entire grid at once. Contrast this to an earlier architecture, in which each storage server required a separate MySQL database and used fixed TCP ports. In that system, it was impossible to perform a realistic test without at least 5 distinct computers. In Tahoe, the integration test suite will spin up a grid with 10 servers, all in a single process, exercise some feature, then shut everything down again, in just a few seconds. This happens dozens of times whenever you run `tox` to run the test suite.

The variety of front-end interfaces are enabled by Twisted's robust suite of well-integrated protocol implementations. We didn't have to write an HTTP client, or server, or the FTP server, or the SSH/SFTP server: these all come "batteries included" with Twisted.

Problems We've Run Into

Our use of Twisted has been fairly smooth. If we were to start again today, we would still begin with Twisted. Our regrets have been minor:

- dependency load: some users (usually packagers) feel that Tahoe depends upon too many libraries. For many years, we tried to avoid adding dependencies because Python's packaging tools were immature, but now `pip` makes this much easier;

- packaging/distribution: it is difficult to build a single-file executable out of a Python application, so currently users must know about Python-specific tools like `pip` and `virtualenv` to get Tahoe installed on their home computers;

- Python 3: Twisted now has excellent support for Python 3, but this took many years of effort. During this time, we became complacent, and the code freely intermixes machine-readable bytes with human-readable strings. Now that py3 is the preferred implementation (and the 2020 end-of-life deadline for py2 is looming), we're struggling to update our code to work under py3.

Daemonization Tools

Twisted provides a convenient tool named `twistd`, which allows long-running applications to be written as plugins, making Twisted responsible for the platform-specific details of daemonization (such as detaching from the controlling tty, logging to a file instead of stdout, and potentially switching to a non-root user after opening privileged listening TCP ports). When Tahoe was started, neither "pip" nor "virtualenv" existed yet, so we built something like them. To combine daemonization with this bespoke dependency installer/manager, the Tahoe command-line tool includes the `tahoe start` and `tahoe stop` subcommands.

These days, we'd probably omit these subcommands, and have users run `twistd` or `twist` (the non-daemonizing form) instead. We would also look for ways to avoid needing a daemon at all.

In the beginning, `twistd` wasn't as easy to manage, so Tahoe used ".tap" files to control it. This was a holdover from a pattern I used in Buildbot, where the first versions regrettably used ".tap" files to record state (a sort of "freeze-dried" copy of the application, which could be thawed out again the next time you wanted to launch it). Tahoe never put dynamic state in there, but the `tahoe create-node` process would create a `.tap` file with the right initialization code to instantiate and launch the new node. Then `tahoe start` was a simple wrapper around `twistd -y node.tap`.

Different kinds of `.tap` files were used to launch different kinds of nodes (Clients, Servers, Introducers, etc.). This was a bad decision. The .tap files contained just a few lines: an import statement and code to instantiate an Application object. Both ended up limiting our ability to rearrange the code base or change its behavior: simply renaming the `Client` class would break all existing deployments. We'd accidentally created a public API (with all the compatibility issues that implies), where the "public" were all the old `.tap` files used by earlier Tahoe installs.

We fixed this by having `tahoe start` ignore the contents of the `.tap` file, and only pay attention to its filename. Most of the node's configuration was already stored in a separate INI-style file named `tahoe.cfg`, so the transition was pretty easy. When `tahoe start` sees `client.tap`, it creates a Client instance (as opposed to an Introducer/etc.), initializes it with the config file, and sets the daemon running.

Internal FileNode Interfaces

Internally, Tahoe defines FileNode objects, which can be created from filecap strings for existing files, or from scratch by uploading some data for the first time. These offer a few simple methods that hide all the details of encryption, erasure coding, server selection, and integrity checking. The download methods are defined in an Interface named IReadable:

```
class IReadable(Interface):

    def get_size():
        """Return the length (in bytes) of this readable object."""

    def read(consumer, offset=0, size=None):
        """Download a portion (possibly all) of the file's contents,
        making them available to the given IConsumer. Return a Deferred
        that fires (with the consumer) when the consumer is unregistered
        (either because the last byte has been given to it, or because the
        consumer threw an exception during write(), possibly because it no
        longer wants to receive data). The portion downloaded will start at
        'offset' and contain 'size' bytes (or the remainder of the file if
        size==None).  """
```

Twisted uses zope.interface for the classes that support Interface definitions (that Interface is really zope.interface.Interface). We use these as a form of type checking: the front end can assert that the object being read is a provider of IReadable. There are multiple kinds of FileNodes, but they all implement the IReadable interface, and the front-end code only uses methods defined on that interface.

The read() interface doesn't return the data directly: instead, it accepts a "consumer" to which it can feed the data as it arrives. This uses Twisted's Producer/Consumer system (described in Chapter 1) to stream data without unnecessary buffering. This allows Tahoe to deliver multi-gigabyte files without using gigabytes of memory.

DirectoryNode objects can be created similarly. These also have methods (defined in IDirectoryNode) to list their children, or follow a child link (by name) to some other node. Mutable directories include methods to add or replace a child by name.

```
class IDirectoryNode(IFilesystemNode):
    """I represent a filesystem node that is a container, with a name-
    to-child mapping, holding the tahoe equivalent of a directory. All
    child names are unicode strings, and all children are some sort of
    IFilesystemNode (a file, subdirectory, or unknown node).
    """
    def list():
        """I return a Deferred that fires with a dictionary mapping child
        name (a unicode string) to (node, metadata_dict) tuples, in which
        'node' is an IFilesystemNode and 'metadata_dict' is a dictionary of
        metadata."""
    def get(name):
        """I return a Deferred  that fires with a specific named child
        node, which is an IFilesystemNode. The child name must be a unicode
        string. I raise NoSuchChildError if I do not have a child by that
        name."""
```

Note that these methods return Deferreds. Directories are stored in files, and files are stored in shares, and shares are stored on servers. We don't know exactly when those servers will respond to our download requests, so we use a Deferred to "wait" for the data to be available.

This graph of node objects is used by each front-end protocol.

Front-End Protocol Integration

To explore how Tahoe takes advantage of Twisted's diverse protocol support, we'll look at several "front-end protocols." These provide a bridge between external programs and the internal IFileNode/IDirectoryNode/IReadable interfaces.

All the protocol handlers make use of an internal object named Client, whose most important method is create_node_from_uri. This takes a filecap or directorycap (as a string), and returns the corresponding FileNode or DirectoryNode object. From here, the caller can use its methods to read or modify the underlying distributed file.

The Web Front End

The Tahoe-LAFS client daemon provides a local HTTP service to control most of its operations. This includes both a human-oriented web application to browse files and folders ("WUI": Web User Interface), and a machine-oriented control interface ("WAPI": Web Application Programming Interface), which we affectionately pronounce "wooey" and "wappy."

Both are implemented through Twisted's built-in `twisted.web` server. A hierarchy of "Resource" objects route requests to some leaf, which implements methods like `render_GET` to process the request details and provide a response. By default, this listens on port 3456, but this can be configured in the `tahoe.cfg` file, by providing a different endpoint descriptor.

Tahoe actually uses the "Nevow" project, which provides a layer on top of raw `twisted.web`, but these days Twisted's built-in functionality is powerful enough on its own, so we're slowly removing Nevow from the code base.

The simplest WAPI call is the GET that retrieves a file. The HTTP client submits a filecap, Tahoe turns this into a `FileNode`, downloads the contents, and returns the data in the HTTP response. The request looks like:

```
curl -X GET http://127.0.0.1:3456/uri/URI:CHK:bz3lwnno6stus:mwmb5vae...
```

This results in a `twisted.web.http.Request` with a "path" array that has two elements: the literal string "`uri,`" and the filecap. Twisted's web server starts with a root resource, upon which you can attach handlers for different names. Our `Root` resource is instantiated with the `Client` object described above, and configured with a handler for the `uri` name:

```
from twisted.web.resource import Resource
class Root(Resource):
    def __init__(self, client):
        ...
        self.putChild("uri", URIHandler(client))
```

All requests that start with `uri/` will get routed to this `URIHandler` resource. When these requests have additional path components (i.e., our filecap), they'll cause the `getChild` method to be called, which is responsible for finding the right Resource to handle the request. We'll create a FileNode or DirectoryNode from the given filecap/dircap, and then we'll wrap it in a web-specific handler object that knows how to deal with HTTP requests:

```python
class URIHandler(Resource):
    def __init__ (self, client):
        self.client = client
    def getChild(self, path, request):
        # 'path' is expected to be a filecap or dircap
        try:
            node = self.client.create_node_from_uri(path)
            return directory.make_handler_for(node,self.client)
        except (TypeError,AssertionError):
            raise WebError("'%s' is not a valid file- or directory- cap" %name)
```

node is the FileNode object that wraps the filecap from the GET request. The handler comes from a helper function that inspects the node's available interfaces and decides what sort of wrapper to create:

```python
def make_handler_for(node, client, parentnode=None, name=None):
    if parentnode:
        assert IDirectoryNode.providedBy(parentnode)
    if IFileNode.providedBy(node):
        return FileNodeHandler(client, node, parentnode, name)
    if IDirectoryNode.providedBy(node):
        return DirectoryNodeHandler(client, node, parentnode, name)
    return UnknownNodeHandler(client, node, parentnode, name)
```

For our example, this returns the FileNodeHandler. This handler has a lot of options, and the actual code in web/filenode.py looks quite different, but a simplified form would read like this:

```python
class FileNodeHandler(Resource):
    def __init__ (self, client, node, parentnode=None, name=None):
        self.node = node
        ...
    @inlineCallbacks
    def render_GET(self, request):
        version = yield self.node.get_best_readable_version()
        filesize = version.get_size()
```

```
first, size, contentsize = 0, None, filesize
... # these will be modified by a Range header, if present
request.setHeader("content-length", b"%d" % contentsize)
yield version.read(request, first, size)
```

Twisted's native web server doesn't allow `Resource` objects to return Deferreds, but Nevow's does, which is convenient. Here's basically what happens:

- First, we ask the FileNode for its best readable version. This isn't needed on immutable files (for which there's only one version anyways), but mutable files might have multiple versions on the grid. "Best" means the most recent. We get back a "version" object that provides the `IReadable` interface.

- Next, we compute the size of the file. For immutable files, the size is embedded in the filecap, so the `get_size()` method lets us compute this immediately. For mutable files, the size was determined when we retrieved the version object.

- We use the file's size and a Range header (if provided) to figure out how much data to read, and what offset to start from.

- We set the Content-Length header to tell the HTTP client how much data to expect.

- The `IReadable`'s `read()` method is called to begin the download. The Request object is also an IConsumer, and the download code builds an IProducer to attach to it. This returns a Deferred that will fire when the last byte of the file has been delivered to the consumer.

- When the last Deferred fires, the server knows it can close the TCP connection, or reset it for the next request.

We've elided many of the details, which are expanded below.

File Types, Content-Type, /name/

Tahoe's storage model maps filecaps to bytestrings, without names, dates, or other metadata. *Directories* contain names and dates, in the table entries that point to their children, but a basic filecap just gives you a bunch of bytes.

However, the HTTP protocol includes a `Content-Type` for each download, which allows the browser to figure out how to render the page (HTML, JPG, or PNG), or what OS metadata to record when saving it to disk. In addition, most browsers assume the last component of the URL path is a filename, and the "save-to-disk" feature will use it as the default filename.

To deal with this mismatch, Tahoe's WAPI has a feature to let you download a filecap with an arbitrary name in the last element of the path. The WUI directory browser puts these special URLs in the HTML of the directory page, so "Save Link As." works correctly. The full URL looks like this:

```
http://127.0.0.1:3456/named/URI:CHK:bz3lwnno6stus:mwmb5vae../kittens.jpg
```

This looks a lot like a directory and a child inside it. To avoid visual confusion, we usually insert an extra funny-looking string into such URLs:

```
http://127.0.0.1:3456/named/URI:CHK:bz3lwn../@@named=/kittens.jpg
```

This is implemented with a `Named` Resource that creates a `FileNodeHandler`, but also remembers the last component of the URL path in `self.filename` (ignoring any intermediate components, like that @@named= string). Then, when we run `render_GET`, we pass this filename into a Twisted utility that maps the filename suffix to a type string, using the equivalent of `/etc/mime.types`. From this, we can set the `Content-Type` and `Content-Encoding` headers.

```
# from twisted.web import static
ctype, encoding = static.getTypeAndEncoding(
    self.filename,
    static.File.contentTypes,
    static.File.contentEncodings,
    defaultType="text/plain")
request.setHeader("content-type", ctype)
if encoding:
    request.setHeader("content-encoding", encoding)
```

Saving to Disk

When you click on a link, the browser will try to render the document that comes back: HTML goes through layout, images get drawn in the window, audio files get played, etc. If it doesn't recognize the file type, it will offer to save the file to disk instead. Tahoe's "WUI" HTML front end offers a way to force this save-to-disk behavior: for any URL that points at a file, just append a ?save=True query argument to the URL. The web server acts on this by adding a Content-Disposition header, which instructs the browser to always save the response, instead of trying to render it:

```
if boolean_of_arg(get_arg(request,"save","False")):
    request.setHeader("content-disposition",
                      'attachment; filename="%s"' % self.filename)
```

Range Headers

The web front end allows HTTP clients to request just a subset of the file by providing a Range header. This is frequently used by streaming media players (like VLC or iTunes) when the "scrubber" control is used to jump around in a movie or audio file. Tahoe's encoding scheme was specifically designed to support this sort of random-access efficiently, by using Merkle hash trees.

Merkle hash trees start by chopping up the data into segments and applying a cryptographic hash function (SHA256) to each segment. Then we hash each pair of segment hashes into a second layer (half the length of the first). This reduction process is repeated until we have a single "root hash" at the top of a binary tree of intermediate hash nodes, with the segments at the bottom. The root hash is stored in the filecap, and we send everything else (segments and intermediate hashes) to the server. During retrieval, any single segment can be validated against the stored root without downloading all the other segments, by asking the server to provide the companion hash nodes for the path from that segment up to the root. This enables fast validation of arbitrary segments with minimum data transfer.

The web front end handles this by parsing the request's Range header, setting the response's Content-Range and Content-Length headers, and modifying the first and size values that we pass into the read() method.

Parsing the Range header is nontrivial, since it can include a list of (potentially overlapping) ranges, which might include the beginning or end of the file, and it might be expressed in various units (not just bytes). Fortunately, servers are allowed to ignore unparsable Range specifications: it's not efficient, but they can just return the entire file, as if the Range header didn't exist. The client is then obligated to ignore the portions of the data they didn't want.

```python
first, size, contentsize = 0,None, filesize
request.setHeader("accept-ranges","bytes")

rangeheader = request.getHeader('range')
if rangeheader:
    ranges = self.parse_range_header(rangeheader)

    # ranges = None means the header didn't parse, so ignore
    # the header as if it didn't exist. If is more than one
    # range, then just return the first for now, until we can
    # generate multipart/byteranges.
    if ranges is not None:
        first, last = ranges[0]

        if first >= filesize:
            raise WebError('First beyond end of file',
                        http.REQUESTED_RANGE_NOT_SATISFIABLE)
        else:
            first = max(0, first)
            last = min(filesize-1, last)

            request.setResponseCode(http.PARTIAL_CONTENT)
            request.setHeader('content-range',"bytes %s-%s/%s" %
                        (str(first), str(last),
                        str(filesize)))
            contentsize = last - first + 1
            size = contentsize

request.setHeader("content-length", b"%d" % contentsize)
```

Error Conversion on the Return Side

Tahoe's internal API throws a variety of exceptions when something goes wrong. For example, if too many servers have failed, the file may not be recoverable (at least not until some servers come back online). We try to map these exceptions into sensible HTTP error codes with an exception handler that runs at the end of the HTTP processing chain. The core of this handler is named humanize_failure(), and looks at the twisted. python.failure.Failure object that wraps all exceptions raised during the processing of a Deferred:

```python
def humanize_failure(f):
    # return text, responsecode
    if f.check(EmptyPathnameComponentError):
        return ("The webapi does not allow empty pathname components, "
                "i.e. a double slash" , http.BAD_REQUEST)
    if f.check(ExistingChildError):
      return ("There was already a child by that name, and you asked me "
              "to not replace it." , http.CONFLICT)
    if f.check(NoSuchChildError):
        quoted_name = quote_output(f.value.args[0], encoding="utf-8")
        return ("No such child: %s" % quoted_name, http.NOT_FOUND)
    if f.check(NotEnoughSharesError):
        t = ("NotEnoughSharesError: This indicates that some "
             "servers were unavailable, or that shares have been "
             "lost to server departure, hard drive failure, or disk "
             "corruption. You should perform a filecheck on "
             "this object to learn more.\n\nThe full error message is:\n"
             "%s" ) % str(f.value)
        return (t, http.GONE)
    ...
```

The first half of the return value is a string to put into the HTTP response body; the second is the HTTP error code itself.

Rendering UI Elements: Nevow Templates

Tahoe's WUI provides a file-browser interface: directory panels, file listings, upload/ download selectors, delete buttons, etc. These are made up of HTML, rendered on the server side from Nevow templates.

The web/ directory contains an XHTML file for each page, with placeholders that are filled in with variables by the DirectoryNodeHandler class. Each placeholder is a namespaced XML element that names a "slot." The directory listing template looks like this:

```
<table class="tahoe-directory"n:render="sequence"n:data="children" >
  <tr n:pattern="header">
    <th>Type</th>
    <th>Filename</th>
    <th>Size</th>
  </tr>
  <tr n:pattern="item"n:render="row" >
    <td><n:slot name="type"/></td>
    <td><n:slot name="filename"/></td>
    <td align="right"><n:slot name="size"/></td>
  </tr>
```

The code that populates this form, in directory.py, loops over all children of the directory being rendered, examines its type, and uses a ctx "context" object to fill in each slot by name. For files, the T.a Nevow tag produces a hyperlink, with the href= attribute pointing at a download URL using the /named/ prefix described earlier:

```
...
elif IImmutableFileNode.providedBy(target):
    dlurl = "%s/named/%s/@@named=/%s"%(root, quoted_uri, nameurl)
    ctx.fillSlots("filename", T.a(href=dlurl, rel="noreferrer")[name])
    ctx.fillSlots("type","FILE")
    ctx.fillSlots("size", target.get_size())
```

Nevow also offers tools to build HTML input forms. These are used to construct the upload file-picker form, and the "make directory" name input element.

The FTP Front End

The front-end protocols allow other applications to access this internal file graph, in some form that matches their existing data model. For example, the FTP front end assigns each "account" (a username / password pair) to a root dircap. When an FTP client connects to this account, they are presented with a filesystem that starts at this directory node, and only extends downward (into child files and subdirectories). In a normal FTP server, all accounts see the same filesystem, but with different permissions (Alice cannot read Bob's files), and different starting directories (Alice starts in /home/ alice, Bob starts in /home/bob). In the Tahoe FTP server, Alice and Bob will have entirely distinct views of the filesystem, which may not overlap at all (unless they have arranged to share some portion of their space).

Tahoe's FTP front end builds upon Twisted's FTP server (`twisted.protocols.ftp`). The FTP server uses Twisted's "Cred" framework for account management (which involves "Portals," "Realms," and "Avatars"). As a result, the server is made up of several components:

- Endpoint: This defines what TCP port the server will listen on, along with options like which network interfaces to use (e.g., the server can be restricted to only listen on 127.0.0.1, the loopback interface).

- `FTPFactory (twisted.protocols.ftp.FTPFactory)`: This provides the overall FTP server. It is a "protocol factory," so it will be invoked each time a new client connects, and it is responsible for building the `Protocol` instance that manages that specific connection. When you tell the Endpoint to start listening, you give it a factory object.

- Checker: This is an object that implements `ICredentialsChecker` and handles authentication, by examining some credentials and (if successful) returning an "Avatar ID." In the FTP protocol, the credentials are a username and password supplied by the user. In SFTP, they include an SSH public key. The "Avatar ID" is just a username. The Tahoe FTP front end can be configured to use an `AccountFileChecker` (in auth.py), which stores the username/ password/rootcap mapping in a local file. It can also use an `AccountURLChecker`, which queries an HTTP server (it POSTs the username and password, and gets the rootcap back in the response). The `AccountURLChecker` was used for centralized account management back at AllMyData.

- Avatar: This is the server-side object that handles a specific user's experience. It is also specific to a service type, so it must implement some particular `Interface`, in this case a Twisted interface named `IFTPShell` (which has methods like `makeDirectory`, `stat`, `list`, and `openForReading`).

- Realm: This is any object that implements Twisted's `IRealm` interface, and is responsible for turning an Avatar ID into an Avatar. The Realm API also deals with multiple interfaces: a client that needs a specific kind of access can ask for a specific `Interface`, and the Realm might return a different Avatar depending on what they ask for. In the Tahoe FTP front end, the realm is a class named `Dispatcher` that knows how to create a root directory node from the account information and wrap it in a handler.

- Portal (`twisted.cred.portal.Portal`): This is a Twisted object that manages the Checkers and the Realms. The `FTPFactory` is configured with a `Portal` instance at construction time, and everything involving authorization is delegated to the portal.

- Handler (`allmydata.frontends.ftpd.Handler`): This is a Tahoe object that implements Twisted's `IFTPShell` and translates FTP concepts into Tahoe concepts.

The Tahoe FTP server code does the following:

- create a `MultiService` that hangs off the top-level Node multiservice;

- hang a `strports.service` off that, listening on the FTP server port;

- configure that listener with an `FTPFactory`;

- configure the factory with a `Portal`;

- create a `Dispatcher` for use as the Portal's "realm";

- add an `AccountFileChecker` and/or an `AccountURLChecker` to the Portal.

When an FTP client connects, the username and password are submitted to the AccountFileChecker, which had previously parsed the accounts file into memory. The account lookup is pretty simple:

```
class FTPAvatarID:
    def __init__ (self, username, rootcap):
        self.username = username
        self.rootcap = rootcap
@implementer(checkers.ICredentialsChecker)
class AccountFileChecker(object):
    def requestAvatarId(self, creds):
        if credentials.IUsernamePassword.providedBy(creds):
            return self._checkPassword(creds)

        ...
    def _checkPassword(self, creds):
        try:
            correct = self.passwords[creds.username]
        except KeyError:
            return defer.fail(error.UnauthorizedLogin())

        d = defer.maybeDeferred(creds.checkPassword, correct)
        d.addCallback(self._cbPasswordMatch, str(creds.username))
        return d

    def _cbPasswordMatch(self, matched, username):
        if matched:
            return self._avatarId(username)
        raise error.UnauthorizedLogin

    def _avatarId(self, username):
        return FTPAvatarID(username,self.rootcaps[username])
```

If the username is not on the list, or if the password doesn't match, requestAvatarId will return a Deferred that errbacks with UnauthorizedLogin, and the FTPFactory will return the appropriate FTP error code. If both are good, it returns an FTPAvatarID object that encapsulates the username and the account's rootcap URI (which is just a string).

When this succeeds, the Portal asks its Realm (i.e., our Dispatcher object) to turn the Avatar ID into a handler. Our realm is also pretty simple:

```
@implementer(portal.IRealm)
class Dispatcher(object):
    def __init__ (self, client):
        self.client = client

    def requestAvatar(self, avatarID, mind, interface):
        assert interface == ftp.IFTPShell
        rootnode = self.client.create_node_from_uri(avatarID.rootcap)
        convergence = self.client.convergence
        s = Handler(self.client, rootnode, avatarID.username, convergence)
        def logout(): pass
        return (interface, s,None)
```

First, we assert that we're being asked for an IFTPShell, not some other interface (which we don't know how to deal with). Then, we use the Tahoe file-graph API to convert the rootcap URI into a directory node. The "convergence secret" is outside the scope of this chapter, but it exists to provide safe deduplication, and is provided to the Handler to let us extend the interface to use distinct convergence secrets for each account.

Then, we build a Handler around the Client (which provides methods to create brand new filenodes) and the rootnode (which provides access to the user's "home directory" and everything below it), and return this to the portal. That's enough to get the FTP server connected.

Later, when the client performs an "ls" command, our handler's list() method will get invoked. Our implementation is responsible for translating the FTP notion of listing a directory (it gets a list of path-name components, relative to the root) into Tahoe's notion (which does a step-wise traversal from the root directory node down into some other dirnode).

```
def list(self, path, keys=()):
    d = self._get_node_and_metadata_for_path(path)
    def _list((node, metadata)):
        if IDirectoryNode.providedBy(node):
            return node.list()
        return { path[-1]: (node, metadata) }
    d.addCallback(_list)
```

```
def _render(children):
    results = []
    for (name, childnode) in children.iteritems():
        results.append( (name.encode("utf-8"),
                            self._populate_row(keys, childnode) ) )
    return results
d.addCallback(_render)
d.addErrback(self._convert_error)
return d
```

We start with a common "follow the path from the root" helper method, which returns a Deferred that eventually fires with the node and metadata for the file or directory named by the path (if the path is foo/bar, then we'll ask our root dirnode for its foo child, expect that child to be a directory, then ask that subdirectory for its bar child). If the path pointed to a directory, we use the Tahoe IDirectoryNode's node. list() method to gets its children: this returns a dictionary that maps child name to (child node, metadata) tuples. If the path pointed to a file, we pretend that it pointed to a directory with only the one file in it.

Then we need to turn this dictionary of children into something the FTP server can accept. In the FTP protocol, the LIST command can ask for different attributes: sometimes the client wants owner/group names, sometimes it wants permissions, sometimes all it cares about is the list of child names. Twisted's IFTPShell interface expresses this by giving the list() method a sequence of "keys" (strings) to indicate which values it wants. Our _populate_row() method turns one child+metadata pair into the correct list of values.

```
def _populate_row(self, keys, (childnode, metadata)):
    values = []
    isdir = bool(IDirectoryNode.providedBy(childnode))
    for key in keys:
        if key == "size":
            if isdir:
                value = 0
            else:
                value = childnode.get_size() or 0
        elif key == "directory":
            value = isdir
```

```
    elif key == "permissions":
        value = IntishPermissions(0600)
    elif key == "hardlinks":
        value = 1
    elif key == "modified":
        if "linkmotime" in metadata.get("tahoe", {}):
            value = metadata["tahoe"]["linkmotime"]
        else:
            value = metadata.get("mtime",0)
    elif key == "owner":
        value = self.username
    elif key == "group":
        value = self.username
    else:
        value = "??"
    values.append(value)
return values
```

For each key that Twisted wants, we translate this into something we can get from Tahoe's IFileNode or IDirectoryNode interfaces. Most of these are simple lookups in the metadata, or are obtained by calling a method on the Node object. One unusual case is permissions: see below for details.

The last step is to attach _convert_error as an errback handler. This converts some Tahoe-specific errors into their closest FTP equivalent, which is more useful than the "internal server error" that the client would get if they weren't converted.

```
def _convert_error(self, f):
    if f.check(NoSuchChildError):
        childname = f.value.args[0].encode("utf-8")
        msg = "'%s' doesn't exist" % childname
        raise ftp.FileNotFoundError(msg)
    if f.check(ExistingChildError):
        msg = f.value.args[0].encode("utf-8")
        raise ftp.FileExistsError(msg)
    return f
```

The SFTP Front End

SFTP is a file-transfer protocol built upon the SSH secure shell encryption layer. It exposes a very POSIX-like API to remote clients: open, seek, read, and write, all on the same filehandle. FTP, on the other hand, only offers all-or-nothing transfer of individual files. FTP is a much better fit for Tahoe's file model, but SFTP is more secure when speaking to remote servers.

The advantage of using Cred is that the same authentication mechanism can be reused with other protocols. FTP and SFTP, despite their differences, use the same basic access model: clients are identified by some credentials, and this gives access to a particular home directory. In Tahoe, both FTP and SFTP use the same FTPAvatarID and AccountFileChecker classes above. AccountFileChecker defines "credentialInterfaces" to cover all the kinds of authentication that might be presented: IUsernamePassword, IUsernameHashedPassword, and ISSHPrivateKey (this is specific to SFTP, and allows users to be identified by their SSH public key, instead of a password).

They only differ in the Realm (our Dispatcher class), which returns a different kind of handler for the two protocols.

Backward-Incompatible Twisted APIs

Tahoe has no notion of Access Control Lists (ACLs), usernames, or read/write/execute permission bits: it follows the object-capability discipline of "if you can reference an object, you can use it." Filecaps are unguessable, so the only way to reference a file is by knowing the filecap, which can only come from someone who uploaded the file originally, or from someone else who learned it from the uploader.

Most files are stored in directories, so access control is managed through directory traversal, which is safe because Tahoe directories do not have "parent" links. You can share one of your own directories with someone else by simply giving them a link: they cannot use this to reach anything "above" the one directory you gave them.

As a result, the FTP server always returns "0600" for the "permissions" field, which means "read and write by the current user only." This value is mostly cosmetic: FTP clients only use it to populate the "mode" column of a long-form (ls -l) directory listing. We could be more accurate here, returning "0400" for immutable objects, but we didn't really care enough to make the change.

However, even a static value caused problems when one of Twisted's APIs changed unexpectedly. In the early days, Twisted used integers to represent file modes/permissions (just like the Unix kernel, and most C programs). Eventually folks realized that this is pretty unix-centric, so in Twisted-11.1.0, a nice, clean `filepath.Permissions` class was created to hold this kind information as a collections of Booleans.

But the FTP server wasn't updated to use it until much later. Up until Twisted-14.0.2, the "permissions" value of `list()` was expected to return an integer. From Twisted-15.0.0 and onward, it was expected to return a `Permissions` instance. Moreover, it *only* accepted a `Permissions` instance: returning an integer would cause an exception.

In effect, the `IFTPShell` interface changed abruptly between 14.0.2 and 15.0.0, which we discovered when we started getting bug reports about FTP `ls` commands failing for folks who had upgraded (we didn't have end-to-end test coverage for this front end, and our personal manual tests were still using Twisted-14.0.2, so we didn't notice the problem ourselves).

Twisted usually does a fantastic job of deprecating APIs for a couple releases before making incompatible changes, but this one slipped through the cracks, probably because the most common implementation of `IFTPShell` is Twisted's built-in `FTPShell` class, which was updated at the same time. So, another way to describe the problem was that `IFTPShell` was modified without a deprecation period, as if it were a private internal API, but in fact it was public.

The easiest way to resolve this would have been to make Tahoe's `setup.py` require `Twisted >= 15.0.0`, and change the code to return a `Permissions` object. But this would have made life more difficult for folks building Tahoe on Linux distributions that included a version of Twisted that was a few years out of date. (Debian 8.0 "jessie" was released in 2015 with Twisted-14.0.2, and wasn't replaced until 2017.) Back then, Tahoe was trying to be compatible with a wide range of Twisted versions. We felt bad about asking users to upgrade their system Twisted just to satisfy Tahoe's enthusiasm for modern fashions.

So, to allow Tahoe work with both old and new Twisteds, we needed to return something that behaved like an integer when necessary, but could behave like a `Permissions` too. When we examined the way that Twisted-14.0.2 used the value, we found that it always did a bitwise AND of the value during the formatting process:

```
# twisted-14.0.2: twisted/protocols/ftp.py line 428
def formatMode(mode):
    return ''.join([mode&(256>>n) and 'rwx'[n % 3] or '-' for n in range(9)])
```

This let us build a helper class that inherited from Permissions, but overrode the binary and method to return an integer if it got used by the older Twisted:

```
# filepath.Permissions was added in Twisted-11.1.0, which we require.
# Twisted <15.0.0 expected an int, and only does '&' on it. Twisted
# >=15.0.0 expects a filepath.Permissions. This satisfies both.

class IntishPermissions(filepath.Permissions):
    def __init__(self, statModeInt):
        self._tahoe_statModeInt = statModeInt
        filepath.Permissions.__init__(self, statModeInt)
    def __and__(self, other):
        return self._tahoe_statModeInt&other
```

These days, the situation is different. We no longer recommend that users install Tahoe (or any Python application) into a system-wide location like /usr/local/bin, nor do we recommend that Tahoe be run against system-provided Python libraries. Instead, users who build from source should be installing Tahoe into a new virtualenv, where it is easy to simply install the latest versions of all dependencies, and they can be safely isolated from the system python.

The pipsi tool makes this quite easy: pipsi install tahoe-lafs will create a Tahoe-specific virtualenv, install Tahoe and all its dependencies into it, then symlink just the tahoe executable into ~/.local/bin/tahoe where it will probably be on your $PATH. pipsi is now the recommended method to install Tahoe from a source tree.

A system-wide install should be done through the OS package manager. For example, apt install tahoe-lafs will get a working /usr/bin/tahoe on modern Debian and Ubuntu releases, and they'll use system-wide dependencies (like Twisted) from /usr/lib/python2.7/dist-packages. The Debian developers (and other packagers) are responsible for making sure the system-wide libraries are compatible with all packaged applications: Tahoe, Magic-Wormhole, Buildbot, Mercurial, Trac, etc. When Tahoe bumps its dependency on Twisted, it is the packagers who must figure this stuff out. And if the system upgrades a library like Twisted, and it contains an unexpected incompatibility, that upgrade can be reverted until Tahoe can be patched to resolve the problem.

Summary

Tahoe-LAFS is a large project, started in 2006 when Twisted itself was not very old. It contains work-arounds for bugs that no longer exist, and techniques that have been superseded by new Twisted features. At times, the code might seem to reflect the developers' historical fears and personal idiosyncrasies better than it serves as a good teaching example.

But it also embeds years of experience working with the Twisted code base "in anger" (not casually). And although Tahoe-LAFS might not be a household name, its core ideas have influenced and been incorporated into numerous other decentralized storage systems (written in Go, Node.js, Rust, and more).

Twisted's central event loop, and the wealth of ready-to-use protocol implementations, have been critical to our feature set. If you really didn't like event-driven systems, you might try to implement something similar with threads and locks (on the client, you'd need a separate thread for writing to each server, a second thread for receiving from each server, a third batch for each front-end request, all of which must carefully use locks against concurrent access). The chances of this working safely are pretty low.

The Python standard library includes some fine protocol implementations, but they're almost all written in a blocking style, limiting them to programs that do only one thing at a time. Hopefully this will change as Python 3 and `asyncio` gather momentum. In the meantime, Twisted is the best tool for a project like this.

References

Tahoe-LAFS home page: `https://tahoe-lafs.org`

- Tahoe-LAFS GitHub page: `https://github.com/tahoe-lafs/tahoe-lafs`

- Nevow: `https://github.com/twisted/nevow`

- Foolscap: `https://foolscap.lothar.com/`

- pipsi: `https://github.com/mitsuhiko/pipsi/`

CHAPTER 7

Magic Wormhole

Magic Wormhole is a secure file-transfer tool, whose motto is "get things from one computer to another, safely." It is most useful for ad hoc one-shot transfer situations, such as:

- You've just sat down next to someone at a conference, and you want to give them a tarball of your favorite project from your laptop.

- You're talking on the phone with someone and need to give them a picture that you're looking at on your computer.

- You've just set up a new account for a coworker and need to get their SSH public key from their computer safely.

- You want to copy your GPG private key from your old computer to your new laptop.

- A colleague on IRC wants you to send them a logfile from your computer.

One distinctive feature of this tool is the use of a **wormhole code**: a short phrase like "4-bravado-waffle" that enables the transfer and must be conveyed from the sending client to the receiving one. When Alice sends a file to Bob, Alice's computer will display this phrase. Alice must somehow get this phrase to Bob: typically, she would speak it to him over the phone, or type it to him over SMS or IRC. The code consists of a number and a few words, and is designed for easy and accurate transcription, even in a noisy environment.

These codes are single use. The security properties are simple: the first recipient who claims the code correctly will get the file, and nobody else. These properties are *strong*: nobody else can get the file because it is encrypted, and only the first correct claim can compute the decryption key. And they depend only upon the behavior of the client software: no server or internet eavesdropper can violate them. Magic Wormhole is unique in combining strong confidentiality with an easy workflow.

The original version of this chapter was revised. A correction to this chapter is available at https://doi.org/10.1007/978-1-4842-3742-7_13

© Mark Williams, Cory Benfield, Brian Warner, Moshe Zadka, Dustin Mitchell, Kevin Samuel, Pierre Tardy 2019
M. Williams et al., *Expert Twisted*, https://doi.org/10.1007/978-1-4842-3742-7_7

What It Looks Like

Magic Wormhole is currently only available as a Python-based command-line tool, but ports to other languages and runtime environments are underway. The most important projects are to develop a GUI application (where you can drag and drop the files to be transferred), and a mobile app.

- 1: Alice runs `wormhole send FILENAME` on her computer, and it tells her the wormhole code ("4-bravado-waffle").

- 2: She then dictates this to Bob over the phone.

- 3: Bob types the wormhole code into his computer.

- 4: The two computers connect, then encrypt and transfer the file.

```
                              2. sender (bash)
% wormhole send catalog.pdf
Sending 143.6 MB file named 'catalog.pdf'
On the other computer, please run: wormhole receive
Wormhole code is: 4-bravado-waffle

Sending (<-8.8.8.8:51133)..
100%|████████████████████████| 144M/144M [00:01<00:00, 76.6MB/s]
File sent.. waiting for confirmation
Confirmation received. Transfer complete.
%
▯
```

Figure 7-1. *Sender Screenshot*

```
                              2. receiver (bash)
% wormhole receive
Enter receive wormhole code: 4-bravado-waffle
Receiving file (143.6 MB) into: catalog.pdf
ok? (y/N): y
Receiving (->tcp:8.8.4.4:53155)..
100%|████████████████████████| 144M/144M [00:02<00:00, 76.4MB/s]
Received file written to catalog.pdf
%
▯
```

Figure 7-2. *Receiver Screenshot*

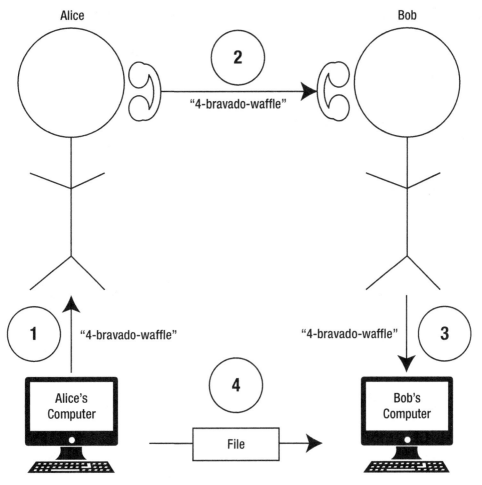

Figure 7-3. *Magic Wormhole Workflow Diagram*

How It Works

Magic Wormhole clients (both sender and receiver) connect to the same **Rendezvous Server** and exchange a handful of short messages. These messages are used to run a special cryptographic key-agreement protocol named **SPAKE2**, which is an authenticated version of the basic Diffie-Hellman key-exchange protocol (see the references below for more detail).

Each side starts their half of the SPAKE2 protocol state machine by feeding it a password: the randomly-generated wormhole code. Their half produces a message to deliver to the other side. When that message is delivered, the other side combines it with their own internal state to produce a session key. When both sides used the same wormhole code, their two session keys will be identical. Each time the protocol is run, they'll get a new random session key. They use this session key to encrypt all subsequent messages, providing a secure connection to figure out the rest of the file transfer details.

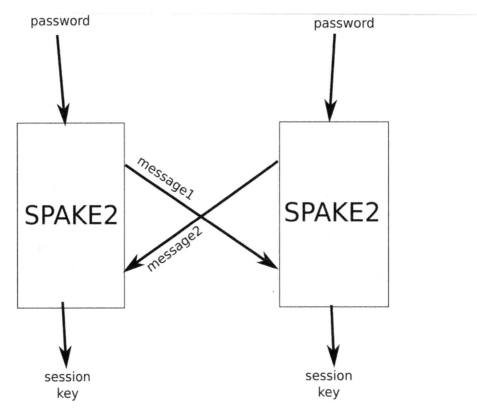

Figure 7-4. SPAKE2 Diagram

Any attacker who tries to intercept the connection will get only one chance to guess the code correctly. If they're wrong, the two session keys will be completely different, and they attacker won't be able to decrypt the rest of the messages. The real clients will notice the mismatch and exit with an error message before trying to send any file data.

Once they establish the secure connection, the magic wormhole clients exchange information about what they want to transfer, and then they work together to establish a **Transit** connection over which the bulk data transfer will take place. This starts with both sides opening a listening TCP network socket. They figure out all the IP addresses that might refer to this socket (there could be multiple ones) and build a list of **connection hints**, which they encrypt with the session key and send through the rendezvous server to the other side.

Each side attempts to make a direct connection to every connection hint it receives. The first attempt that succeeds is used for the file transfer. This works if both sides are on the same local network (for example, when both computers are on the same conference WiFi). Since they both try to connect to each other (regardless of which side is sending the file), this also works if at least one of the machines is a server with a public IP address. In practice, this appears to establish a direct connection about two-thirds of the time.

If both machines are behind different NAT firewalls, all the direct connections will fail. In this case, they fall back to using a central **transit relay** server that basically glues the two inbound TCP connections together.

In all cases, the file data is encrypted by the session key, so neither the rendezvous server nor the transit relay gets to see the contents of the file.

This same protocol can be used in other applications by importing the `wormhole` library and making API calls. For example, an encrypted instant-messaging application like Signal or Wire could use this to securely add a friend's public key to your address book: instead of copying a large key string, you would instead tell your friend a wormhole code.

Network Protocols, Transfer Latency, Client Compatibility

The total transfer time, from the moment the sender launches the tool, to the last byte arriving at the receiver, is roughly the sum of three phases:

- waiting for the receiver to finish typing in the wormhole code;
- performing key agreement and negotiating a transit connection;
- transferring the file over the encrypted channel.

The first phase depends upon the humans: the program will cheerfully wait several days for the receiver to finally type in the wormhole code. The last phase depends upon the size of the file and the speed of the network. Only the middle phase is really under the control of the protocol, so we want to make it as fast as possible. We try to minimize the number of messages that must be exchanged, and use a low-latency real-time protocol to accelerate this phase.

The rendezvous server effectively provides a persistent broadcast channel (i.e., a "pubsub" server) for each pair of clients. The sender connects first, leaves a message for the receiver, and waits for a response. Later, when the human on the receiving side finally starts up their wormhole program, the receiver will connect and collect that message, and send a few of its own. If either client has a network problem, their connection might get dropped, and it must be reestablished.

Network Protocols and Client Compatibility

Twisted makes it quite easy to build custom protocols over TCP or UDP, as seen in the first chapter of this book. We could have built a simple TCP-based protocol for the rendezvous connection. But when we think about the future, we'd like to see Magic Wormhole clients in other languages and runtime environments, like web pages or mobile operating systems. The protocol we build for a command-line Twisted application might not be easy to implement in other languages, or it might require network access that's forbidden to those programs:

- Web browsers can do WebSockets and WebRTC, but not raw TCP connections.

- Browser extensions can do everything a web page can, and more, but must be implemented in specialized JavaScript where binary protocols are not very natural.

- iOS/Android can do HTTP, but power management may prohibit long-lived connections, and non-HTTP requests might not activate the radios.

So, for cross-runtime compatibility, we must stick to things that a web browser can do.

The simplest such protocol would do plain HTTP GETs and POSTs, using the excellent `treq` package, which provides a `requests`-like API to Twisted-based programs. However, it isn't clear how frequently the client ought to poll the server: we might poll once per second, wasting a lot of bandwidth to check for a response that won't happen for an hour. Or we might save bandwidth by only checking once a minute, at the cost of adding 60 seconds of latency to a utility that should only take a second or two. Even polling once per second adds an unnecessary delay. With a real-time connection, the connection completes as fast as the network can carry the messages.

One trick to reduce this latency is "HTTP long polling" (sometimes known as COMET). In this approach, the magic wormhole client would make a GET or a POST as usual, but the relay server would pretend to take a really long time to deliver the response (in fact, the server would just stall the response until the other client connects to receive the file). One limitation is that the server must usually respond *somehow*, usually with a "please try again" error, within 30–60 seconds, or the client HTTP library may give up. Also, back-to-back messages (like the second and third messages sent by the clients) aren't delivered immediately: the time it takes to send a request must be added to the latency of each message.

Another web-compatible real-time technique is called "Server Sent Events," which is exposed to web content as the `EventSource` JavaScript object. This is a more principled way to do long polling: the client does a regular GET, but sets the `Accept` request header to the special value `text/event-stream` to tell the server that the connection should be kept open. The response is expected to contain a stream of encoded events, each on a single line. This is pretty easy to implement on the server; however, there is no off-the-shelf library for Twisted. The messages only travel in one direction (server to client), but that's all we need for our protocol because we can use POSTs in the upstream direction. The biggest downside is that some web browsers (in particular IE and Edge) don't support it.

Our solution is to use **WebSockets**. This is a well-standardized protocol, implemented in most browsers, and available as a library in many programming languages. It's easy to use from Python and Twisted, thanks to the excellent **Autobahn** library (described in the next chapter). The connection looks just like a long-lived HTTP session, which makes it easier to integrate with existing HTTP stacks (and makes it more likely to work through proxies and TLS terminators). Keepalives are handled automatically. And it is a fast, real-time protocol, so messages are delivered as quickly as possible.

If we didn't have Autobahn, we might reconsider. WebSockets are somewhat complicated to implement because they use a special kind of framing (to prevent confused servers from misinterpreting the traffic as some other protocol: you wouldn't want an attacker's web page to make your browser send DELETE commands to your company's internal FTP server).

In the future, the rendezvous server will probably speak multiple protocols, not just WebSockets. WebRTC is the most compelling, because it includes support for ICE and STUN. These are protocols to perform "NAT hole-punching", so two clients can make a direct Transit connection despite both of them being behind firewalls. WebRTC is mostly used for audio/videochat, but it includes APIs specifically for ordinary data transfer. And WebRTC is well-supported by most browsers. A browser-to-browser Magic Wormhole would be fairly easy to build and might perform better than the current CLI tool.

The problem is that support *outside* a browser environment is minimal, partially because of the audio/video focus. Most libraries seem to spend all their energy trying to support the audio codecs and video compression algorithms, leaving them less time for the basic connectivity layer. The most promising ones I've seen are written in C++, for which Python bindings are second class, making build and packaging difficult.

One other contender is the **libp2p** protocol developed for IPFS. This relies upon a swarm of nodes in a large distributed hash table (DHT), rather than a central server, but has been well tested, and has good implementations in at least Go and JavaScript. A Python version of libp2p could be very promising.

Server Architecture

The Rendezvous Server is written as a `twisted.application.service.MultiService`, with a listening port for the main WebSocket connection.

WebSockets are basically HTTP, and the Autobahn library makes it possible to use the same port for both. In the future this will let us host the pages and other assets of a web-based version of Magic Wormhole from the same origin as the rendezvous service. To set this up, the Rendezvous Server looks like this:

```
from twisted.application import service
from twisted.web import static, resource
from autobahn.twisted.resource import WebSocketResource
from .rendezvous_websocket import WebSocketRendezvousFactory
```

```python
class Root(resource.Resource):
    def __init__ (self):
        resource.Resource.__init__(self)
        self.putChild(b"", static.Data(b"Wormhole Relay\n", "text/plain"))

class RelayServer(service.MultiService):
    def __init__ (self, rendezvous_web_port):
        service.MultiService.__init__(self)
        ...
        root = Root()
        wsrf = WebSocketRendezvousFactory(None, self._rendezvous)
        root.putChild(b"v1", WebSocketResource(wsrf))
```

self._rendezvous is our Rendezvous object that provides the internal API for the Rendezvous Server actions: adding messages to a channel, subscribing to channels, etc. When we add additional protocols, they will all use this same object.

WebSocketResource is Autobahn's class for adding a WebSocket handler at any HTTP endpoint. We attach it as the "v1" child of Root, so if our server is on magic-wormhole. io, then the Rendezvous service will live at a URL of ws://magic-wormhole.io/v1. We reserve v2/ and the like for future versions of the protocol.

The WebSocketResource must be given a factory: we use our WebSocketRendezvous Factory from a neighboring module. This factory produces Protocol instances of our WebSocketRendezvous class, which has an onMessage method that examines the payload of each message, parses the contents, and invokes the appropriate action:

```python
def onMessage(self, payload, isBinary):
    msg = bytes_to_dict(payload)
    try:
        if "type" not in msg:
            raise Error("missing 'type'")
        self.send("ack", id=msg.get("id"))

        mtype = msg["type"]
        if mtype == "ping":
            return self.handle_ping(msg)
        if mtype == "bind":
            return self.handle_bind(msg)
        ...
```

261

Persistent Database

When both clients are connected at the same time, the rendezvous server delivers messages from one to the other right away. But at least the initial message must be buffered while waiting for the second client to connect: sometimes for just a few seconds, but sometimes for hours or days.

Early versions of the rendezvous server held these messages in memory. But then each time the host was rebooted (e.g., to upgrade the operating system), these messages were lost, and any clients waiting at that moment would fail.

To fix this, the server was rewritten to store all messages in an SQLite database. Every time a message arrives, the first thing the server does is to append it to a table. Once the message is safely stored, a copy is forwarded to the other client. The Rendezvous object wraps a database connection, and each method performs SELECTs and INSERTs.

The clients were also rewritten to tolerate losing a connection, as described in the next section, with state machines that retransmit any message that hasn't been acknowledged by the server.

An interesting side effect of this work was that it enables an "offline mode": two clients can exchange messages without ever being connected at the same time. While this doesn't enable a direct file-exchange operation, it *does* allow use cases like exchanging public keys for a messaging application.

Transit Client: Cancelable Deferreds

After a session key is computed, the wormhole clients can communicate securely, but all their data is still being relayed by the rendezvous server. This is too slow for the bulk file-transfer phase: every byte must go up to the server, and then back down to the other client. It would be faster (and cheaper) to use a direct connection. However, sometimes the clients cannot make a direct connection (e.g., they are both behind NAT boxes), in which case they must use a "transit relay" server. The **Transit Client** is responsible for making the best connection that is possible.

As described earlier, the clients each open a listening TCP port, figure out their IP addresses, then send the address+port to the other side (through the encrypted rendezvous channel). To accommodate future connection mechanisms (perhaps WebRTC), this is generalized as a set of "connection hints" of various types. The current client recognizes three kinds of hints: direct TCP, transit-relay TCP, and Tor hidden-service TCP. Each hint includes a priority, so a client can encourage the use of cheaper connections.

Both sides initiate connections to every hint that they can recognize, starting with the high-priority hints first. Any hints that use the transit relay are delayed by a few seconds, to favor a direct connection.

The first connection that completes the negotiation process will win the race, at which point we use defer.cancel() to abandon all the losers. Those might still be waiting to start (sitting in the two-second delay imposed on relay connections), or trying to complete DNS resolution, or connected but waiting for negotiation to finish.

Deferred cancellation neatly handles all of these cases, because it gives the original creator of the Deferred an opportunity to avoid doing some work that's now going to be ignored anyway. And if the Deferred has chained to another, the cancel() call follows this chain and gets delivered to the first Deferred that has not yet fired. For us, that means canceling a contender that is waiting for a socket to connect will cancel the connection attempt. Or canceling one that is connected but still waiting for a connection handshake will shut down the connection instead.

By structuring each step of the process as another Deferred, we don't need to keep track of those steps: a single cancel() will do the right thing.

We manage this race with a utility function in src/wormhole/transit.py:

```python
class _ThereCanBeOnlyOne:
    """Accept a list of contender Deferreds, and return a summary Deferred.
    When the first contender fires successfully, cancel the rest and fire the
    summary with the winning contender's result. If all error, errback the summary.
    """

    def __init__(self, contenders):
        self._remaining = set(contenders)
        self._winner_d = defer.Deferred(self._cancel)
        self._first_success = None
        self._first_failure = None
        self._have_winner = False
        self._fired = False

def _cancel(self, _):
    for d in list(self._remaining):
        d.cancel()
    # since that will errback everything in _remaining, we'll have
    # hit _maybe_done() and fired self._winner_d by this point
```

```
def run(self):
    for d in list(self._remaining):
        d.addBoth(self._remove, d)
        d.addCallbacks(self._succeeded,self._failed)
        d.addCallback(self._maybe_done)
    return self._winner_d

def _remove(self, res, d):
    self._remaining.remove(d)
    return res

def _succeeded(self, res):
    self._have_winner = True
    self._first_success = res
    for d in list(self._remaining):
        d.cancel()

def _failed(self, f):
    if self._first_failure is None:
        self._first_failure = f

def _maybe_done(self, _):
    if self._remaining:
        return
    if self._fired:
        return self._fired = True
    if self._have_winner:
        self._winner_d.callback(self._first_success)
    else:
        self._winner_d.errback(self._first_failure)

def there_can_be_only_one(contenders):
    return _ThereCanBeOnlyOne(contenders).run()
```

This is exposed as a function, not a class. We need to turn a collection of Deferreds into a single new Deferred, and a class constructor can only return the new instance (not a Deferred). If we exposed _ThereCanBeOnlyOne as the main API, callers would be forced to use an awkward d = ClassXYZ(args).run() syntax (precisely the syntax we hide inside our function). This would add several opportunities for mistakes:

- What if they call run() twice?

- What if they subclass it? what sort of compatibility are we promising?

Note that if *all* the contender Deferreds fail, the summary Deferred will fail too. In this case, the errback function will receive whatever Failure instance was delivered with the first contender failure. The idea here is to report common-mode failures usefully. Each target will probably behave in one of three ways:

- successful connection (maybe fast or maybe slow);

- fail because of something specific to the target: it uses an IP address that we can't reach, or a network filter blocks the packets;

- fail because of something not specific to the target, for example, we aren't even connected to the internet;

If we're in the latter case, all the connection failures will be the same, so it doesn't matter which one we report. Recording the first should be enough to let the user figure out what went wrong.

Transit Relay Server

The code for the Transit Relay is in the magic-wormhole-transit-relay package. It currently uses a custom TCP protocol, but I hope to add a WebSockets interface to enable browser-based clients to use it too.

The core of the relay is a Protocol for which pairs of instances (one per client) are linked together. Each instance has a "buddy," and every time data arrives, that same data is written out to the buddy:

```python
class TransitConnection(protocol.Protocol):
    def dataReceived(self, data):
        if self._sent_ok:
            self._total_sent += len(data)
            self._buddy.transport.write(data)
            return
        ...
```

```python
def buddy_connected(self, them):
    self._buddy = them
    ...
    # Connect the two as a producer/consumer pair. We use streaming=True,
    # so this expects the IPushProducer interface, and uses
    # pauseProducing() to throttle, and resumeProducing() to unthrottle.
    self._buddy.transport.registerProducer(self.transport,True)
    # The Transit object calls buddy_connected() on both protocols, so
    # there will be two producer/consumer pairs.

def buddy_disconnected(self):
    self._buddy = None
    self.transport.loseConnection()

def connectionLost(self, reason):
    if self._buddy:
        self._buddy.buddy_disconnected()
    ...
```

The rest of the code has to do with identifying exactly which connections should be paired together. Transit clients write a handshake string as soon as they connect, and the relay looks for two clients that wrote the same handshake. The remainder of the dataReceived method implements a state machine that waits for the handshake to arrive, then compares it against other connections to find a match.

When the buddies are linked, we establish a Producer/Consumer relationship between them: Alice's TCP transport is registered as a producer for Bob's, and vice versa. When Alice's upstream link is faster than Bob's downstream link, the TCP Transport connected to Bob's TransitConnection will fill up. It will then call pauseProducing() on Alice's Transport, which will remove her TCP socket from the reactor's readable list (until resumeProducing() is called). This means the relay won't read from that socket for a while, causing the kernel's inbound buffer to fill, at which point the kernel's TCP stack shrinks the TCP window advertisement, which tells Alice's computer to stop sending data until it catches up.

The net result is that Alice observes a transfer rate that is no greater than what Bob can handle. Without this Producer/Consumer linkage, Alice would write data to the relay as fast as her connection allows, and the relay would have to buffer all of it until Bob caught up. Before we added this, the relay would occasionally run out of memory when people sent very large files to very slow recipients.

Wormhole Client Architecture

On the client side, the `wormhole` package provides a `Wormhole` library to establish wormhole-style connections through the server, a `Transit` library to make encrypted direct TCP connections (possibly through a relay), and a command-line tool to drive the file-transfer requests. Most of the code is in the `Wormhole` library.

The `Wormhole` object is built with a simple factory function, and has a Deferred-based API to allocate a wormhole code, discover what code was selected, and then send/receive messages:

```
import wormhole

@inlineCallbacks
def run():
    w = wormhole.create(appid, relay_url, reactor)
    w.allocate_code()
    code = yield w.get_code()
    print "wormhole code:", code
    w.send_message(b"outbound message")
    inbound = yield w.get_message()
    yield w.close()
```

We use a `create` factory function, not a class constructor, to build our Wormhole object. This lets us keep the actual class private, so we can change the implementation details without causing compability breaks in the future. For example, there are actually two flavors of Wormhole objects. The default has a Deferred-based interface, but if you pass an optional `delegate=` argument into `create`, you get an alternate one that makes calls to the delegate object intead of firing a Deferred.

`create` takes a Reactor, rather than importing one internally, to allow the calling application to control which type of reactor is used. This also makes unit tests easier to write, because we can pass in a fake reactor where, for example, network sockets are stubbed out, or one where we get explicit control over the clock.

Internally, our `Wormhole` object uses over a dozen small state machines, each of which is responsible for a small part of the connection and key-negotiation process. For example, the short integer at the beginning of a wormhole code (the "4" in `4-bravado-waffle`) is called a *Nameplate*, and these are allocated, used, and released, all by a single dedicated state machine. Likewise, the server hosts a *Mailbox* where the two clients can exchange messages: each client has a state machine that manages their view of this Mailbox, and knows when they want it to be opened or closed, and ensures that all messages are sent at the right time.

Deferreds vs State Machines, One-Shot Observer

While the basic message flow is pretty simple, the full protocol is fairly complex. This complexity stems from a design goal of tolerating connection failures (and subsequent reconnections), as well as server shutdowns (and subsequent restarts).

Each resource that the client might allocate or reserve must be freed at the right time. So, the process of claiming Nameplates and Mailboxes is carefully designed to always move forward, despite connections coming and going.

It is further complicated by another design goal: applications that use the library can save their state to disk, shut down completely, then restart at a later time and pick up where they left off. This is intended for messaging applications that get started and shut down all the time. For this to work, the application needs to know when a wormhole message has arrived, and how to serialize the protocol's state (along with everything else in the application). Such applications must use the **Delegate** API.

Deferreds are a good choice for dataflow-driven systems in which any given action can happen exactly once, but they are hard to serialize. And for states that might roll forward and then roll back, or for events which can occur multiple times (more of a "stream" interface), state machines might be better. Earlier versions of the wormhole code used more Deferreds, and it was harder to handle connections being lost and restarted. In the current version, Deferreds are only used for the top-level API. Everything else is a state machine.

The Wormhole object uses over a dozen interlocking state machines, all of which are implemented with **Automat**. Automat is not a part of Twisted per se, but it was written by members of the Twisted community, and one of its first use cases was Twisted's ClientService (this is a utility that maintains a connection to a given endpoint, reconnecting any time the connection is lost, or when the connection process fails; Magic Wormhole uses ClientService for the connection to the Rendezvous server).

As a specific example, Figure 7-5 shows the **Allocator** state machine, which manages the allocation of Nameplates. These are allocated by the rendezvous server upon request by the sending side (unless the sender and receiver have decided upon a code offline, in which case both sides type the code into their clients directly).

At any given moment, the connection to the rendezvous server is either established or not, and the transitions between these two states causes a connected or lost message to be dispatched to most state machines, including the Allocator. The allocator remains in one of the two "idle" states (S0A idle+disconnected, or S0B idle+connected) until/unless it is needed. If the higher-level code decides that a nameplate is required, it sends the allocate event. If the Allocator was connected at that moment, it tells the Rendezvous Connector to transmit an allocate message (the box labelled RC. tx_allocate), then moves to state S1B where it waits for a response. When the response arrives (rx_allocated), it will choose random words that make up the rest of the code, inform the Code state machine that one has been allocated (C.allocated()), and move to the terminal S2: done state.

Until the rx_allocated response is received, we can't know if the request was delivered successfully or not. So we must 1: make sure to retransmit the request each time the connection is reestablished; and 2: make sure the request is idempotent, so that the server reacts to two or more requests the same way it would react to a single request. This ensures that the server behaves correctly in both cases.

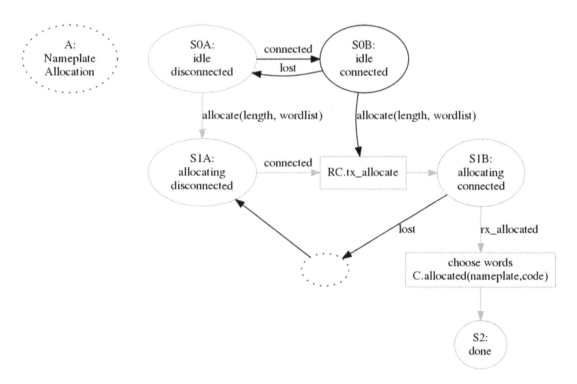

Figure 7-5. *Allocator state machine*

We might be asked to allocate a nameplate before the connection has been established. The path from S1A to S1B is where the `allocate` request is transmitted in either case: connecting before discovering the need to allocate, and reconnecting after sending the allocation request but not yet hearing the response.

This pattern appears in most of our state machines. For more complex examples, look at the Nameplate or the Mailbox machines, which create or subscribe to a named channel on the rendezvous server. In both cases, the states line up into two columns: either "disconnected" on the left, or "connected" on the right. The vertical position within the column indicates what we've accomplished so far (or what we still need to do). Losing a connection moves us from right to left. Establishing a connection moves us from left to right, and generally sends a new request message (or retransmits an earlier one). Receiving a response moves us downward, as does being instructed to achieve something from a higher-level state machine.

The top-level **Boss** machine is where the state machines give way to Deferreds. Applications that import the magic wormhole library can ask for a Deferred that will fire when an important event occurs. For example, an application can create a Wormhole object and allocate a code like this:

```
from twisted.internet import reactor
from wormhole.cli.public_relay import RENDEZVOUS_RELAY
import wormhole
# set APPID to something application-specific

w = wormhole.create(APPID, RENDEZVOUS_RELAY, reactor)
w.allocate_code()
d = w.get_code()
def allocated_code(code):
    print("the wormhole code is:{}".format(code))
d.addCallback(allocated_code)
```

The Allocator state machine delivers the `allocated` messages to the Code machine (`C.allocated`). The Code machine will deliver the code to the Boss (`B.got_code`), the Boss machine will deliver it to the Wormhole object (`W.got_code`), and the Wormhole object will deliver it to any waiting Deferreds (which were constructed by calling get_code()).

One-Shot Observers

The following excerpt from src/wormhole/wormhole.py shows the "one-shot observer" pattern used to manage the delivery of wormhole codes, both from allocation (described above) and interactive input:

```
@implementer(IWormhole, IDeferredWormhole)
class _DeferredWormhole(object):
    def __init__(self):
        self._code = None
        self._code_observers = []
        self._observer_result = None
        ...

    def get_code(self):
        if self._observer_result is not None:
            return defer.fail(self._observer_result)
        if self._code is not None:
            return defer.succeed(self._code)
        d=defer.Deferred()
        self._code_observers.append(d)
        return d

    def got_code(self, code):
        self._code = code
        for d in self._code_observers:
            d.callback(code)
        self._code_observers[:] = []

    def closed(self, result):
        if isinstance(result,Exception):
            self._observer_result = failure.Failure(result)
        else:
            # pending Deferreds get an error
            self._observer_result = WormholeClosed(result)
        ...
        for d in self._code_observers:
            d.errback(self._observer_result)
```

get_code() might be called any number of times. For the standard CLI filetransfer tool, the sending client allocates the code, and waits for get_code() to fire so it can display the code to the user (who must dictate it to the receiver). The receiving client is *told* the code (either as an invocation argument, or via interactive input, with tab completion on the words), so it doesn't bother calling get_code(). Other applications might have reasons to call it multiple times.

We want all these queries to get the same answer (or error). And we want their callback chains to be independent.

Promises/Futures vs. Deferreds

Futures come from the Actor model, by Carl Hewitt, and languages like Joule and E, and other early object-capability systems (in which they're known as Promises). They represent a value that is not available *yet*, but which (might) resolve to something eventually, or might "break" and never refer to anything.

This lets programs talk about things that don't yet exist. This might seem unhelpful, but there are plenty of useful things that can be done with not-yet-existent things. You can schedule work to happen when they *do* become available, and you can pass them into functions that can themselves schedule this work. In more advanced systems, **Promise Pipelining** lets you send messages *to* a Promise, and if that promise actually lives on a different computer entirely, the message will chase the promise to the target system, which can cut out several roundtrips. In general, they help programmers describe their future intentions to the compiler or interpreter, so it can better plan out what to do.

Deferreds are closely related, but are unique to Twisted. They serve more as a callback management tool than a fully fledged Promise. To explore how they differ, we should first explain how real Promises work.

In E, the object-capability language that most fully explored Promises, there is a function named makePromiseResolverPair(), which returns two *separate* objects: a Promise and a Resolver. The only way to resolve the promise is with the Resolver, and the only way to learn of the resolution is with the Promise. The language provides a special syntax, the "when" block, which lets the programmer write code that will execute only after the promise has been resolved to some concrete value. If Magic Wormhole were written in E, the get_code() method would return a Promise, and it would be displayed to the user like this:

```
p = w.get_code();
when (p) {
    writeln("The code is:", p);
}
```

Promises are available in modern JavaScript (ES6), thanks to the sizable overlap between the object-capability community and the TC39 standards organization. These Promises do not have any special syntax to wait for resolution, instead relying upon JavaScript's convenient anonymous functions (including the **arrow function** syntax introduced in ES6). The corresponding JavaScript code would look like:

```
p=w.get_code();
p.then(code=>{console.log("The code is:",code);});
```

A significant difference between E's Promises, JS Promises, and Twisted's Deferreds is in how you chain them together. The Javascript then() method returns a *new* Promise, which fires if and when the callback function finishes (if the callback returns an intermediate promise, the then() promise won't fire until the intermediate one fires). So, given a single "parent" promise, you can build two separate processing chains like this:

```
p=w.get_code();
function format_code(code){
    return slow_formatter_that_returns_a_promise(code);
}
p.then(format_code).then(formatted => {console.log(formatted);});
function notify_user(code){
    return display_box_and_wait_for_approval(code);
}
p.then(notify_user).then(approved => {console.log("code delivered!");});
```

In JavaScript, these two actions will run "in parallel," or at least neither will interfere with the other.

Twisted's Deferreds, on the other hand, build a chain of callbacks *without* creating additional Deferreds.

```
d1=w.get_code()
d=d1.addCallback(format_code)
assert d1 is d # addCallback returns the same Deferred!
```

This looks a bit like the JavaScript "attribute construction" pattern, common in web frameworks (e.g., d3.js, jQuery) that build up an object across many attribute-invocation calls:

```
s = d3.scale()
     .linear()
     .domain([0,100])
     .range([2,40]);
```

This chaining behavior of Deferreds can cause surprises, especially when trying to create parallel lines of execution:

```
d1 = w.get_code()
d1.addCallback(format_code).addCallback(print_formatted)
# wrong!
d1.addCallback(notify_user).addCallback(log_delivery)
```

In that example, notify_user is only called *after* print_formatted finishes, and it won't be called with the code: instead it will get whatever value print_formatted *returned*. Our coding pattern (two lines, each of which starts with d1.addCallback) is deceptive. In fact, the code above is exactly equivalent to:

```
d1 = w.get_code()
d1.addCallback(format_code)
d1.addCallback(print_formatted)
d1.addCallback(notify_user) # even more obviously wrong!
d1.addCallback(log_delivery)
```

Instead, we need a new Deferred that will fire with the same value but lets us establish a new chain of execution:

```
def fanout(parent_deferred, count):
    child_deferreds = [Deferred() for i in range(count)]
    def fire(result):
        for d in child_deferreds:
            d.callback(result)
    parent_deferred.addBoth(fire)
    return child_deferreds
```

```
d1 = w.get_code()
d2, d3 = fanout(d1,2)
d2.addCallback(format_code)
d2.addCallback(print_formatted)
d3.addCallback(notify_user)
d3.addCallback(log_delivery)
```

This is enough of a nuisance that in my projects, I usually create a utility class named OneShotObserverList. This "observer" has a when_fired() method (that returns a new, independent Deferred), and a fire() method (which fires them all). when_fired() can be called either before or after fire().

The Magic Wormhole code quoted above (get_code() / got_code()) is a subset of the full OneShotObserverList. There are several ways that the connection process might fail, but they all call closed() with a Failure instance (a successful/intentional close will call closed() with a non-Failure, which is then wrapped in a WormholeClosed exception). This code ensures that every Deferred returned by get_code() will be fired exactly once, with either success (and the code), or a Failure.

Eventual-Send, Synchronous Testing

Another aspect of Promises that comes from E and the object-capability community is the **eventual send**. This is a facility to queue a method invocation for some subsequent turn of the event loop. In Twisted, this is basically a reactor.callLater(0, callable, argument). In E and JavaScript, Promises automatically provide this guarantee for their callbacks.

Eventual send is a simple and robust way to avoid a number of ordering hazards. For example, imagine a general observer pattern (with more functionality than the simple OneShotObserverList described above):

```
class Observer:
    def __init__ (self):
        self.observers = set()
    def subscribe(self, callback):
        self.observers.add(callback)
    def unsubscribe(self, callback):
        self.observers.remove(callback)
```

```
def publish(self, data):
    for ob in self.observers:
        ob(data)
```

Now, what happens if one of the callback functions invokes `subscribe` or `unsubscribe`, modifying the list of observers while in the middle of the loop? Depending upon how iteration works, the newly added callback might receive the current event, or it might not. In Java, the iterator might even throw a `ConcurrentModificationException`.

Reentrancy is another potential surprise: if some callback publishes a new message to the same observer, then the `publish` function will be invoked a second time while the first invocation is still running, which can violate many common assumptions the programmer might have made (especially if the function keeps state in instance variables). Finally, if a callback raises an exception, do the remaining observers see the event, or are they bypassed?

These unexpected interactions are collectively known as "plan-coordination hazards," and the consequences include dropped events, duplicated events, non-deterministic ordering, and infinite loops.

Meticulous programming can avoid many of these failure modes: we could duplicate the observer list before iteration, catch/discard exceptions in the callbacks, and use a flag to detect reentrant calls. But it is far simpler and more robust to use an eventual send with each call:

```
def publish(self, data):
    for ob in self.observers:
        reactor.callLater(0, ob, data)
```

I've used this with great success in many projects (Foolscap, Tahoe-LAFS), and it removes entire classes of bugs. The downside is that testing becomes more difficult, since the effects of an eventual send cannot be checked synchronously. In addition, the lack of causal stack traces makes debugging tricky: if the callback raises an exception, the traceback doesn't make it clear *why* that function was called. Deferreds have similar concerns, for which the `defer.setDebugging(True)` function can help.

With Magic Wormhole, I've been experimenting with using synchronous unit tests instead of eventual send.

Asynchronous Testing with Deferreds

Twisted has a unit test system named **Trial**, which builds upon the stdlib `unittest` package by providing specialized methods for handling Deferreds. The most obvious feature is that a test case can return a Deferred, and the test runner will wait for it to fire before declaring success (or allowing the next test to run). When combined with `inlineCallbacks`, this makes it easy to test that certain things happen in a specific order:

```
@inlineCallbacks
def test_allocate_default(self):
    w = wormhole.create(APPID,self.relayurl, reactor)
    w.allocate_code()
    code = yield w.get_code()
    mo = re.search(r"^\d+-\w+-\w+$", code)
    self.assert_(mo, code)
    # w.close() fails because we closed before connecting
    yield self.assertFailure(w.close(), LonelyError)
```

In that test, `w.allocate_code()` initiates the allocation of a code, and `w.get_code()` returns a Deferred that will eventually fire with the complete code. In between, the Wormhole object must contact the server and allocate a nameplate (the test launches a local rendezvous server in `setUp()`, rather than relying upon the real server). The `yield w.get_code()` takes that Deferred and waits for it to finish, then assigns the result to `code` so we can test its structure later.

Of course, what really happens is that the test function returns a Deferred and goes back to the event loop, then at some point in the future the server's response arrives and causes the function to be resumed where it left off. If a bug prevents the `get_code()` Deferred from being fired, the test will wait quietly for two minutes (the default timeout), then declare an error.

The `self.assertFailure()` clause takes a Deferred and a list (`*args`) of exception types. It waits for the Deferred to resolve, then requires that it was errbacked with one of those exceptions: if the Deferred's `.callback()` is invoked (i.e., not an error), `assertFailure` flunks the test. And if the Deferred's `.errback()` is invoked with the *wrong* kind of error, it also flunks the test.

For us, this serves three purposes. The Wormhole API requires that you call `w.close()` when you're done, and `close` returns a Deferred that fires when everything is fully shut down. We use this to avoid moving on to the next test until everything has stopped moving from the previous one (all network sockets are shut down, all timers have been retired), which also avoids triggering an "unclean reactor" error from Trial.

This Deferred also gives applications a way to discover connection errors. In this test, we're only running a single client, so there's nobody for it to connect to, and the `close` Deferred will be errbacked with `LonelyError`. We use `assertFailure` to make sure that no *other* error happened, which catches all the usual coding errors that our unit tests are designed to find, like maybe a `NameError` because we misspelled a method somewhere.

The third purpose is that it keeps the overall test from being flunked. In other tests, where the wormhole connects successfully, we use a simple `yield w.close()` at the end of the test. But in this case, the `LonelyError` errback would look like a problem to Trial, which would mark the test as failed. Using `assertFailure` tells Trial that it's ok for this Deferred to fail, as long as it fails in a very specific way.

Synchronous Testing with Deferreds

`test_allocate_default` is really an **integration test**, which is exercising multiple pieces of the system at once (including the rendezvous server and the loopback network interface). These tests tend to be thorough but somewhat slow. They also don't provide predictable coverage.

Tests that wait for a Deferred to happen (either by returning one from the test, yielding one in the middle of an `@inlineCallbacks` function, or calling `assertFailure`) imply that you aren't entirely sure quite *when* that event will happen. This separation of concerns is fine when an application is waiting for a library to do something: the details of what will trigger the callback are the library's job, not the application. But during unit tests, you should know exactly what to expect.

Trial offers three Deferred-managing tools that do *not* wait for the Deferred to fire: `successResultOf`, `failureResultOf`, and `assertNoResult`. These assert that the Deferred is currently in a specific state, rather than waiting for a transition to occur.

They are most commonly used with the `Mock` class, to reach "into" some code under test, to provoke specific internal transitions at a known time.

As an example, we'll look at the tests of Magic Wormhole's `tor` support. This feature adds an argument to the command-line tools, which causes all connections to be routed through a Tor daemon, so `wormhole send --tor` won't reveal your IP address to the rendezvous server (or the recipient). The details of finding (or launching) a suitable Tor daemon are encapsulated in a `TorManager` class, and depends upon the external `txtorcon` library. We can replace `txtorcon` with a `Mock`, then we exercise everything above it to make sure our `TorManager` code behaves as expected.

These tests exercise all of our Tor code, without actually talking to a real Tor daemon (which would clearly be slow, unreliable, and unportable). They accomplish this by assuming that `txtorcon` works as advertised. We don't assert anything about what `txtorcon` actually does: instead we record and inspect everything we told `txtorcon` to do, then we simulate the correct `txtorcon` responses and examine everything that our own code does in reaction to those responses.

The simplest test checks to see what happens when `txtorcon` is not installed: normal operation should not be affected, but trying to use `--tor` should cause an error message. To make this easier to simulate, the `tor_manager.py` module is written to handle an import error by setting the `txtorcon` variable to None:

```python
# tor_manager.py
try:
    import txtorcon
except ImportError:
    txtorcon = None
```

This module has a `get_tor()` function, which is defined to return a Deferred that either fires with a `TorManager` object, or with a `NoTorError` Failure. It returns a Deferred because, in normal use, it must establish a connection to the Tor control port before anything else can happen, and that takes time. But in this specific case, we know it should resolve immediately (with `NoTorError`), because we discover the `ImportError` without waiting for anything. So, the test looks like this:

```python
from ..tor_manager import get_tor
class Tor(unittest.TestCase):
    def test_no_txtorcon(self):
        with mock.patch("wormhole.tor_manager.txtorcon",None):
            d = get_tor(None)
        self.failureResultOf(d, NoTorError)
```

The mock.patch ensures that the txtorcon variable is None, even though the txtorcon package is always importable during tests (our setup.py marks txtorcon as a dependency in the [dev] extra). The Deferred returned by get_tor() is already in the errback state by the time our test regains control. self.failureResultOf(d, *errortypes) asserts that the given Deferred has already failed, with one of the given error classes. And because failureResultOf tests the Deferred immediately, it returns immediately. Our test_no_txtorcon does not return a Deferred, nor does it use @inlineCallbacks.

A similar test exercises the precondition checks inside get_tor(). For each typecheck that this function does, we exercise it with a call. For example, the launch_tor= argument is a Boolean flag that says whether the tor_manager should spawn a new copy of Tor, or try to use a preexisting one. If we pass in a value that isn't True or False, we should expect the Deferred to fire with a TypeError:

```
def test_bad_args(self):
    d = get_tor(None, launch_tor="not boolean")
    f = self.failureResultOf(d,TypeError)
    self.assertEqual(str(f.value), "launch_tor= must be boolean")
```

This entire test runs synchronously, without waiting for any Deferreds. A collection of tests like this exercises every line and every branch in the tor_manager module in 11 milliseconds.

Another common test is to make sure that a Deferred has *not* fired yet, because we haven't yet triggered the condition that would allow it to fire. This is usually followed by a line that triggers the event, then an assertion that the Deferred is either resolved successfully (with some specific value), or has failed (with some specific exception).

The magic wormhole Transit class manages the (hopefully direct) client-to-client TCP connections used for bulk data transfer. Each side listens on a port and builds a list of "connection hints" based on every IP address it might possibly have (including several local addresses that are unlikely to be reachable). Each side then initiates connections to all of their peer's hints at the same time. The first one to connect successfully and perform the right handshake is declared the winner, and all the others are canceled.

A utility function named there_can_be_only_one() (described earlier) is used to manage this race. It takes a number of individual Deferreds, and returns a single Deferred that fires when the first has succeeded. Twisted has some utility functions that do something similar (DeferredList has been around forever), but we needed something that would cancel all the losing contenders.

To test this, we use Trial's `assertNoResult(d)` and `value = successResultOf(d)` features:

```
class Highlander(unittest.TestCase):
    def test_one_winner(self):
        cancelled = set()
        contenders = [Deferred(lambda d, i=i: cancelled.add(i))
                      for i in range(5)]
        d = transit.there_can_be_only_one(contenders)
        self.assertNoResult(d)
        contenders[0].errback(ValueError())
        self.assertNoResult(d)
        contenders[1].errback(TypeError())
        self.assertNoResult(d)
        contenders[2].callback("yay")
        self.assertEqual(self.successResultOf(d),"yay")
        self.assertEqual(cancelled, set([3,4]))
```

In this test, we make sure that the combined Deferred has not fired right away, and also that it does not fire even when some of the component Deferreds have failed. When a component member does succeed, we check that both the combined Deferred has fired with the correct value, and that the remaining contenders have been canceled.

`successResultOf()` and `failureResultOf()` have one catch: you can't call them multiple times on the same Deferred, because internally they add a callback to the Deferred, which interferes with any subsequent callbacks (including additional calls to `successResultOf`). There's no good reason to do this, but it might cause you some confusion if you have a subroutine that checks the state of a Deferred, and you use that subroutine multiple times. However, `assertNoResult` can be called as many times as you like.

Synchronous Testing and Eventual Send

The Twisted community has been moving toward this immediate/mocked style for several years. I've only recently started using it, but I'm pleased with the results: my tests are faster, more thorough, and more deterministic. However I'm still torn: there's a lot of value in using eventual send. In `there_can_be_only_one()`, the contender Deferreds are mostly independent of the callbacks attached to the result, but I'm still worried about bugs, and I'd feel more comfortable if the callback was executed on a different turn of the event loop.

But anything involving the actual Reactor is difficult to test without waiting for a Deferred to fire. So, I'm looking for ways to combine this immediate test style with an eventual-send utility.

When I first started using eventual send, and Glyph saw what I was doing with reactor.callLater(0, f), he wrote me a better version, which we use in both Foolscap and Tahoe-LAFS. It maintains a separate queue of callbacks, and only has one callLater outstanding at any given moment: this is more efficient if there are thousands of active calls, and avoids depending upon reactor.callLater maintaining the activation order of equal-value timers.

The nice feature of his eventually() is that it comes with a special function named flushEventualQueue(), which repeatedly cycles the queue until it is empty. This should allow tests to be written like this:

```python
class Highlander(unittest.TestCase):
    def test_one_winner(self):
        cancelled = set()
        contenders = [Deferred(lambda d, i=i: cancelled.add(i))
                        for i in range(5)]
        d = transit.there_can_be_only_one(contenders)
        flushEventualQueue()
        self.assertNoResult(d)
        contenders[0].errback(ValueError())
        flushEventualQueue()
        self.assertNoResult(d)
        contenders[1].errback(TypeError())
        flushEventualQueue()
        self.assertNoResult(d)
        contenders[2].callback("yay")
        flushEventualQueue()
        self.assertEqual(self.successResultOf(d),"yay")
        self.assertEqual(cancelled, set([3,4]))
```

The downside is that flushEventualQueue lives on a singleton instance of the eventual-send manager, which has all the problems of using an ambient reactor. To handle this cleanly, there_can_be_only_one() should be given this manager as an argument, just like modern Twisted code passes the Reactor *into* functions that need it, rather than importing one directly. In fact, if we were to rely upon `reactor.callLater(0)`, we could test this code with a `Clock()` instance and manually cycle the time forward to flush the queue. Future versions of the code will probably use this pattern.

Summary

Magic Wormhole is a file-transfer application with strong security properties that stem from the SPAKE2 cryptographic algorithm at its core, with a library API for embedding into other applications. It uses Twisted to manage multiple simultaneous TCP connections, which usually enables fast direct transfers between the two clients. The Autobahn library provides WebSocket connections that will enable compatibility with future browser-based clients. The test suite uses Twisted utility functions to examine the state of each Deferred as they are cycled through their operating phases, allowing fast synchronous tests.

References

- Magic Wormhole home page: `http://magic-wormhole.io`

- GitHub development page: `https://github.com/warner/magic-wormhole`

- SPAKE2: `http://www.lothar.com/blog/54-spake2-random-elements/`

- WebSockets: `https://developer.mozilla.org/en-US/docs/Web/API/WebSockets_API`

- requests: `http://python-requests.org/`

- treq: `https://github.com/twisted/treq`

- Autobahn: `https://crossbar.io/autobahn/`

- libp2p: `https://libp2p.io/`

- Automat: `https://github.com/glyph/Automat`

- Futures: `https://en.wikipedia.org/wiki/Future_(programming)`

- JavaScript Promises: `https://developer.mozilla.org/en-US/docs/Web/JavaScript/Guide/Using_promises`

- E Promises: `http://wiki.erights.org/wiki/Promise`

- Eventual Send: `https://en.wikipedia.org/wiki/E_(programming_language)`

- Plan-Coordination Hazards: `http://erights.org/talks/thesis/`

- eventual() utility: `https://github.com/warner/foolscap/blob/master/src/foolscap/eventual.py`

CHAPTER 8

Push Data to Browsers and Micro-services with WebSocket

Why WebSocket?

WebSocket started as a competitor of HTTP AJAX requests. When we needed real-time communication from the browser or data push from the server, they came out as a nice alternative to legacy solutions such as long polling or comet. Because they were using a persistent connection and no headers, they were the fastest and lightest option if you had a lot of small messages to exchange.

Today though, HTTP2 is being more and more adopted and does have a persistent connection and data push.

So why WebSocket?

Well, first, WebSocket APIs target application code, not just server code. So, on all implementations, you can hook on the connection life cycle, react to disconnection, attach data to the session, etc. A very handy feature to create robust interactions and pleasant user experiences.

Then, while HTTP2 does have compressed headers, WebSocket has no headers at all, making the whole footprint even lower. In fact, HTTP2 implementations force encryption even for non-sensitive data, while in WebSocket you have the choice on where and when to spend your machine resources, and activate SSL or not.

What's more, HTTP2 servers tend to use push to send static resources (CSS, images, JS, etc.) to the browsers, but it's not generally used for pushing application data. This is where WebSocket shines: pushing notifications to users, propagating events, signaling changes. . .

© Mark Williams, Cory Benfield, Brian Warner, Moshe Zadka, Dustin Mitchell, Kevin Samuel, Pierre Tardy 2019
M. Williams et al., *Expert Twisted*, https://doi.org/10.1007/978-1-4842-3742-7_8

However, there is one strange thing about WebSocket: it is not tied to a domain name, and browsers don't need any special setup for doing CORS. You can actually connect from a web page to a local WebSocket server on your computer without any warning. It can be seen as a pro, or a con, depending on what you need to do.

All those characteristics make WebSocket a great tool for your website notifications, chat, trading, multi-player games, or real-time charts and graphs. Needing less to say, you don't have to limit yourself to that, as you can leverage it as a link between all your components, and make it the communication layer that coordinates your whole system.

This means that your web server can talk to your caching processes or your authentication platform through WebSocket. Or that you can manage a herd of IoT[1] devices. After all, the Raspberry Pi has de facto Python support.

Overall, WebSocket is a safe bet now, as it is available in most major browsers, down to, and including IE10. That's about 94% of the market, according to caniuse.com. Worst case scenario, you can find shims for the few remaining browsers. As the WebSocket and HTTP handshakes are compatible, it will likely work on any network that lets through HTTP. You can even share the 80 and 443 ports between the two protocols.

WebSocket and Twisted

On the server side, WebSocket is now broadly supported by popular languages, but it does require asynchronous programming because of the persistent connections. Since you may end up with a lot of clients connected simultaneously, threads may not be the best solution to code a WebSocket server. Asynchronous IO, however, is a perfect fit; and Twisted is a welcoming platform in that regard.

The even better news is that you can use WebSocket outside the browser, so that all the components on your servers can talk to each other in real time. This will allow you to create your very own micro-service architecture, decoupling features to distribute them on smaller components, or propagating information instead of querying a central database for everything.

To demonstrate how to benefit from WebSocket in a Twisted environment, we are going to use the Autobahn ecosystem. Autobahn is a collection of libraries under MIT license, written in different languages, allowing you to create WebSocket clients and servers. It also comes with a test suite to check the level of standard compliance of any WebSocket system.

And there is more.

---

[1]Internet of Things.

You can, of course, build your own communication conventions using WebSocket; and Autobahn certainly helps you doing so. But eventually you'll end up doing exactly the same as everyone else and reinvent a (most probably square) wheel.

Indeed, WebSocket use cases can broadly be classified in two categories:

- Calling remote code and getting a result. Like a better, faster, lighter AJAX. Well, it's been done for decades, and it is called "RPC," for Remote Procedure Calls.

- Sending messages to signal other parts of the system, something happened. Same here, it's actually a very common pattern often called "PUB/SUB," for Publish/Subscribe.

We'll go into more details about what this means for you later. But for now, the important part is that doing this properly requires a lot of well-designed code to handle serialization, authentication, routing, error handling, and edge cases.

Knowing this, the authors of Autobahn decided to create a higher-level protocol, called WAMP, for "WebSocket Application Messaging Protocol"[2]. It's a documented open standard registered by IANA[], and it can basically do all the heavy lifting for you, if you so desire.

The best thing is, you can use WAMP everywhere WebSocket is supported, which means pretty much everywhere, for everything. No need to mangle with HTTP here, MQTT there, and AMQP for the rest. One protocol to rule them all. And less hassle.

Luckily, the Python Autobahn library supports both raw WebSocket and WAMP, using Twisted. This is what we are going to go through with this chapter. Hence before we start, install the autobahn package, for example using pip:

```
pip install autobahn[twisted]
```

As usual, it's recommended that you create a Python 3 virtualenv for this. The Autobahn version we are going to use for this chapter – 17.10.1 – will, anyway, work with Python 2.7 and 3.3+. It can even run on PyPy and Jython, and supports asyncio in case you don't want to stick only to Twisted. For this chapter, of course, we will stick to Twisted, with Python 3 examples.

Since WebSocket is an interesting front-end technology for websites, we are going to use a bit of JavaScript later. However, WebSocket doesn't need the web to be useful, as is a fine protocol to communicate between server processes on its own.

---

[2]Not to be confused with the "Windows Apache MySQL PHP" stack that was popular during the pre-AJAX web.

Raw WebSocket, from Python to Python

The "hello world" from the network world, being an echo server, is what we are going to make first. While Twisted now supports async / await constructs, we are going to stick with coroutines to allow a broader range of Python 3 support.

Here is what a WebSocket echo server looks like, using autobahn:

```python
import uuid

from autobahn.twisted.websocket import (
    WebSocketServerProtocol,
    WebSocketServerFactory
)

class EchoServerProtocol(WebSocketServerProtocol):

    def onConnect(self, request):
        """Called when a client is connecting to us"""
        # Print the IP address of the client this protocol instance is serving
        print(u"Client connecting:{0}".format(request.peer))

    def onOpen(self):
        """Called when the WebSocket connection has been opened"""
        print(u"WebSocket connection open.")

    def onMessage(self, payload, isBinary):
        """Called for each WebSocket message received from this client

            Params:

                payload (str|bytes): the content of the message
                isBinary (bool): whether the message contains (False) encoded text
                            or non-textual data (True). Default is False.
        """
        # Simply prints any message we receive
        if isBinary:
            # This is a binary message and can contain pretty much anything.
            # Here we recreate the UUID from the bytes the client sent us.
            uid=uuid.UUID(bytes=payload)
```

```python
        print(u"UUID received:{}".format(uid))
    else:
        # This is encoded text. Please note that it is NOT decoded for you,
        # isBinary is merely a courtesy flag manually set by the client
        # on each message. You must know the charset used (here utf8),
        # and call ".decode()" on the bytes object to get a string object.
        print(u"Text message received:{}".format(payload.decode( 'utf8')))

    # It's an echo server, so let's send back everything it receives
    self.sendMessage(payload, isBinary)

def onClose(self, wasClean, code, reason):
    """Called when the WebSocket connection for this client closes

        Params:

            wasClean (bool): whether we were told the connection was going
                              to be closed or if it just happened.
            code (int): any code among WebSocketClientProtocol.CLOSE_*
            reason (str): a message stating the reason the connection
                          was closed, in plain English.
    """

    print(u"WebSocket connection closed:{0}".format(reason))

if __name__ == '__main__':

    from twisted.internet import reactor

    # The WebSocket protocol netloc is WS. So WebSocket URLs look exactly
    # like HTTP URLs, but replacing HTTP with WS.
    factory=WebSocketServerFactory(u"ws://127.0.0.1:9000")
    factory.protocol=EchoServerProtocol

    print(u"Listening on ws://127.0.0.1:9000")
    reactor.listenTCP(9000,  factory)
    reactor.run()
```

Run it in a terminal by simply doing:

```
$ python echo_websocket_server.py
Listening on ws://127.0.0.1:9000
```

Assuming "echo_websocket_server.py" is the name you gave to the script, obviously. Here is what a WebSocket echo client looks like, using autobahn:

```python
# coding: utf8
import uuid

from autobahn.twisted.util import sleep
from autobahn.twisted.websocket import (
    WebSocketClientProtocol,
    WebSocketClientFactory
)

from twisted.internet.defer import Deferred, inlineCallbacks

class EchoClientProtocol(WebSocketClientProtocol):

    def onConnect(self, response):
        # Print the server ip address we are connected to
        print(u"Server connected:{0}".format(response.peer))

    @inlineCallbacks
    def onOpen(self):

        print("WebSocket connection open.")

        # Send messages every second
        i=0
        while True:

            # Send a text message. You MUST encode it manually.
            self.sendMessage(u"© Hellø wørld{}!".format(i).encode('utf8'))
            # If you send non-text data, signal it by setting "isBinary". Here
            # we create a unique random ID, and send it as bytes.
            self.sendMessage(uuid.uuid4().bytes, isBinary=True)
            i+=1
            yield sleep(1)
```

```python
    def onMessage(self, payload, isBinary):
        # Let's not convert the messages so you can see their raw form
        if isBinary:
            print(u"Binary message received:{!r}bytes".format(payload))
        else:
            print(u"Encoded text received:{!r}".format(payload))

    def onClose(self, wasClean, code, reason):
        print(u"WebSocket connection closed:{0}".format(reason))

if __name__ == '__main__':

    from twisted.internet import reactor

    factory=WebSocketClientFactory(u"ws://127.0.0.1:9000")
    factory.protocol=EchoClientProtocol

    reactor.connectTCP(u"127.0.0.1",9000, factory)
    reactor.run()
```

Run the code in a second terminal by doing:

```
python echo_websocket_client.py
```

It is important that you run the client after you started the server, as those simple examples don't implement fancy connection detection or reconnection.

Immediately after that, you will see something like this on the client console:

```
WebSocket connection open.
Encoded text received: b'\xc2\xa9 Hell\xc3\xb8 w\xc3\xb8rld 0 !'
Binary message received: b'\xecA\xd9u\xa3\xa1K\xc3\x95\xd5\xba~\x11ss\xa6' bytes
Encoded text received: b'\xc2\xa9 Hell\xc3\xb8 w\xc3\xb8rld 1 !'
Binary message received: b'\xb3NAv\xb30Oo\x97\xaf\xde\xeaD\xc8\x92F' bytes
Encoded text received: b'\xc2\xa9 Hell\xc3\xb8 w\xc3\xb8rld 2 !'
Binary message received: b'\xc7\xda\xb6h\xbd\xbaC\xe8\x84\x7f\xce:,\x15\
                         xc4$' bytes
Encoded text received: b'\xc2\xa9 Hell\xc3\xb8 w\xc3\xb8rld 3 !'
Binary message received: b'qw\x8c@\xd3\x18D\xb7\xb90;\xee9Y\x91z' bytes
```

And on the server console:

```
WebSocket connection open.
Text message received: © Hellø wørld 0 !
UUID received: d5b48566-4b20-4167-8c18-3c5b7199860b
Text message received: © Hellø wørld 1 !
UUID received: 3e1c0fe6-ba73-4cd4-b7ea-3288eab5d9f6
Text message received: © Hellø wørld 2 !
UUID received: 40c3678a-e5e4-4fce-9be8-6c354ded9cbc
Text message received: © Hellø wørld 3 !
UUID received: eda0c047-468b-464e-aa02-1242e99a1b57
```

This means the server and the client are exchanging messages.

Also please note that in the server example, we only answered messages. Nonetheless, it's allowed to call "self.sendMessage()" even when we have not received any message, therefore pushing data to the client.

Let's do exactly that, but with a web example.

Raw WebSocket, Between Python and JavaScript

Pushing data to the browser is a classic use case for WebSocket. The limited number of pages we have don't not allow us to show off the traditional chat example. However, any chat needs to signal how many people are online. Here is what a naive implementation might look like.

First, let's create a Python server.

```python
from autobahn.twisted.websocket import (
    WebSocketServerProtocol,
    WebSocketServerFactory
)

class SignalingServerProtocol(WebSocketServerProtocol):

    connected_clients=[]

    def onOpen(self):
        # Every time we receive a WebSocket connection, we store the
        # reference to the connected client in a class attribute
```

```python
        # shared among all Protocol instances. It's a naive implementation
        # but perfect as a simple example.
        self.connected_clients.append(self)
        self.broadcast(str(len(self.connected_clients)))

    def broadcast(self, message):
        """ Send a message to all connected clients

            Params:
                message (str): the message to send
        """
        for client in self.connected_clients:
            client.sendMessage(message.encode('utf8'))

    def onClose(self, wasClean, code, reason):
        # If a client disconnect, we remove the reference from the class
        # attribute.
        self.connected_clients.remove(self)
        self.broadcast(str(len(self.connected_clients)))

if __name__ == '__main__':

    from twisted.internet import reactor

    factory = WebSocketServerFactory(u"ws://127.0.0.1:9000")
    factory.protocol = SignalingServerProtocol

    print(u"Listening on ws://127.0.0.1:9000")
    reactor.listenTCP(9000, factory)
    reactor.run()
```

Again, run it doing:

```
python signaling_websocket_server.py
```

Now for the HTML + JS part:

```html
<!DOCTYPEhtml> <html><head></head><body>

<h1>Connected users: <span id="count">...</span></h1>
```

```
// Short url to a CDN version of the autobahn.js lib
// Visit https://github.com/crossbario/autobahn-js
// for the real deal
<script src="http://goo.gl/1pfDD1"></script>
<script>

  /* If you are using an old browser, this part of the code may look
     different. This will work starting from IE11
     and will require vendor prefixes or shims in other cases.*/
  var sock = new WebSocket("ws://127.0.0.1:9000");

  /* Like with the Python version, you can then hook on sock.onopen() or
     sock.onclose() if you wish. But for this example with only need
     to react to receiving messages: */

  sock.onmessage = function(e){
    var span = document.getElementById('count');
    span.innerHTML=e.data;
  }

</script>
</body></html>
```

All you have to do is to open the file with this HTML code in your web browser.

If you open this file in your browser, you will get a page stating "Connected users: x," with x adjusting every time you open a new tab with the same page, or close one.

You'll notice that even browsers with strict CORS policy, such as Google Chrome, are not preventing the connection from the "file://" protocol like they would do with an AJAX request. WebSocket works in any context, with remote or local domain names, even if the file is not served from a web server.

More Powerful WebSocket with WAMP

WebSocket is a simple yet powerful tool; however, it's still quite low level. Should you create a full-blown system using WebSocket, you'll eventually end up coding:

- A way to pair up two messages, to mimic the HTTP request / response cycle.

- Some swappable back end for serialization, with JSON or msgpack, or else.

- A convention to manage errors, and a workflow to debug them.

- Boilerplate to broadcast messages, including only to a subset of clients.

- Authentication, and something to bridge your session ID from HTTP cookies / token to WebSocket.

- A permission system so that all clients can't do or see everything.

And you would have rewritten a nonstandard, less documented, and untested alternative to WAMP.

WAMP is an answer to all of this, in a clean and proven way. It runs on top of WebSocket, so it shares all its characteristics and inherits from all its benefits. It also adds a lot of goodies:

- You can define functions and declare them public on the network. Then any client can call those functions from anywhere (yes, remotely) and get the result. It's the RPC part of WAMP, and you can see it as a replacement for AJAX requests on steroids, or a much easier CORBA/XMLRPC/SOAP.

- You can define events. Some code can say "hey, I'm interested in that event" from anywhere (again, yes, remotely). Now another code anywhere can then say "hey, it happened," and all interested clients are notified. It's the PUB/SUB part of WAMP, and you can use it like an even easier RabbitMQ.

- All errors are automatically propagated through the network. So if your client X call a function on client Y that fails, you will get the error back in client X.

- Identification and Authentication are part of the specs and can blend in with your own HTTP session mechanism.

- Everything is namespaced. And you can filter on them, use wildcards, set permissions, and even add load balancing to the mix.

Now we won't see most of that in this short chapter, but at least I will try to give you a taste of what RPC and PUB/SUB can do for you.

WAMP is a routed protocol, which means that every time you make a WAMP call, it does not go directly to the code that will handle it. Instead, it goes through a WAMP compatible router, which then ensures the distribution of the messages back and forth to the proper pieces of code.

In that sense, WAMP is not a client-server architecture: any code that makes a WAMP call is a client. So, all your code, including web pages, processes on your servers, external service, anything that speaks WAMP, will be clients – or the WAMP router – talking to each other.

This makes the WAMP router a single point of failure, and a potential bottleneck for performance. Luckily the reference implementation, Crossbar.io, is a robust and fast Twisted powered software. It also means you can install it with a simple pip command, and to run our next example, you need to do so:

```
pip install crossbar
```

If you are using Windows, you may need the win32api dependency. In that case, install it as well before starting.[3]

The command crossbar should now be available to you[4]:

```
$ crossbar version

   __   __ __ __ __   __   __
  /  `| _)/  \/ _ `/_`| _) /\ | _)  |/  \
  \__,|  \\_/._ /._ /|_)/~~\|  \.|\__/

Crossbar.io       : 17.11.1 (Crossbar.io COMMUNITY)
  Autobahn        : 17.10.1 (with JSON, MessagePack, CBOR, UBJSON)
  Twisted         : 17.9.0-EPollReactor
  LMDB            : 0.93/lmdb-0.9.18
  Python          : 3.6.2/CPython
OS                : Linux-4.4.0-98-generic-x86_64-with-Ubuntu-16.04-xenial
Machine           : x86_64
Release key       : RWT/n6IQ4dKesCP8YwwJiWH3OST8eq5D21ih4EFbJZazzsqEX6CmaT3k
```

---

[3]Binaries are listed on the project page: https://github.com/mhammond/pywin32.

[4]If you can't or don't want to install a crossbar instance, you can find one for demo purpose listed on https://crossbar.io/docs/Demo-Instance/. In that case, you can use it instead of "ws://127.0.0.1:8080/ws". But you'll still need to pip install pyopenssl service_identity to use it.

Crossbar.io wears many hats and can do so many things, so a configuration file is needed to tell what you want to do. Thankfully, it can generate a basic one automatically:

```
crossbar init
```

This will create a web and .crossbar directories, as well as a README file. You can ignore, or even delete web and README. What we are interested in is the .crossbar/config.json that has been created for us. You don't need to modify it to run this example, as by default it just "allows everything." If you open it, you'll find a great number of settings that, without context, will be hard to make sense of. To understand the basics of WAMP though, you don't need to dig that deep, so we will just carry on.

Next on our list is just to run the crossbar router. You need to run it on the same directory that contains the .crossbar directory:

```
$ crossbar start
2017-11-23T19:06:43+0200 [Controller  11424] New node key pair generated!
2017-11-23T19:06:43+0200 [Controller  11424] File permissions on node public key fixed!
2017-11-23T19:06:43+0200 [Controller  11424] File permissions on node private key fixed!
2017-11-23T19:06:43+0200 [Controller  11424]     __  __  __  __  __  __       __  __

2017-11-23T19:06:43+0200 [Controller  11424]    / `|_)/ \/_`/_`|_) /\ |_) |/ \
2017-11-23T19:06:43+0200 [Controller  11424]    \_,| \\_/._/._/|_)/~~\| \.|\_/
2017-11-23T19:06:43+0200 [Controller  11424]
2017-11-23T19:06:43+0200 [Controller  11424] Version:   Crossbar.io COMMUNITY 17.11.1
2017-11-23T19:06:43+0200 [Controller  11424] Public Key:
81da0aa76f36d4de2abcd1ce5b238d00a

...
```

You can picture Crossbar.io as Apache or Nginx: it's a piece of software that you configure and then run, and the rest of your code revolves around it. Crossbar.io is actually perfectly capable of being a static web server, a WSGI server, and even a process manager. But we are just going to use it for its WAMP capabilities. And for that, you don't need to do anything else. Let it run in the background, and focus on your client's code.

Now the beauty of WAMP is that the clients don't need to know each other. They just need to know about the router. By default, it listens on `localhost:8080` and defines a "realm" (a group of clients that can see each other) named `realm1`. So, all we have to do to use the router is connect to it using that information.

To illustrate the fact that WAMP clients don't need to know each other, or that you are not in a client/server architecture anymore, I am going to use two web pages in our first example.

One page will have an input field and a "sum" button. The other one is another input field, and it declares a `sum()` function as available for remote calling. When you click on the "sum" button, it will send the value of the first input to the second page, which will call `sum()` on both the received value and the local one, then send back the result.

Without writing any server-side code

First page, first client:

```html
<!DOCTYPEhtml> <html><head></head><body>

   <form name="sumForm"><input type="text"name="number"value="3"></form>

   <script src="http://goo.gl/1pfDD1"></script>

   <script>

   // Connection to the WAMP router
   var connection = new autobahn.Connection({
     url:"ws://127.0.0.1:8080/ws",
     realm:"realm1"
   });

   // Callback for when the connection is established
   connection.onopen = function (session,details){
     // We register a function under the name "sum", so that any WAMP
     // client on "realm1" can call it remotly. This is RPC.
     session.register('sum', function(a){
       // It's just a regular function, really. But the parameters and
       // return value must be serializable. By default to JSON.
       return parseInt(a) + parseInt(document.sumForm.number.value);
     });
   }
```

```
    // Start the connection
    connection.open();

  </script>
</body></html>
```

If you open a file with this code in a web browser, you will notice that the Crossbar.io console logs something about a new connected client:

```
2017-11-23T20:11:41+0200 [Router 13613] session "5770155719510781" joined
realm "realm1"
```

Now a second page, and another JS client:

```
<!DOCTYPEhtml> <html><head></head><body>

<form name="sumForm"method="post" >
  <input type="text"name="number"value="5">
  <button name="sumButton">Sum!</button>
  <span id="sumResult">...</span>
</form>

<script src="http://goo.gl/1pfDD1"></script>
<script>

  var connection = new autobahn.Connection({
    url:"ws://127.0.0.1:8080/ws",
    realm:"realm1"
  });

  connection.onopen = function (session,details){
    // When we submit the form (e.g: click on the button), call "sum()"
    // We don't need to know where "sum()" is declared or how it will run,
    // just that something exists under this name.
    document.sumForm.addEventListener('submit', function(e){
      e.preventDefault();
      // The first parameter is the namespace of the function. The second is
      // the arguments passed to the function. This returns a promise which
      // we use to set the value of our span when the results comes back
      session.call('sum',[document.sumForm.number.value]).then(
```

```
      function(result){
         document.getElementById('sumResult').innerHTML = result;
      });
   })
  }
  connection.open();

</script>

</body></html>
```

Again, the router reacts.

You can now press the "Sum!" button from the second page, which will happily call the code from the second page and get the result almost immediately. This, of course, works from and to Python as well. Obviously, this example is a basic one and does not take into consideration robustness or security. But I hope you get the general picture. You can use this mechanism, routed RPC, to define and call code anywhere on any browser or any process on any server that is connected to the router.

Now RPC alone is useful, but its little sibling, PUB/SUB, is another nice tool on its own. To demonstrate it, I'll add a Python client (which would actually be on the Crossbar server).

This Python client surveys a directory, and every second, scans all files in it. For each file extension it finds in the directory, it sends an event with a list of all matching files. Useless? Maybe. Very cool? Certainly!

```python
import os

from twisted.internet.defer import inlineCallbacks
from twisted.logger import Logger

from autobahn.twisted.util import sleep
from autobahn.twisted.wamp import ApplicationSession
from autobahn.twisted.wamp import ApplicationRunner

class DirectoryLister(ApplicationSession):

    log = Logger()

    @inlineCallbacks
```

```python
    def onJoin(self, details):
        while True:

            # List files and group them by extension
            files = {}
            for f in os.listdir('.'):
                file, ext = os.path.splitext(f)
                if ext.strip():
                    files.setdefault(ext, []).append(f)

            # Send one event named "filewithext.xxx" for each file extension
            # with "xxx" being the extension. We attach the list of files
            # to the events so that every clients interested in the event
            # can get the file list.
            # This is the "publish" part of "PUB/SUB".
            for ext, names in files.items():
                # Note that there is no need to declare the event before
                # using it. You can publish events as you go.
                yield self.publish('filewithext' +ext , names)

            yield sleep(1)

# The ApplicationRunner will take care starting everything for us.
if __name__ == '__main__':
    runner=ApplicationRunner(url=u"ws://localhost:8080/ws", realm=u"realm1")
    print(u"Connecting to ws://localhost:8080/ws")
    runner.run(DirectoryLister)
```

Run the code as before with:

```
python directory_lister.py
```

It will start listing everything in the current directory and publish events about the files it finds.

Now we need a client to say it is interested in those events. We can create a Python one or a JS one. Since everything is a client in WAMP, let's create a JS one to see clients from both languages.

```html
<!DOCTYPEhtml> <html><head></head><body>

  <div id="files">...</div>

  <script src="http://goo.gl/1pfDD1"></script>

  <script>

    // Connection to the WAMP router
    var connection = new autobahn.Connection({
      url:"ws://127.0.0.1:8080/ws",
      realm:"realm1"
    });

    connection.onopen = function (session,details){

      // Populate the HTML page with a list of files
      var div=document.getElementById('files');
      div.innerHTML="";
      function listFile(params,meta,event){
        var ul=document.getElementById(event.topic);
        if (!ul){
          div.innerHTML += "<ul id='" + event.topic + "'></ul>";
          ul=document.getElementById(event.topic);
        }
        ul.innerHTML="";
        params[0].forEach(function(f){
          ul.innerHTML += "<li>" + f + "</li>";
        })
      }

      // We tell the router we are interested in events with this name.
      // This is the "subscribe" part of "PUB/SUB".
      session.subscribe('filewithext.py',listFile);
      // Any client, like this Web page, can subscribe to an arbitrary number
      // of events. So here we say we are interested in events about files
      // with the ".py" extension and the ".txt" extension.
      session.subscribe('filewithext.txt',listFile);
    }
```

```
    connection.open();

  </script>
</body></html>
```

In my directory, I then have at least a file with a .py extension and a file with an .html extension: my two clients. For the sake of the demonstration, I'll create an empty text file called empty.txt next to them. This way we should at least have three events every second.

If you open this as a web page, you'll notice it will start listing the files like:

- empty.txt

- directory_lister.py

If you add or remove files, you'll see that change in real time. If you create a new JS client with a different set of subscriptions, it will display a different file listing.

Summary

As you would expect, we only scratched the surface of what you can do with WebSocket, Twisted, Autobahn, and WAMP.

Try to edit the given examples to make them do more, or combine them, to get a sense of what's going on. To feel more comfortable with this code, you should add some logging to it.

For the WebSocket examples, in the `if __name__ == "__main__"` section, add:

```
import sys
from twisted.python import log

log.startLogging(sys.stdout)
...
```

For the WAMP examples, in the body of the Application session class:

```
from twisted.logger import Logger
...

class TheAppClass(ApplicationSession):
    log=Logger()
    ...
```

If you want to explore further, here are some ideas:

- Convert the example to use `async` / `await` constructs for a more modern experience.

- Try other forms of messages such as streaming.

- Give more reliability to your code by leveraging auto-connect or load balancing (Twisted / WAMP only).

- Write a client in yet another language: Java, C#, PHP. You have WebSocket and WAMP clients for a lot of popular platforms.

- Look for security features: SSL, Authentication, Permissions. . . They are hard to set up, but quite solid.

- Learn more about Crossbar.io (which is also Twisted): process management, WSGI server, static file handling. You will be surprised by all the things it can do.

CHAPTER 9

Applications with asyncio and Twisted

The `asyncio` package, included with Python implementations since version 3.4, standardizes a suite of APIs for asynchronous, event-driven network programs. In addition to shipping its own concurrency and networking primitives, `asyncio` also specifies an event loop interface that provides a common denominator for asynchronous libraries and frameworks. This shared substrate allows applications to use Twisted and `asyncio` together in the same process.

In this chapter, we'll learn how to compose Twisted's APIs with `asyncio`'s by writing a simple HTTP proxy with `treq`, a high-level HTTP client built on top of Twisted; and `aiohttp`, an HTTP client and server library built on top of `asyncio`.

`asyncio` and its ecosystem are still evolving. New APIs have been developed and idioms adopted as more people use `asyncio` in more situations. As a result, our HTTP proxy is a case study and not a recipe for integrating Twisted and `asyncio`. We'll begin with an introduction to the fundamental and stable concepts that enable cross-compatibility between the two that lays out a path for integrating future iterations of `asyncio` and its libraries with Twisted.

Core Concepts

`asyncio` and Twisted share many design and implementation details, partially because Twisted's community participated in `asyncio`'s development. PEP 3156, which describes `asyncio`, drew from PEP 3153, which in turn was written by a member of Twisted's development team. Consequently, `asyncio` borrows Twisted's protocols, transports, producers, and consumers and presents a familiar environment to Twisted programmers.

© Mark Williams, Cory Benfield, Brian Warner, Moshe Zadka, Dustin Mitchell, Kevin Samuel, Pierre Tardy 2019
M. Williams et al., *Expert Twisted*, https://doi.org/10.1007/978-1-4842-3742-7_9

This common ancestry, however, is largely irrelevant to the process of integrating libraries that *use* asyncio with those that use Twisted. Instead, two concepts necessary to any event-driven framework form the interface at which they meet: *promises* that represent values before they're available and *event loops* that schedule I/O.

Promises

By now you're familiar with Twisted's Deferreds, which allow developers to associate business logic and error handling with values before they become available. Deferreds are known generically in computer science literature and other communities as *promises*. As Chapter 2 explains, promises ease the development of event-driven programs by externalizing the composition of callbacks without special support from the host language.

asyncio's foundational promise implementation is its asyncio.Future class. Unlike Deferreds, Futures do *not* run their callbacks synchronously; instead, Future. add_done_callback schedules a callback to be run in the next iteration of the event loop. Compare the behavior of Deferreds and Futures in the following example when run on Python 3.4 or later:

```
>>> from twisted.defer import Deferred
>>> d = Deferred()
>>> d.addCallback(print)
<Deferred at 0x1234567890>
>>> d.callback("value")
>>> value
>>> from asyncio import Future
>>> f.add_done_callback(print)
>>> f.set_result("value")
>>>
```

Deferred.addCallback and Future.add_done_callback both arrange for a function to be run against the value represented by the respective promise abstraction when that value becomes available. Deferred.callback, however, immediately runs all associated callbacks, while Future.set_result makes no progress until an event loop begins its next iteration.

On the one hand, this eliminates the possibility for re-entrancy bugs that exist with `Deferred`, because all `asyncio` code can assume that adding a callback will not result in its being run immediately, even if the `Future` already has a value. On the other hand, all `asyncio` code must be run with an event loop, which complicates both its use and its design. For example: With what event loop did the `Future` we named `f` above schedule its `print` callback? We have to look at `asyncio`'s event loop system and how it differs from Twisted's reactor to answer this question.

Event Loops

As explained in Chapter 1, Twisted calls its event loop a *reactor*. In Chapter 3, we used `twisted.internet.task.react` and Twisted application framework to manage the creation and provisioning of the reactor for our feed aggregation application. Both of these ways to get a reactor are preferred to importing it in application code as `twisted.internet.reactor`. That's because the selection of a reactor depends on the context in which it's used; different platforms provide their own I/O multiplexing primitives, so that Twisted applications that run on macOS should use `kqueue` while those run on Linux should use `epoll`; tests might prefer a stub reactor implementation to minimize the impact on shared operating resources; and, as we'll see, applications might want to combine Twisted with other frameworks by running it on top of another event loop. Code that imports the reactor instead of accepting it as an argument to callables cannot itself be imported before reactor selection, which significantly complicates its use. For this reason, Twisted introduced APIs like `react` to facilitate parameterizing applications on a reactor.

While Twisted had to develop new APIs to manage reactor selection and installation, from the beginning `asyncio` included *event loop policies* that serve this purpose. `asyncio` includes a default policy that developers can replace with `asyncio.set_event_loop_policy` and retrieve with `asyncio.get_event_loop_policy`.

The default policy ties event loops to threads; `asyncio.get_event_loop` returns the loop for the current thread, creating it if necessary, while `asyncio.set_event_loop` sets it.

This is how our example `Future` associated itself with an event loop. `asyncio.Future` initializer accepts an event loop via the keyword-only `loop` argument; if this remains `None`, the `Future` retrieves the default policy's current loop with `asyncio.get_event_loop`.

Historically `asyncio` expected its users to explicitly pass the current event loop where it was needed, with the result that a bug in get_event_loop caused unexpected behavior when the function was called anywhere below module level. As of Python 3.5.3, however, get_event_loop was made to reliably return the running event loop when run inside callbacks. More recent `asyncio` code favors get_event_loop over explicit references passed down through the call stack or set as instance variables.

In addition to their pervasiveness, `asyncio`'s event loops differ from Twisted's reactors in terms of functionality. Reactors, for example, can run *system event triggers* at defined points in their life cycle. Twisted often manages resources that must be allocated before any application code is run and explicitly released before the process shuts down with `IReactorCore.addSystemEventTrigger`; for example, the lifetime of thread pool used by Twisted's default DNS resolver is tied to the lifetime of the reactor via a `shutdown` event trigger. At the time of this writing, `asyncio`'s event loops do not have an equivalent API.

Guidelines

Because of the differences between `asyncio.Futures` and Twisted's `Deferreds` and between the two libraries' event loops, it's necessary to follow specific guidelines when combining the two.

1. Always run the Twisted reactor on top of an `asyncio` event loop.

2. When calling `asyncio` code from Twisted, convert `Futures` to `Deferreds` with `Deferred.fromFuture`. Wrap coroutines in `asyncio.Tasks` and convert these to `Deferreds` like `Futures`.

3. When calling Twisted from `asyncio`, convert `Deferreds` to `Futures` with `Deferred.asFuture`. Pass the active `asyncio` event loop as this method's argument.

The first guideline follows from the fact that `IReactorCore`'s API is larger than that of `asyncio`'s event loops. The second and third, however, require familiarity with `asyncio`'s coroutines, `Futures`, and `Tasks` and the differences between them.

We saw above that `Futures` function equivalently to `Deferreds`. We also learned in Chapter 2 that *coroutines* – functions and methods defined with `async def` – are a *language feature*; they are not implicitly tied to `asyncio` or Twisted or any other library. Recall that a coroutine may `await` a *future-like object*, and that `Deferreds` are future-like objects, so a coroutine may `await` a `Deferred`.

Unsurprisingly, `asyncio.Futures` are also future-like objects, so coroutines can await them, too. Idiomatic `asyncio` code rarely explicitly creates `Futures` to `await`, however, preferring to directly `await` other coroutines. Consider the following example:

```
>>> import asyncio
>>> from twisted.internet import defer, task, reactor
>>> aiosleep=asyncio.sleep(1.0, loop=asyncio.get_event_loop())
>>> txsleep=task.deferLater(reactor,1.0, lambda:None)
>>> asyncio.iscoroutine(aiosleep)
True
>>> isinstance(txsleep, defer.Deferred)
True
```

`aiosleep` is an object that will pause an `asyncio` coroutine for at least one second, while `txsleep` does the same for Twisted code that uses `Deferreds`. While `txsleep` is a `Deferred` like any other, `aiosleep` is in fact a coroutine suitable for `awaiting` by other coroutines.

`aiosleep`, like all coroutines, *must* be `awaited` to make any progress. This makes them ill-suited for "fire and forget"-type background operations that should run without blocking their caller while they resolve to a value. This differs from the `txsleep` `Deferred`, which will fire after approximately 1 second regardless of whether or not it has any callbacks or errbacks.

`asyncio` provides a solution in the form of `Tasks`. A Task wraps a coroutine in a `Future` and `awaits` that `Future` on behalf of its creator. `Tasks` allow `asyncio.gather` to simultaenously `await` multiple coroutines. The following code, for example, will run only for 4 seconds instead of 6:

```
import asyncio


sleeps = asyncio.gather(asyncio.sleep(2), asyncio.sleep(4))
asyncio.get_event_loop().run_until_complete(sleeps)
```

Twisted's `Deferreds` can be linked with asyncio's `Futures` with `Deferred.fromFuture` and as`Future`. Using `asyncios` Task creation APIs, like `asyncio.AbstractEventLoop.create_task` and `asyncio.ensure_future`, enables coroutines that await `asyncio` objects to interoperate with Twisted through `Deferred`'s Future-aware interfaces.

Exactly how asyncio and Twisted can be made to cooperate is best explained by an example. The following code demonstrates all three of our interoperability guidelines:

```
import asyncio
from twisted.internet import asyncioreactor
loop = asyncio.get_event_loop()
asyncioreactor.install(loop)
from twisted.internet import defer, task

originalFuture = asyncio.Future(loop=loop)
originalDeferred = defer.Deferred()
originalCoroutine = asyncio.sleep(3.0)

deferredFromFuture = defer.Deferred.fromFuture(originalFuture)
deferredFromFuture.addCallback(print,"from deferredFromFuture")
deferredFromCoroutine = defer.Deferred.fromFuture(
    loop.create_task(originalCoroutine))
deferredFromCoroutine.addCallback(print,"from deferredFromCoroutine")
futureFromDeferred = originalDeferred.asFuture(loop)
futureFromDeferred.add_done_callback(
    lambda result: print(result,"from futureFromDeferred"))

@task.react
def main(reactor):
    reactor.callLater(1.0, originalFuture.set_result, "1")
    reactor.callLater(2.0, originalDeferred.callback, "2")
    return deferredFromCoroutine
```

We begin by setting up Twisted's asyncio reactor with asyncioreactor.install. This function accepts an asyncio event loop as its argument to which it will bind the Twisted reactor. As explained above, asyncio.get_event_loop requests that the global (and in this case default) event loop policy create and cache a new loop retrievable by later get_event_loop calls.

originalFuture, originalCoroutine, and originalDeferred represent the three kinds of objects we'll convert to and from Deferreds: a Future, a coroutine that awaits asyncio code, and a Deferred.

Next, we link `originalFuture` with a `Deferred` via the `Deferred.fromFuture` class method and add a `print` invocation as a callback to the new `Deferred`. Remember that the first argument to a callback is the `Deferred`'s result, while additional arguments are any passed to `addCallback`.

We have to wrap `originalCoroutine` in a `Task` with `create_task` before passing it to `Deferred.fromFuture`; after that, however, we proceed as we did with `deferredFromFuture`.

As we saw above, `Futures`, unlike `Deferreds`, only make progress when an `asyncio` event loop is running, and `asyncio` can have multiple event loops at any time. Associating `originalDeferred` with a `Future` via `asFuture` consequently requires an explicit reference to an event loop. After providing this, we arrange for an informative print callback to run when `originalDeferred`, and thus `futureFromDeferred`, resolves to a value. This is complicated by `Future.add_done_callback`, which only accepts single-argument callbacks. We use a `lambda` to print both the result and an informative message.

None of these objects will make any progress without an event loop, so we use `task.react` to run the reactor for us. We schedule `originalFuture` to resolve to `"1"` after at least one second and `originalDeferred` to resolve to `"2"` after at least two. Finally, we terminate the reactor when `deferredFromCoroutine`, and thus `originalCoroutine`, completes.

Running this program should produce the following output:

```
1 from deferredFromFuture
<Future finished result='2'> from futureFromDeferred
None from deferredFromCoroutine
```

The first line corresponds to the `print` callback we added to `deferredFromFuture`, the second to `futureFromDeferred`'s callback (note that `Future` callbacks receive their `Future` as their argument), and the third to `deferredFromCoroutine`'s callback.

This example illustrates the three guidelines necessary to integrating `asyncio` and Twisted in an abstract way that's hard to apply to real-world problems. As we explained, however, it's not possible to give more specific advice that's still generally applicable. But since we now know the players, we can see how they perform together with a case study.

Case Study: A Proxy with aiohttp and treq

aiohttp (https://aiohttp.readthedocs.io) is a mature HTTP client and server library for asyncio that runs on Python 3.4 and later.

treq, as we saw in Chapter 3, is a high-level HTTP client library built on top of Twisted.

We can use these together to build a simple HTTP proxy. Clients configured to use an HTTP proxy send all requests to it; the proxy then relays these requests to the desired target and sends its response back to the client. We'll use the server portion of aiohttp to talk to clients and treq to retrieve pages on their behalf.

HTTP proxies are used to filter and cache content and to mediate POSTs, PUTs, and all other HTTP methods. We'll consider ours a success when it just relays GET requests back and forth to clients!

Let's begin by running the simplest aiohttp server possible under Twisted. Create a new virtual environment *with Python 3.4 or later*, install aiohttp, Twisted, and treq, and then run the following program:

```python
import asyncio
from twisted.internet import asyncioreactor

asyncioreactor.install(asyncio.get_event_loop())

from aiohttp import web
from twisted.internet import defer, task

app = web.Application()

async def handle(request):
    return web.Response(text=str(request.url))

app.router.add_get('/{path:.*}', handle)

async def serve():
    runner = web.AppRunner(app)
    await runner.setup()
    site = web.TCPSite(runner, 'localhost',8000)
    await site.start()

def asDeferred(f):
    return defer.Deferred.fromFuture(asyncio.ensure_future(f))
```

```
@task.react
@defer.inlineCallbacks
def main(reactor):
    yield asDeferred(serve())
    yield defer.Deferred()
```

We begin, as we did in our previous example, by installing the asyncio Twisted reactor and wrapping it around a cached event loop.

Next, we import aiohttp's web module and construct an Application, the fundamental web application abstraction provided by the library. We add a regular-expression *route* to it that matches all URLs (.*) and set the *handle* coroutine as its handler. This coroutine accepts a aiohttp.web.Request instance representing the client's request as its argument and returns its URL as a response.

The serve coroutine contructs the AppRunner and Site objects necessary to set up our application and bind it to a network port.

Our application, its handler, and the serve coroutine are drawn directly from aiohttp's documentation, and would remain exactly the same if we weren't using Twisted at all. The interoperation that we started with our installation of the asyncio reactor is realized in the main function run by task.react. This, as usual, is a Deferred, though this time it is one that uses inlineCallbacks. We could have written this as a async def-style coroutine and converted it to a Deferred with ensureDeferred; we've chosen instead to use inlineCallbacks to show how different styles can be used interchangeably.

The asDeferred helper function accepts either a coroutine or a Future. It then uses asyncio.ensure_future to ensure that whatever it received becomes a Future; if it's a coroutine, this evaluates to a Task, and if it's a Future, it's evaluated to the same object. The result can then be passed to Deferred.fromFuture.

We use this to wrap the serve coroutine in a Deferred, and then block the reactor forever by waiting on a Deferred that will never fire.

Running this program will run our simple URL echoing service under Twisted. Visiting http://localhost:8000 in a browser will return the URL you used to access it; adding path elements, like http://localhost:8000/a/b/c, will result in a different URL.

Now that we have the basics down, we can implement our proxy:

```
import asyncio
from twisted.internet import asyncioreactor

asyncioreactor.install(asyncio.get_event_loop())
```

```python
from aiohttp import web
from twisted.internet import defer, task

app = web.Application()

async def handle(request):
    url=str(request.url)
    headers = Headers({k: request.headers.getall(k)
                        for k in request.headers})
    proxyResponse = await asFuture(treq.get(url, headers=headers))
    print("URL:", url,"code:", proxyResponse.code)
    response = web.StreamResponse(status=proxyResponse.code)
    for key, values in proxyResponse.headers.getAllRawHeaders():
        for value in values:
            response.headers.add(key.decode(), value.decode())
    await response.prepare(request)
    body = await asFuture(proxyResponse.content())
    await response.write(body)
    await response.write_eof()
    return response

app.router.add_get('/{path:.*}', handle)

async def serve():
    runner = web.AppRunner(app)
    await runner.setup()
    site = web.TCPSite(runner, 'localhost',8000)
    await site.start()

def asFuture(d):
    return d.asFuture(asyncio.get_event_loop())

def asDeferred(f):
    return defer.Deferred.fromFuture(asyncio.ensure_future(f))

@task.react @defer.inlineCallbacks
def main(reactor):
    yield asDeferred(serve())
    yield defer.Deferred()
```

The code above differs from our miminal `aiohttp` implementation in two places: the `handle` function and a new `asFuture` helper.

The `handle` function begins by extracting the target URL from the client's request. Recall that clients of HTTP proxies specify their target by providing a full URL in their request line; `aiohttp` makes a parsed representation of this available as `request.url`.

Next, we recover all the client's header values from the `aiohttp` request and convert them to a `twisted.web.http_headers.Headers` instance so that they can be included in the outbound `treq` request. HTTP headers can be multi-valued, and `aiohttp` handles this with a case-insensitive multi-dictionary; `request.headers.getall(key)` returns a list of all the values for that header key in the request. The resulting dictionary maps keys to lists of their values, which matches Twisted's `Headers` initializer. Note that `aiohttp` decodes headers into text, while Twisted's `Headers` work in terms of bytes; fortunately, Twisted will automatically encode textual header keys and values to bytes automatically.

Once we've prepared a replica of the client's headers suitable for use with `treq`, we issue our GET request. At this point, the `asyncio` event loop is scheduling our `handle` coroutine, so whatever we `await` must be `asyncio` compatible. `treq`, however, works in terms of `Deferreds`, which *can* be awaited but fail with an error when `asyncio` attempts to schedule them. The solution is to wrap the `Deferred` in a `Future` associated with the same event loop that's scheduled our `handler`.

This is exactly what the `asFuture` helper does. Because we bound our reactor to a global event loop with `get_event_loop` at the beginning of our program, all subsequent calls to `get_event_loop` will return the same loop. This includes calls inside `aiohttp` and calls inside our own code, which is how `asFuture` binds the enclosing `Future` with the correct event loop.

As we saw in our example, `asyncio` awaits `Futures` that wrap `Deferreds` exactly as Twisted would await the `Deferreds` themselves. Consequently, our handler resumes and assigns the `treq` response object to `proxyResponse`. At this point, we print out a message detailing the URL retrieved and its status code.

Next, we construct an `aiohttp.web.StreamResponse` and provide it with the same status code we received from the target URL so that the client will see the same code the proxy did. We also reverse the header translation, copying Twisted's `Header` keys and values into our `StreamResponse`'s headers. `twisted.web.http_headers.Headers.getAllRawHeaders` represents header keys and values as bytes, so we must decode them for `StreamResponse`'s sake.

We then send the response's envelope with `StreamResponse.prepare` back to the client. All that's left is to receive and send back the body, which we do with treq's Response's `content` method; this is again a `Deferred`, so we have to wrap it in `asFuture` for asyncio's sake.

Here an excerpt of what our program outputs when we configure a web browser to use it as an HTTP proxy and visit `http://twistedmatrix.com/`:

```
URL: http://twistedmatrix.com/ code: 200
URL: http://twistedmatrix.com/trac/chrome/common/css/bootstrap.min.css code:200
URL: http://twistedmatrix.com/trac/chrome/common/css/trac.css code: 200
...
```

Summary

In this chapter we learned how to composed Twisted and `asyncio` in a single application. Because the two share the core concepts of *promises* and *event loops*, it's possible to run Twisted on top of `asyncio`.

Using `asyncio` and Twisted together requires following three guidelines: Always run the reactor on top of `asyncio`'s event loop; convert `Futures` to `Deferreds` with `Deferred.asFuture` when calling `asyncio` from Twisted; and vice versa with `Deferred.fromFuture` when calling Twisted from `asyncio`.

Because `asyncio` is still evolving, it's not possible to provide more specific integration guidelines. Instead, we applied what we learned to a case study: a simple GET-only HTTP proxy with `aiohttp` and `treq`. While minimal, our proxy resembled a real application closely enough that we learned how to put those guidelines to work and bridged the gap between two of Python's asynchronous programming communities.

CHAPTER 10

Buildbot and Twisted

Buildbot is a framework for automating software build, test, and release processes. It is a popular choice for organizations and projects with complex and unusual build, test, and release requirements. The framework is heavily customizable and ships with "batteries included," including support for lots of version-control systems, build and test frameworks, and status displays. Since it is written in Python, Buildbot can easily be extended with purpose-specific implementations of key components. We compare Buildbot to Django: it provides the basis on which to build complex, customized applications, but it is not as simple to set up or use as tools like Joomla or WordPress.

History of Buildbot

Brian Warner wrote the predecessor to Buildbot in 2000–2001, when he was working at a router company. He was tired of hassling his coworkers each morning when they'd checked code into CVS that worked on their Solaris boxes but not on his Linux machine.

It was initially closed source, and used `asyncore` and `pickle` to implement an RPC system in which the workers drove the whole process. The central buildmaster only accepted status information from the workers to render it on a web-based waterfall display. It was modeled closely on Mozilla's "Tinderbox."

In the process of looking for examples of `asyncore`, Brian discovered Twisted, and found that it was already more advanced and growing quickly. After leaving the router company in early 2002, he built a clean re-implementation of the build system, in part as a way to learn Twisted, and the result became Buildbot.

Until about 2009, Buildbot had no database back end. Before that time, databases were fairly hard to deploy, and storing data directly on disk was not uncommon and seemed an efficient solution. Everything was smaller scale: disks were fast, networks were slow, and a "big" CI application only ran tens of parallel builds.

317

© Mark Williams, Cory Benfield, Brian Warner, Moshe Zadka, Dustin Mitchell, Kevin Samuel, Pierre Tardy 2019
M. Williams et al., *Expert Twisted*, https://doi.org/10.1007/978-1-4842-3742-7_10

Starting in 2009, Mozilla began using Buildbot, and the organization's needs quickly outstripped this simple model. Within a few years, Mozilla was operating thousands of workers and more than 50 buildmasters. To support this, they engaged Brian to add a partial database back end to allow the buildmasters to coordinate their work. This database implementation did not store the results of builds – that remained in pickle files on individual buildmasters.

The web interface was entirely synchronous, rendering static HTML representations of build results. As such, displaying some pages could block the buildmaster for several minutes while it loaded results from the database and from pickle files. At Mozilla, just viewing a "waterfall" page could cause an outage, so access to those pages was not permitted.

About this time, Dustin Mitchell took over maintenance of the project and began organizing a long effort to modernize the application. This effort succeeded with the release of Buildbot 0.9.0 in October of 2016. The project aimed to refashion Buildbot as a database-backed server application presenting an HTTP API and hosting an interactive front-end web application. In a multi-master configuration, build results are now available from any master, updated "live" as results come in from workers. The HTTP API supports integration with other CI tools, and new well-defined, asynchronous interfaces support development of third-party plugins.

Nine was no easy project – it took a half decade of hard work by a team of developers including Pierre Tardy, Tom Prince, Amber Yust, and Mikhail Sobolev. It also involved solving a lot of tricky problems relating to asynchronous Python, as described in the rest of this chapter.

The Evolution of Buildbot's Async Python

Twisted already had good protocol support, including Perspective Broker, when Brian began writing Buildbot. Its reactor and Deferred handling were well-developed and built on solid theoretical foundations. However, "async" was still a relatively unknown concept in mainstream software development, and asynchronous code lived up to the name "Twisted Python."

As an example, let's look at Buildbot's `Builder.startBuild` method, as it existed around 2005 (it has since been rewritten). It performed two asynchronous operations in sequence, first pinging the selected worker, then calling that worker's `startBuild` method. This was implemented with a series of instance methods:

```python
# buildbot/process/builder.py @ 41cdf5a
class SlaveBuilder(pb.Referenceable):
    def attached(self, slave, remote, commands):
        # ...
        d = self.remote.callRemote("setMaster",self)
        d.addErrback(self._attachFailure,"Builder.setMaster")
        d.addCallback(self._attached2)
        return d

    def _attached2(self, res):
        d = self.remote.callRemote("print","attached")
        d.addErrback(self._attachFailure,"Builder.print 'attached'")
        d.addCallback(self._attached3)
        return d

    def _attached3(self, res):
        # now we say they're really attached
        return self

    def _attachFailure(self, why, where):
        assert type(where) is str
        log.msg(where)
        log.err(why)
        return why
```

This clunky syntax required careful threading of variables through multiple methods, made control flow hard to follow, and polluted the method namespace. This led to lots of interesting bugs with unhandled errors mysteriously disappearing or callbacks firing in unexpected order. Conditionals and loops that involved asynchronous operations were extremely difficult to get right and therefore, debug properly.

We are now accustomed to referring to functions as asynchronous (meaning they return a Deferred) and synchronous (meaning they do not). In these dark ages, the distinction was not so clear, and there were functions in Buildbot that could return a Deferred or an immediate value, depending on the circumstances. Needless to say, such functions were difficult to call correctly and were refactored to be strictly synchronous or asynchronous.

As Twisted matured, and more importantly as Python grew additional features like generators, decorators, and yield expressions, the situation gradually improved. Twisted's deferredGenerator allowed control flow to be written in a normal Python style with if, while, and for statements. Its syntax was still clunky, requiring three lines of code to perform an asynchronous operation and failing in obscure ways if any of those lines were omitted:

```python
# buildbot/buildslave/base.py @ 8b4e7a9
class BotBase(service.MultiService):
    @defer.deferredGenerator
    def remote_setBuilderList(self, wanted):
        retval = {}
        # ...
        dl = defer.DeferredList([
            defer.maybeDeferred(self.builders[name].disownServiceParent)
            for name in to_remove])
        wfd = defer.waitForDeferred(dl)
        yield wfd
        wfd.getResult()
        # ...
        yield retval # return value
```

With Python 2.5 and the introduction of yield expressions, Twisted implemented inlineCallbacks. These are similar to deferredGenerator, but use only one line to perform an asynchronous operation:

```python
# master/buildbot/data/buildrequests.py @ 8b4e7a9
class BuildRequestEndpoint(Db2DataMixin, base.Endpoint):
    @defer.inlineCallbacks
    def get(self, resultSpec, kwargs):
        buildrequest = yield self.master.db.buildrequests.getBuildRequest(k
        wargs['buildrequestid
        if buildrequest:
            defer.returnValue((yield self.db2data(buildrequest)))
        defer.returnValue(None)
```

This approach is much more forgiving, except that it is very easy to forget to yield a Deferred. Such errors cause the asynchronous operation to execute "in parallel" with the calling function, and often don't cause any issues until that operation fails and the calling function continues undeterred. Several such insidious errors have survived extensive testing and persisted over Buildbot releases.

As Twisted and Buildbot move to Python 3, Python's `async`/`await` syntax will provide a more natural way of writing asynchronous Python, although it will not solve the issue of a forgotten `await`. The function above reads even more naturally with this syntax:

```python
class BuildRequestEndpoint(Db2DataMixin, base.Endpoint):
    async def get(self, resultSpec, kwargs):
        buildrequest = await self.master.db.buildrequests.getBuildRequest
        (kwargs['buildrequestid'])
        if buildrequest:
            return (await self.db2data(buildrequest))
        return None
```

Historically, asynchronous Python has been used only for performance-critical network applications, with the majority of Python applications built on a synchronous model. The NodeJS community has shown that standardized, interoperable asynchronous, can lead to a vibrant ecosystem of libraries, utilities, and frameworks that can be freely combined. Python now has `async`/`await`, and `asyncio` enables code written for Twisted to interoperate with code written for other asynchronous frameworks, facilitating similar growth.

Migrating Synchronous APIs

In the early days, the Buildbot master ran as a single process and stored its status in pickle files on disk. It read from and wrote to those files synchronously, so most operations within the master did not involve Deferreds.

Around 2010, as continuous integration caught on in the software development community and Buildbot installations began to grow, pickle files did not scale. The time had come to add a database back end, and we were faced with a choice: convert all of those status functions to return Deferreds, or make synchronous database calls from the main thread, blocking other operations until they complete. The first option was appealing, but when a function is modified to return a Deferred, then every function that calls it must also be modified to return a Deferred, rippling through the code base. Buildbot is a framework, so most installations contain lots of custom code that calls Buildbot functions. Making those functions return a Deferred constituted a breaking change and would require users to rewrite and retest their custom code.

In the interest of expediency, we decided to make most database calls on the main thread. Most of the data about build status – results, steps, and logs – was left on-disk. While this allowed us to ship the feature on time, it had predictable performance issues. In fact, in larger installations such as Mozilla's, database queries could stall the master for so long that workers would time out, cancel running builds, and try to reconnect.

This situation repeated itself with many other APIs in Buildbot, as we added new functionality to code that was once simple and synchronous. If we could begin again without any compatibility requirements, we would make every exposed API method asynchronous, and accept a Deferred on every call into user code.

Async Build Steps

Build steps were particularly difficult to make asynchronous. While Buildbot includes a number of "canned" build steps for common tasks, we allow users to implement their own steps as well. Such custom build steps call a number of methods as a step executes to add log output, update status, and so on. Historically, all of those calls were synchronous, since they updated state in memory that was later flushed to disk.

Buildbot 0.9 eliminated those on-disk data structures, and now stores everything in the database. It also provides "live" updates, so caching build step results until the step was completed was not an option. Thus, all of the synchronous methods to update status became asynchronous – but existing custom build steps called them synchronously!

Our approach to solving this problem was an unusual one: define "old-style" (synchronous) and "new-style" build steps, with different behavior for each. When executing old-style build steps, Buildbot gathers all of the otherwise-unhandled Deferreds from these methods and, when the step is otherwise complete, waits until all have fired. Since most of the methods are providing information about the step's progress, callers do not expect any return value. We added a simple method to distinguish old and new build step implementations and only activate the compatibility mechanism for old steps. The strategy is remarkably successful, and for the minority of custom build steps for which it fails, the solution is easy: rewrite as a new-style build step.

We developed this compatibility mechanism before rewriting the built-in build steps in the "new" style. This provided an opportunity to test and refine the mechanism before rewriting all of the built-in steps in the more reliable new style.

Buildbot's Code

Buildbot is unusual for an asynchronous application. Most such applications focus on a request/response cycle, with asynchronous programming permitting a much higher degree of parallelism than a thread-based, synchronous model. Buildbot, on the other hand, maintains long-term connections between the master and its attached workers and performs sequential operations on those workers. Even the process of accepting a new connection from a worker involves a complex sequence of operations to check for duplicate workers, interrogate the new worker's features, and set it up to perform builds.

A synchronous approach to building this sort of application would involve a thread for each worker, plus threads for any other service objects such as schedulers or change sources. Even a modest installation of such an approach might then have thousands of threads, with all of the scheduling and concurrency issues that entails.

Async Utilities

While Twisted provides a broad variety of useful asynchronous tools, Buildbot has found a few behaviors not supported by those tools. Just like queues and locks support building synchronous, threaded applications, these tools support building asynchronous applications.

Debounce

A production-scale Buildbot master may be communicating with hundreds of workers, receiving events with updated status and log data. These events are often easy to coalesce – for example, several lines of log data can be combined into one chunk – but must be handled in a timely fashion to support live logging and dynamic status updates.

The fix is to "debounce" these events, calling the handler only once when several events occur in rapid succession. A debounced method specifies a delay, and guarantees that the decorated method will be called at least once within that period, but can coalesce multiple calls within that time.

Debouncing can cause intermittent errors by allowing a method to execute at a time when it no longer makes sense. For example, it does not make sense to continue adding log lines to a build step if the step has been marked complete. To avoid this issue, debounced methods have a "stop" method that will wait (asynchronously) for any pending invocations, thus supporting clean state transitions.

Async Services

As Buildbot is based on the excellent Twisted Application Framework, this framework provides (among other features) IService and IServiceCollection interfaces that can be used to create a hierarchy of services. Buildbot arranges the buildmaster service at the top of this hierarchy, with managers for workers, change sources, and so on, added as child services. Workers and change sources are added as children of their respective managers.

This design has been critical to the structure of Buildbot applications: supporting application startup and shutdown. More importantly, it allows Buildbot to dynamically reconfigure itself at runtime. For example, if the configuration is modified to add an additional worker, the reconfiguration process creates a new worker service and adds it as a child of the worker manager.

There's just one problem with the application framework: startService is synchronous.

As we have services that handle talking to the database or to the message queue, it is critical for us that service startup is properly serialized by the Application framework. With this serialization, we can be sure that all the workers, builders, etc., are properly registered in the database, and listening to their requested message queues before we start the build requests distribution. For example, when a reconfiguration adds a new worker, that worker must be added to the database. The worker has not truly started until that asynchronous operation is complete.

While initialization dependency could be seen as an orthogonal problem as services dependencies, it has been quite handy for us to make startService asynchronous.

```
class AsyncMultiService(AsyncService, service.MultiService):

    def startService(self):
        service.Service.startService(self)
        dl = []
```

```
    # if a service attaches another service during the reconfiguration
    # then the service will be started twice, so we don't use iter, but rather
    # copy in a list
    for svc in list(self):
        # handle any deferreds, passing up errors and success
        dl.append(defer.maybeDeferred(svc.startService))
    return defer.gatherResults(dl, consumeErrors=True)
[...]
```

Buildbot adds an AsyncMultiService subclass of MultiService that supports asynchronous startService methods among its child services. It handles the edge cases around adding and removing services, meaning that addService, setServiceParent, and disownServiceParent are also made asynchronous.

We had the luxury of rewriting this functionality because we control all calls to addService and startService. Twisted itself could not easily make this change without introducing an entirely new, mutually incompatible class hierarchy.

In fact, since Twisted makes the call to the top-level service's startService method, some care is required to handle asynchronous behavior in this case. Buildbot's top-level service is BuildMaster, and its startService method returns a Deferred that never fails, using a try/except to catch any errors and stop the reactor. Since the reactor is not yet running at startup, startService begins by waiting for reactor startup:

```
class BuildMaster(...):

    @defer.inlineCallbacks
    def startService(self):
        [...]
        # we want to wait until the reactor is running, so we can call
        # reactor.stop() for fatal errors
        d = defer.Deferred()
        self.reactor.callWhenRunning(d.callback, None)
        yield d

        startup_succeed = False
        try:
            [...]
        except:
```

```
f = failure.Failure()
log.err(f, 'while starting BuildMaster')
self.reactor.stop()
```

What our system does not handle well is dependencies between peer services. For example, WorkerManager is dependent on the MessageQueueConnector, but both are children of the masterService. The MessageQueueConnector manages an externally backed message queue, and cannot accept any messages or registration request until the connection to the broker is done. Such registration requests are needed by the WorkerManager. Both services are started in parallel, being the children of the same service. As of now this has been resolved by optimistically queuing any messages or registration request until the connection is maintained. We could improve our system by adding an initialization dependency layer that is different from the service hierarchy. The design of such system is not easy to do if you want to have an efficient and simple interface, which does not require to rewrite all the startService of all our services.

An alternative design, one used in the ClientService class introduced in Twisted 16.1.0, is to return immediately from startService while allowing the startup process to run in parallel. This design requires that service startup cannot fail, or that some other mechanism of communicating failure be developed. Buildbot relies on the straightforward error behavior of AsyncMultiService to handle runtime reconfigurations, which must fail gracefully when the new configuration has an error. For ClientService, connections retry indefinitely, so the startup process never truly fails, even if it never truly completes. The immediate-return approach also requires careful consideration of the case where a service's method is called before startup has completed, generally by guarding each method to wait until startup has completed.

LRU Cache

Caching is critical to scaling any application, and Buildbot is no different. A common cache eviction strategy is least-recently-used (LRU), where cache entries that have not been used recently are discarded when space is required for new entries. A cache "hit" occurs when a request can be satisfied from data in the cache; a cache "miss" requires fetching the data from its source.

LRU caches are common, and several distributions are available on PyPI implementing them. However, at the time they were all synchronous and designed for use in a threaded environment.

In an asynchronous implementation, a cache miss will involve waiting for a fetch and additional requests for the same cache entry may arrive during the wait. These requests should not trigger additional fetches, but should wait for the same fetch to complete. This requires some careful handling of Deferreds, particularly around error handling.

Eventual

There are lots of cases where we want to call some function but don't care about the result or exactly when it is called. In an asynchronous system, it is best to invoke such functions later, when the current reactor iteration is complete. This allows a more fair distribution of work, with the reactor able to handle other events before invoking the functions.

A simple approach is to call `reactor.callLater(0, callableForLater)`; this is equivalent to Node's `process.nextTick`. However, this has the drawback of being difficult to test. Depending on the scheduling of the test, `callableForLater` may not be complete before the test finishes, resulting in intermittent test failures. This approach also fails to handle any exceptions or errbacks from `callableForLater`.

Buildbot's `buildbot.util.eventual.eventually` wraps `reactor.callLater`. It provides an extra `flushEventualQueue` method that tests can use to wait for all pending function calls to complete. And it handles errors in the called functions by logging them to the Twisted log.

Interfacing with Synchronous Code

Unlike the JS ecosystem, asynchronous is not the default and only way of doing I/O operations in Python. The Python ecosystem has grown over time with lots of very useful and well-thought-out libraries, and most of them are synchronous. Buildbot, being an integration tool, would have liked to use all these libraries.

We developed several best practices to use these synchronous libraries from our asynchronous core.

SQLAlchemy

SQLAlchemy is a well-known library that abstracts SQL to Python. It supports several SQL dialects, and make it easier to support several database back ends. SQLAlchemy provides a Pythonic SQL generation DSL (Domain Specific Language), which allows it to store and reuse SQL snippets, and also automatically handles the necessary SQL injection protection.

As of now, Buildbot supports SQLite, MySQL, and PostgreSQL.

SQLAlchemy has the concept of database connection pool; the SQL engine will reuse its connection to the database from request to request. In Buildbot, we map this connection pool to a `threadpool`, and each database operation is then operated inside a thread.

All of our database operations are implemented in a dedicated `db` module, and follow the same pattern.

- The database component code must derive from `buildbot.db.base.DBConnectorComponent`.

- Each public method is meant to be called from asynchronous code, and returns a `Deferred`.

- We use a nested function that accesses the Python scope of the asynchronous method inside our sync code in order to avoid passing around our parameters.

- We jump from the asynchronous world to synchronous world using `self.db.pool.do(..)`.

- We always prepend functions or methods names that are meant to be use blocking code with the `thd` prefix.

```python
class StepsConnectorComponent(base.DBConnectorComponent):

    def getStep(self, stepid=None, buildid=None, number=None, name=None):
        # create shortcut handle to the database table
        tbl = self.db.model.steps

        # we precompute the query inside the mainthread to fast exit in
        # case of error
```

```
if stepid is not None:
    wc = (tbl.c.id == stepid)
else:
    if buildid is None:
        return defer.fail(RuntimeError('must supply either stepid
        or buildid'))
    if number is not None:
        wc = (tbl.c.number == number)
    elif name is not None:
        wc = (tbl.c.name == name)
    else:
        return defer.fail(RuntimeError('must supply either number
        or name'))
    wc = wc & (tbl.c.buildid == buildid)

# this function could appear in a profile, so better give it a
meaningful name
def thdGetStep(conn):
    q = self.db.model.steps.select(whereclause=wc)
    # the next line does sync IO and block. That is why we need to
    be in a threadpool.
    res = conn.execute(q)
    row = res.fetchone()

    rv = None
    if row:
        rv = self._stepdictFromRow(row) res.close()
    return rv
return self.db.pool.do(thdGetStep)
```

requests

A lot of tools Buildbot interacts with are controllable via an HTTP API. Like Python's
urllib, Twisted has its own http client library, twisted.web.client. However, the
excellent python-requests library has proven to be very well crafted. It has a very simple
and powerful API emphasizing convention over configuration (hence the "HTTP for
humans" motto), connection pooling, keepalive, proxy support, and – importantly for
ensuring reliability in automation – automatic retries.

Naturally, a Python programmer will want to use similar APIs within Buildbot. But requests is a synchronous API, because humans like synchronous.

There is the treq library that implements the requests API using Twisted client, but it does not have all the reliability features of requests yet.

Initially, the Buildbot community wrote the txrequests library, which is a simple wrapper around a requests session that makes every requests in a ThreadPool, similar to what we've done with SQLAlchemy. Then Buildbot implemented a HttpClientService that abstracts the requests API, and allows the choice of the treq or txrequests back end.

Several important features were implemented for HTTPClientService, which was the result of our experience writing code using txrequests: It abstracts the differences between the two implementations, using whichever is installed. The service includes a unit test framework, which allows us to test our components without relying on a fake HTTP server. It also supports sharing sessions between components, so, for example, two components that interface with GitHub can use the same HTTP sessions.

```
class GitHubStatusPush(http.HttpStatusPushBase):

    @defer.inlineCallbacks
    def reconfigService(self, token, startDescription=None,
                        endDescription=None, context=None, baseURL=None,
                        verbose=False,**kwargs):
        yield http.HttpStatusPushBase.reconfigService(self,**kwargs)

        [...]
        self._http = yield httpclientservice.HTTPClientService.getService(
            self.master, baseURL, headers={
                'Authorization': 'token ' + token,
                'User-Agent': 'Buildbot'
            },
            debug=self.debug, verify=self.verify)
        self.verbose = verbose

    [...]
    def createStatus(self,
                     repo_user, repo_name, sha, state, target_url=None,
                     context=None, issue=None, description=None):
        payload = {'state': state}
```

```
        if description is not None:
            payload['description'] = description

        if target_url is not None:
            payload['target_url'] = target_url

        if context is not None:
            payload['context'] = context

        return self._http.post(
            '/'.join(['/repos', repo_user, repo_name, 'statuses', sha]),
            json=payload)
    [...]

class TestGitHubStatusPush(unittest.TestCase, ReporterTestMixin):
    [...]
    @defer.inlineCallbacks
    def setUp(self):
        self.master = fakemaster.make_master(testcase=self,
                                             wantData=True, wantDb=True,
                                             wantMq=True)

        yield self.master.startService()
        # getFakeService will patch the HTTPClientService, and make sure any
        # further HTTPClientService configuration will have same arguments.
        self._http = yield fakehttpclientservice.HTTPClientService.
        getFakeService(
            self.master,self,
            HOSTED_BASE_URL, headers={
                'Authorization': 'token XXYYZZ',
                'User-Agent': 'Buildbot'
            },
            debug=None, verify=None)
        self.sp = GitHubStatusPush('XXYYZZ')
        yield self.sp.setServiceParent(self.master)

    @defer.inlineCallbacks
    def test_basic(self):
        build = yield self.setupBuildResults(SUCCESS)
```

```
    # we make sure proper calls to txrequests have been made
    self._http.expect(
        'post',
        '/repos/buildbot/buildbot/statuses/d34db33fd43db33f',
        json={'state': 'pending',
            'target_url': 'http://localhost:8080/#builders/79/builds/0',
            'description': 'Build started.', 'context': 'buildbot/
            Builder0'})
# this will eventually make a http request, which will be checked
against expectations
self.sp.buildFinished(build)
```

Docker

Another example of a library we use is the official Python docker library. It is another synchronous library, which makes use of python-requests in order to implement the Docker HTTP protocol.

The Docker protocol is complex and might change frequently, so we decided against custom building a client using our HTTPClientService framework. But the official Docker API library is synchronous, so we needed to wrap it in such a way that it would not block the main thread.

We just used twisted.internet.threads.deferToThread to achieve this wrapping. This utility function uses the default shared thread pool, which Twisted manages automatically.

```
class DockerBaseWorker(AbstractLatentWorker): [...]
    def stop_instance(self, fast=False):
        if self.instance is None:
            # be gentle. Something may just be trying to alert us that an
            # instance never attached, and it's because, somehow, we never
            # started.
            return defer.succeed(None)
        instance = self.instance
        self.instance = None
        return threads.deferToThread(self._thd_stop_instance, instance, fast)
```

```
def _thd_stop_instance(self, instance, fast):
    docker_client = self._getDockerClient()
    log.msg('Stopping container %s... ' % instance[ 'Id'][:6])
    docker_client.stop(instance['Id'])
    if not fast:
        docker_client.wait(instance['Id'])
    docker_client.remove_container(instance['Id'], v=True, force=True)
    if self.image  is None:
        try:
            docker_client.remove_image(image=instance['image'])
        except docker.errors.APIError as e:
            log.msg('Error while removing the image: %s ', e)
```

Concurrent Access to Shared Resources

Concurrent programming is a hard computer science domain, with lots of traps. When you run several programs in parallel, you need to make sure that they do not work on the same data at the same time. With Twisted, it is easy to have the same function running at the same time in two different deferred chains (or `inlineCallbacks` generators or coroutines). This typical problem is called re-entrancy. Of course, with asynchronous programming, the function will not really run twice at the same time. It runs in the "reactor" thread. So, in principle, you can do any read-modify-write of a shared state without having to care for concurrency.

That is true. . . until you reach the following limitations:

Yield as a Concurrency Barrier

You can rationalize Twisted as cooperative multitasking, until you do some I/O operations. At that point, `yield`, `await`, and `d.addCallback()` become your concurrency barriers. You need to take care of not modifying shared state across those statements.

```
class MyClass(object):
    [...]
    # The following function cannot be called several times in parallel,
    as it will be modifying
```

```
    # self.data attribute between "yield"
    # It is not safe for reentrancy
    def unsafeFetchAllData(self, n):
        self.data = []
        for i in range(n):
            # during the yield, the context of the main thread could change
            up to the
            # point where the function is called again.
            current_data = yield self.fetchOneData(i)
            # BAD! modifying the shared state accross yield!
            self.data.append(current_data)

    # A correct implementation which does not involve locks is
    def safeFetchAllData(self, n):
        # we prepare the data in a local variable
        data = []
        for i in range(n):
            current_data = yield self.fetchOneData(i)
            data.append(current_data)
        # even if several fetchAllData is called several times in
        parallel, self.data will always be coherent.
        self.data = data
```

Thread-Pool Functions Should Not Mutate State

Sometimes you need to do some heavy calculation or use a library that is doing blocking I/O. You usually want to do those operations inside a helper thread different from the "reactor" thread, to avoid having to hang the reactor during the long processing.

So, when using threads, you have to think about protecting your shared state from concurrent access. There is, however, a simple rule that we follow in Buildbot in order to avoid using any kind of threading mutexes. All our functions or methods running in non-reactor threads must have no side effects on the application state. Instead, they communicate with the rest of the application only through function parameters and return values.

```python
from twisted.internet import defer
from twisted.internet import threads

class MyClass(object):
    [...]
    def unsafeFetchAllData(self, n):
        def thdfetchAllData():
            # BAD! modifying the shared state from a thread!
            self.data = []
            for i in range(n):
                with open("hugefile-{}.dat".format(i)) as f:
                    for line in f:
                        self.data.append(line)
        return threads.deferToThread(thdfetchAllData)

    @defer.inlineCallbacks
    def safeFetchAllData(self, n):
        def thdfetchAllData():
            data = []
            for i in range(n):
                with open("hugefile-{}.dat".format(i)) as f:
                    for line in f:
                        data.append(line)
            # we don't modify state, but rather pass the results to the
            # main thread
            return data
        data = yield threads.deferToThread(thdfetchAllData)
        self.data = data
```

This example involves loading data from large files, but any synchronous operation, or any operation for which no asynchronous library is available, would follow the same pattern.

DeferredLocks

In our experience, following the two previous best practices will keep you safe from 99% of concurrency issues. For the remaining 1%, Twisted has great concurrency primitives. You should, however, think twice before using them as it often hides design issues.

- DeferredSemaphore implements a semaphore, the case where at most N concurrent access to the same resource can happen.

- DeferredLock implements a simple Lock. It is equivalent a DeferredSemaphore with N==1 but has a simpler implementation.

- DeferredQueue implements a queue that can be read via Deferred.

The source code for these classes is instructive and worth reading. Unlike their threaded counterparts, the implementations are very simple, thanks to asynchronous principles. In cases where they are missing features, it is usually simple to extend or re-implement them with the required features. For example, DeferredQueue does not provide a way to determine the length of a queue, a critical feature for monitoring production services.

Testing

Automated testing is a necessity for any serious software engineering effort today, but this was not the case 15 years ago, especially in the open source world. Tools such as Buildbot, Jenkins, and Travis-CI have improved the situation dramatically, and it is now rare to find an open source library or application that does not have at least rudimentary tests.

Buildbot's test suite has had a rocky history. Early versions of the application had a collection of integration-style tests, but were flaky, difficult to understand, and had poor code-base coverage. At some point, these proved more trouble than they were worth, and we chose to delete them entirely and began again with a unit-testing focus. We have since written new unit tests for some of the existing code, but more importantly, required that new or refactored code come with new tests. With several years of hard work, Buildbot's line coverage is now about 90%, with much of the untested code being retained only for backward compatibility. Such coverage is critical for a framework like Buildbot, where no single installation exercises even a fraction of the framework's code.

Twisted's testing framework, Trial is indispensable for testing a heavily asynchronous code base. With years of experience of asynchronous testing, Trial's feature list sets the standard for asynchronous test frameworks.

Test cases are asynchronous by default, which means they can return a Deferred. The test framework makes sure the Deferred is waited for, and runs each test case within a new instance of the reactor infrastructure. Trial also has the concept of SynchronousTestCase, which skips the reactor setup and runs even faster.

Failing to handle a Deferred is a common mistake. Trial introduces the principle of the "dirty reactor" in order to try and catch a certain class of unhandled Deferred.

For example, consider this code:

```
@defer.inlineCallbcks
def writeRecord(self, record):
    db = yield self.getDbConnection()
    db.append(self.table, record) # BAD: forgotten yield
```

and accompanying test:

```
@defer.inlineCallbacks
def test_writeRecord(self):
    record = ('foo', 'bar')
    yield self.filer.writeRecord(record)
```

On completion of this test's Deferred, Trial will examine the reactor's list of pending I/O and timers. If the append operation has not yet completed, the pending socket read or write operation will cause a DirtyReactor exception. Any Deferred that is garbage collected in an unhandled failed state will also be flagged as a test failure. Unfortunately, if an unhandled operation completes successfully before the test does, Trial cannot detect the error. This makes unclean reactor errors intermittent, causing some frustration for users and developers.

Python 3.5's coroutines add features in the language to better track such programming mistakes (RuntimeError: coroutine [...] was never awaited), but these will only work with coroutines.

Fakes

Unit testing requires good isolation of the units being tested. Most Buildbot components depend on other components, including the database, message queue, and data API. The convention in Buildbot is to include a reference to the `BuildMaster` instance as `self.master` on every service object. Other objects are then available via properties of the master such as `self.master.data.buildrequests`. For testing purposes, the `buildbot.test.fake.fakemaster.FakeMaster` class defines a fake master that can provide access to a similar array of fake components.

Many of these fake components are simple dummy classes instrumented for testing. The risk with such fakes is that they do not faithfully reproduce the behavior of the real component. For small components, this risk is generally small, and with due care we can be confident they are correct.

The database API, however, is a complex component with dozens of methods and complex interactions. One option is to always test against a database – Buildbot supports SQLite, which is built into Python, so this is not a great burden on developers. However, it is slow to tear down and set up even an in-memory database for each test. Instead, Buildbot sports a full implementation of the DB API using only simple Python data structures. To ensure its fidelity to the real database API, it must pass the same unit tests as the real implementation. The result is a fake that is guaranteed to give reliable results for unit tests of components that depend on it – a "verified fake." This fake is faster than the production code, while also providing highly reliable test results.

Summary

Buildbot is a large, mature code base that has grown up with Twisted since its early days. Its history demonstrates the journey – and some of the wrong turns – of asynchronous Python over the last decade. And its latest releases provide a trove of practical, real-life Twisted code.

CHAPTER 11

Twisted and HTTP/2

Introduction

HTTP/2 is the latest revision of the venerable protocol that underlies almost all of the world wide web: the HyperText Transfer Protocol, HTTP. Originally developed by Tim Berners-Lee at CERN (the European Organization for Nuclear Research) in 1989, HTTP has been the engine of the web ever since. The dominance of the protocol is so complete that almost everything that most people think of as "the Internet" is in fact part of the world wide web, and so uses HTTP.

At its core, HTTP is the protocol that allows your browser to communicate with a website. It provides a formal encoding for your browser to request "resources," such as a web page or image, and for servers to provide those resources in response. It also supports uploading data. While its most common use is for websites, HTTP is also commonly used for machine-to-machine communication through the use of "web APIs," which let programmers write applications that interact with data stored on other computers. Most major companies you have heard of run a web API!

Early on, the protocol went through multiple revisions, but the protocol solidified into its most common form in 1996 with the publication of RFC 1945 by the Internet Engineering Task Force (IETF). This represented a vision for the first long-term version of the protocol and established its well-known properties. These include its text-based, human-readable nature; its reliance on a dictionary of verbs with well-defined behaviors, such as GET, POST, and DELETE; and its tools for managing caching of content. HTTP/1.0 was followed swiftly by HTTP/1.1, an incremental release that provided a number of improvements to the expressiveness and efficiency of the protocol. HTTP/1.1 was first specified in RFC 2068 in 1997 and was updated in the famous RFC 2616 in 1999. This version of HTTP was then left almost entirely

© Mark Williams, Cory Benfield, Brian Warner, Moshe Zadka, Dustin Mitchell, Kevin Samuel, Pierre Tardy 2019
M. Williams et al., *Expert Twisted*, https://doi.org/10.1007/978-1-4842-3742-7_11

unchanged for 15 years.[1] All of the fantastic software and services that came of age in this time were built on top of this 1990s-era protocol.

Unfortunately, HTTP/1.1 has a number of shortcomings that rendered it increasingly ill-suited to the web of the 2010s. As a text-based protocol, it's extremely verbose, requiring the transmission of many more bytes than are strictly required. It also lacks any form of multiplexing,[2] meaning each HTTP request/response pair in flight at any time requires a dedicated TCP connection, which causes problems that are further explored below. It's also complex and slow to parse in comparison to most binary protocols.

The combination of these shortcomings cause HTTP/1.1 connections to have problems with latency, bandwidth, and operating system resource usage. These concerns led Google to begin experimenting with alternatives to HTTP/1.1 that maintained the same semantics but used a different wire format to transmit the data. After a few years of testing this experimental protocol, called SPDY,[3] it became clear that the protocol offered solutions to many of HTTP/1.1's problems, and the IETF HTTP Working Group resolved to use SPDY as the basis of a new revision to the HTTP protocol: version 2.

HTTP/2 contains many improvements over HTTP/1.1. It changes the protocol from being text-based to using a stream of length-prefixed binary frames. It adds a special form of compression suitable for use with HTTP headers, vastly reducing the overhead associated with a given HTTP request or response. It provides multiplexing and flow control to allow multiple HTTP request/response dialogs to take place over a single TCP connection. And, finally, it adds explicit support for negotiating extensions, giving HTTP/2 the option of being much more easily extended in the future than HTTP/1.1 is.

---

[1]HTTP/1.1 was updated in RFC 7230 and its related RFCs in 2014. This was not a substantial revision to the protocol: instead, the goal was to codify the way HTTP/1.1 had been deployed in the wild over the intervening 15 years.

[2]HTTP/1.1 does define a concept called "pipelining," which allows a user-agent to submit multiple requests without waiting for a response to the previous one. In principle, pipelining provides some form of multiplexing support. Unfortunately, pipelining is a bad solution to the issue and suffers from a number of problems. The most severe is that servers are required to respond to requests in the order they were delivered. If the server needs to generate a large response, this can cause long waits for a response to a subsequent request. Additionally, if a server receives a request that has a side effect (e.g., changing some data), it is required to stop processing all other requests on that pipelined connection until that request has been fully processed, unless it can prove those other requests are safe. In practice, these limitations are so onerous that none of the major browsers have enabled support for pipelining, and so it has never been widely deployed.

[3]Pronounced "speedy."

Since being standardized in 2015, HTTP/2 has become extremely successful. All major browsers support it as do most major web servers, and it is rapidly becoming the primary protocol used on the web, supplanting HTTP/1.1. This wide deployment means that developers will want to be able to take advantage of the protocol in their own applications, including those built on Twisted directly.

Twisted contains a HTTP server. In 2016 work began to extend this HTTP server that provides HTTP/1.1 support to provide HTTP/2 support alongside it, with the initial release of this functionality landing in Twisted 16.3 in July 2016. The rest of this chapter will discuss how this implementation was built, its key features, and cover several useful techniques for asynchronous programming that this implementation uses.

Design Goals

The HTTP/2 integration work in Twisted had a number of specific design goals from the very beginning.

Seamless Integration

The first and most-important design goal of the HTTP/2 project was to integrate it as seamlessly as possible with Twisted's existing web server, which is a part of `twisted.web`. The ideal outcome for the project would be for existing Twisted Web applications to enable HTTP/2 support with zero code changes. This would enable the widest possible access to HTTP/2 for existing and new web applications with an extremely low barrier to entry.

Happily, HTTP/2 was designed to have the same "semantics" as HTTP/1.1. This means that any valid HTTP/1.1 message had to have at least one exactly equivalent representation in HTTP/2. Even though the specific arrangement of bytes sent on the network are different, the abstract meaning of the HTTP session can be conveyed exactly in both HTTP/1.1 and HTTP/2. This meant that it would be possible, at least in principle, to allow users of `twisted.web` to transparently enable HTTP/2 without any code changes.

This kind of "seamless" integration is made possible in Twisted by the extensive use of interfaces to define an abstraction layer. An interface is a formal description of the functions you can call on a family of related objects. For example, you could describe a "vehicle" interface using zope.interface like so:

```
from zope.interface import interface

class IVehicle(Interface):
    def turn_on():
        pass

    def turn_off():
        pass
```

With this interface defined, you can write programs that can operate any kind of vehicle by programming against the interface, rather than against a specific implementation. Interfaces like this are a form of *polymorphism* (a term used in object-oriented programming) that is an alternative to class-based inheritance. This section will not explore the idea of interfaces for polymorphism any further, except to say that defining interfaces for your objects allows you to write code that can use alternative implementations of the same interface very gracefully.

In the case of HTTP, in principle we could define a set of interfaces for working with HTTP at the semantic level (without reference to the specific wire format) and have users write code against those interfaces. For example, you could have a HTTPServer interface that exposes an interface that operates in terms of general HTTPRequest and HTTPRespose objects, and that shields the user code from the specific properties of the underlying connection.

Unfortunately defining interfaces in this way is not always simple to do, and in practice a number of difficulties were encountered that needed to be resolved to make this design goal achievable. These will be covered more later in this chapter. Once these difficulties were resolved, however, we were able to construct a final implementation that was *almost* completely seamlessly meshed with the existing HTTP/1.1 implementation.

The end result was that as of Twisted 16.3 any application using twisted.web could get automatic HTTP/2 support by installing the optional http2 extra when installing or upgrading Twisted. Twisted would then feature detect all of the relevant features from the operating system and, assuming that everything was in order, HTTP/2 would automatically be used where possible.

Most-Optimized Behavior by Default

HTTP/2 is a complex protocol with a number of tunable parameters that can affect the efficiency of the protocol. Frame sizes, priority management, compression strategies, concurrent stream limits, even buffer sizes all play a part in tuning the efficiency of the protocol.

Because HTTP/2 support in Twisted was planned to be transparent to the user, it is highly likely that the majority of users will not notice it is there. As a result, it is vitally important that the protocol behave as efficiently as it can by default. This is because if users are not aware that a feature is present, they cannot be expected to reasonably configure that feature for their use case.

This is a general lesson with feature development that follows on from the previous design goal: features that are intended to be completely seamless and transparent must also have sensible defaults that apply to the widest range of use cases. If they do not, users will experience suboptimal behavior from their software without knowing, and if they are eventually made aware of this behavior, they'll have to engage in complex profiling and debugging in order to trace it.

For this reason, Twisted's HTTP/2 support needs to tread a fine line. The default configuration needs to perform well in almost all circumstances without substantial overhead, with a minimal goal of performing at least as well as the HTTP/1.1 implementation. Otherwise this feature will end up punishing users that enable it, making it completely worthless.

Separating Concerns and Reusing Code

The final, and most important, design goal was to avoid reinventing too many wheels. A substantial anti-pattern when designing networked applications is to build custom components, rather than to glue in preexisting implementations of solved problems. This is particularly tempting when working with frameworks like Twisted, which tend to require care when integrating preexisting solutions to avoid blocking the event loop. The reason for this is that the specific mechanisms to use to avoid blocking the event loop usually differ from framework to framework, and so it is profoundly tempting to write custom code for each framework: the cost of doing so is that it is impossible to reuse large chunks of code across multiple frameworks.

Fortunately, the Python ecosystem already contained a "sans-io" HTTP/2 implementation. This is a protocol stack that can be used to parse and serialize the HTTP/2 protocol but that does not understand anything about I/O. Implementations like this are designed to be glued into frameworks like Twisted, and they allow a substantial amount of code reuse.

This is one of the most-important design patterns in network programming, and so bears repeating: wherever possible, you should strive to separate your protocol parser from your specific I/O implementation. Your protocol parser should operate only on in-memory buffers of bytes, whether consuming or producing them, and should have no mechanism to either obtain bytes from the network or provide them to the network. This design pattern allows you to much more easily transport your protocol parser from one I/O pattern to another, as well as making it vastly easier to test and extend your protocol parser.

Having this design goal changes the nature of the work. The Twisted HTTP/2 implementation handles the portions of the HTTP/2 protocol that require writing bytes to and from the network, setting and handling timers, and translating the HTTP/2 events into the twisted.web interface. The sans-io HTTP/2 implementation is responsible for parsing the byte stream into HTTP/2 events, and turning the function calls from twisted.web into bytes to emit.

This code reuse also allows more time to be spent optimizing the portions of the implementation where Twisted can add the most value. Twisted's implementation focuses heavily on reducing the latency of data reaching the network, propagating backpressure efficiently, and reducing unnecessary system calls or I/O overhead. This is much easier to do when the core protocol logic is factored out into a separate project.

In general, when working on "standard" problems, this is the best approach to use. It shrinks the size of the code base, avoids spending too much engineering time solving problems that have already been solved, and allows you to focus on improving the efficiency and scalability of your solution.

Implementation Concerns

Once the design goals were decided, work could begin on the code. While for many developers this is the fun part, it's also often where a number of unforeseen surprises can occur. Additionally, it's common to find that there are aspects of a design that are simple enough when discussed conceptually, but that become substantially more tricky when they are translated into code. This section covers a number of specific concerns that relate to the concrete implementation.

What Is a Connection Anyway? The Value of Standard Interfaces

In twisted.web, there are a number of objects that cooperate to implement HTTP support. The simplest version of this relates the underlying TCP Transport to the HTTPChannel and Request objects. This relationship is shown in Figure 11-1.

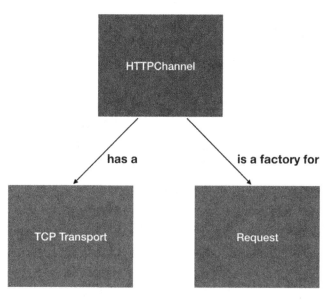

Figure 11-1. *The three most-important objects to provide HTTP support in Twisted*

When implementing HTTP/2 support, we discovered that the standard Twisted HTTP request handler (twisted.web.http.Request) expects to be passed a reference to the HTTP connection handling object in the form of twisted.web.http.HTTPChannel (or something with a similar interface: frustratingly, the expected interface was never codified). In the constructor for Request it reached into the channel it was just passed and pulled out the transport attribute to save on itself. All subsequent calls to Request. write to write out the response body would be proxied through to transport.write. transport.write would invoke the write function on whatever the transport object was. This object will be something that implements twisted.internet.interfaces. ITransport: another of those zope.interface interfaces used extensively within Twisted. In this case, ITransport is a particularly common interface that is used to represent any kind of writable data transport. This is commonly a low-level stream protocol such as TCP, but can in practice be anything that provides a stream writing interface. In the old HTTP/1 model, this would almost always be the underlying TCP transport.

This layering violation ends up working just fine for HTTP/1.1 because once the response headers are sent, the response body can be treated as just an arbitrary byte stream. However, this very much does not work for HTTP/2: multiplexing, priority, and flow control all make it extremely important to prevent applications making arbitrary writes to the TCP connection.

As part of the HTTP/2 work, then, we needed to clean this up. However, we couldn't simply remove these properties: they're part of the public API of the Request and need to be preserved.[4]

The most straightforward change was to make the HTTP/1.1 twisted.web.http. HTTPChannel object an implementer of ITransport that proxied most of its methods through to its underlying transport. This ensures that the HTTPChannel does a better job of encapsulating its own resources by ensuring that users do not need to reach inside it to write the response body, and also resolves some semantic issues with the previous design. Essentially, a HTTPChannel should *be* a transport for responses, rather than an object that *has* a transport down in which responses can be sent. Of course, due to the backward compatibility policy, HTTPChannel could not have its transport property removed, so it does not truly encapsulate the transport, but discouraging its use is an important first step.

Once this was done, the internal implementation of Request could be changed to use the HTTPChannel for every call that originally went to the transport. Essentially every instance of self.transport in the body of a Request method was changed to self. channel. This ensured that Twisted's default implementation of HTTP request handling now appropriately respected the intended abstraction between TCP connection and HTTP connection.

Unfortunately, we couldn't create a clean break here due to Twisted's compatibility policy. A large number of HTTP/1.1 applications created with Twisted Web already existed, and some number of them inevitably directly wrote to the transport (or otherwise handled the transport, for example, to reach in and retrieve TLS certificates). For this reason, the transport property could not be removed from the HTTPChannel and would also need to be present on whatever object was provided as the HTTP/2 equivalent.

---

[4]The virtues of backward compatibility are better explained in https://twistedmatrix.com/ documents/current/core/development/policy/compatibility-policy.html.

As discussed in the previous section, the multiplexing in HTTP/2 requires multiple cooperating objects to provide the needed abstractions. This also means that there are two separate objects that *together* provide the same interface as HTTPChannel. The Request only needs a subset of the HTTPChannel interface. That portion of the interface was placed on the H2Stream for compatibility purposes.

Due to the need for Request to get the transport property from its channel, H2Stream needs a transport property as well. However, there is no need for the HTTP/2 code to continue to make the same abstraction violation available as the HTTP/1.1 code has: given that there are no legacy API requirements, it just needs to be possible to access the property. For this reason, all H2Stream objects have a transport property that is always set to None.

This is a good example of a situation that could have been made much easier by the existence of standard interfaces between the Request and HTTPChannel objects. When originally created, it was not foreseen that it may be necessary to have each of these objects support multiple possible implementations of their partner object, so the interfaces used between these two objects were not formally defined. This lack of formal definition means that the *effective* interface of these objects is their entire API surface: all methods and all properties.

This kind of broad and implicit interface leads to enormous difficulty when attempting to create extra abstraction layers. If the person re-implementing an object needs to completely emulate its entire public API, it gets substantially harder to offer alternative implementations and to build appropriate abstractions.

However, on the positive side, the majority of the effective interface that Request needed from HTTPChannel *was* defined, in the form of ITransport. Because Request spent the majority of its time writing to the transport of HTTPChannel, and because that transport could only reasonably be assumed to be an implementer of ITransport, it was very easy to identify what methods needed to be added to HTTPChannel and what their behaviors should be. Once this was done, it was a simple matter to identify what the effective API H2Stream needed to present was.

Due to a lack of focus on extensibility during the early years of Twisted Web, integrating HTTP/2 was harder than it needed to be. However, it could have been a lot worse: thanks to the wide usage of interfaces throughout all of Twisted's code, fixing these abstraction violations was a much more tractable problem than it could otherwise have been.

This should be an important lesson to future engineers: when the system is designed, it will likely be designed in terms of high-level interfaces between components. These interfaces should be codified in the code, because they provide extremely helpful guidance about what each component expects of the others and allows much more tractable extension and enhancement of components in future.

Multiplexing and Priority

One of the most complex parts of HTTP/2 is its multiplexing support. This core feature of HTTP/2 was introduced to allow multiple HTTP request/response pairs to use the same TCP connection by sending and receiving them simultaneously on the same TCP connection. This approach has a number of advantages over HTTP/1.1's use of multiple concurrent TCP connections:

1. It uses fewer system resources. Each TCP connection takes up a file descriptor in the operating system of both the client and the server, which increases the amount of work both operating systems must do to keep track of network connections. It also increases the amount of memory used in both the kernel, which must allocate data structures to keep track of the connections, and in Twisted applications, which allocate a number of data structures to manage each transport.

2. It leads to better throughput and higher data transfer rates. The most widely-deployed TCP congestion control algorithms were designed with the expectation that there would be no more than one TCP connection between any two hosts at any one time.[5] The result of having many connections between the two hosts, particularly if they're all transmitting bulk data (a usage pattern common on the web), is that the throughput of the multiple concurrent connections fails to reach the maximum possible throughput on the link.

---

[5]More specifically, the algorithms assume that packet loss events for each TCP connection on the system are independent: that a packet loss event on one connection does not have anything to do with the behavior of the others. For multiple TCP connections between the same two hosts doing bulk data transfer this assumption does not hold: packet loss events most often occur because the link is saturated, and as a result packet loss will likely occur on most or all of the TCP connections all at once. This causes all the TCP connections to halve their data throughput all at once, leaving the link underutilized for long periods of time.

3. It keeps connections "hotter." If TCP connections become idle for a long period of time they are prone to being closed (either by middleboxes or either peer) or to returning to a "slow-start" state where previous knowledge of the congestion on the link is discarded. In either case, when that connection comes to be reused it will have a long period of low throughput as the TCP slow-start phase progresses and, if the connection was closed, it will also have the added latency of the TCP and TLS handshakes. "Hot" connections, which are connections that are in constant or almost-constant use, avoid both of these problems, which reduces latency and increases throughput.

Multiplexing is achieved in HTTP/2 by dividing a single HTTP/2 connection into a number of bidirectional "streams." Each stream carries a single HTTP request and its associated response. This is achieved very simply, by giving each stream a unique identifier and ensuring that each frame of data that belongs to that stream carries that stream identifier. This allows the single ordered stream of data provided by a TCP connection to be divided up into multiple logical streams of data, as shown in Figure 11-2.

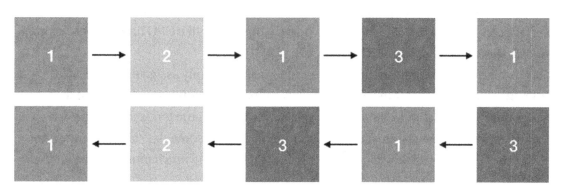

Figure 11-2. *Streams are interspersed blocks of data. They can be interleaved in any order.*

However, simply tagging all the data with its appropriate stream identifier is not enough. To explain why, consider what might happen with a hypothetical website that acts as a cloud picture gallery. This website has two purposes: it displays images, and it accepts user input to make changes to them. Each user input triggers an API request/response: additionally, the user scrolling or editing will cause the server to stream down another image file.

The API requests/responses will typically be very small: for example, they may be JSON documents that consist of only a few hundred bytes. The images are proportionally much larger: maybe many megabytes in size. Additionally, the images require no computation to generate: they're stored on disk, and so their data is constantly available for the web server to serve.

A possible problem, then, is that the server may completely fill the HTTP/2 connection with data for the image streams, blocking the data for the API responses. The API responses form a proportionally small fraction of the data that needs to be sent, but that data is much higher *priority* than the data for the images. Users are probably willing to wait for thumbnails to load, but they are much less likely to be willing to wait for all the images to download until they see the effects of their UI interactions.

This problem exists for most multiplexed data transfer media: How do we ensure that the highest priority data arrives as soon as possible while ensuring the connection is always maximally utilized? There are many possible solutions to this problem, but HTTP/2 uses a scheme that involves clients setting *stream priorities*.

Stream priorities allow clients to inform the server about the relative importance of the data on different streams. The intent of this data is to allow servers to decide how to apportion its scarce resources to the different requests the client is making. In general, the primary resource that servers have to dole out is bandwidth, but more complex servers can also use this information to portion out things like CPU time, file descriptors, or disk space: really any limited resource.

The simplest possible stream priority scheme is to simply assign each stream a numerical priority. A stream with a higher number is more important than one with a lower number, and should be served first. This kind of scheme tends to struggle due to its lack of expressiveness: while it allows you to indicate that some data is more important than other data, it critically fails to allow you to express *how much* more important that data is.

The simplest possible scheme that works pretty well is to give every stream a numerical weight. This weight reflects the stream's relative importance: if stream X has twice the *weight* of stream Y, then it is roughly twice as important to serve. The advantage of this approach is that it can be used to hand resources out proportionally: in the prior example, stream X should be allocated twice the resources of stream Y. This allows clients to signal that they believe that it is more important to get a timely response to stream X than to stream Y, and exactly how important they believe it is.

This simple approach was used by HTTP/2's predecessor protocol, SPDY. However, when it came time to specify HTTP/2, the HTTP Working Group believed that this approach was insufficiently expressive and that it left a few use cases out. In particular, it did not allow the client to easily express the constraint "only use your resources on stream A if you cannot use them on stream B for some reason." Put another way, this allows the client to say "Stream A is worthless without the result of stream B, so don't spend any time on A unless stream B is blocked for some reason."

For this reason, HTTP/2 has a much more complex priority system. This system allows the client to specify a *tree* of priorities, where each node in the tree *depends upon* its parent node above it. These priorities do not affect "control" data, such as HTTP headers: they are only used to indicate the priority of the requested resource.

For Twisted's web server, it is extremely difficult for us to apportion most of the non-bandwidth resources discussed above, as we do not have sufficient insight into the user's application to know exactly what questions we should ask. As a result, we can only divide up the bandwidth. To do this as performantly as possible in Twisted, we make a simple approximation to dividing up the bandwidth: we divide up the frames instead. For example, if we have streams A and B with weights 32 and 64 respectively, a perfect implementation of the priority algorithm would allocate stream A 1/3 of the bandwidth and stream B the other 2/3. Accurately doing this would require splitting up data that arrives in each call the user makes to `transport.write`, which would entail repeatedly copying that data into and out of buffers. This kind of repeated slicing and copying of memory is extremely slow without a high-performance buffer to use for this purpose (something not available in Twisted at the time of development and not in scope for this work), which means we want to avoid it as much as possible.

To avoid doing this slicing we can keep the data as-written and instead give each stream a number of *frames* equal to its relative weight. Each time there is room in the send buffer for more data to be sent, the Twisted implementation will check which of the streams that have data to send should send next, based on the stream weighting. We then send a single data chunk up to the maximum frame size[6] for that stream, and then rinse and repeat. This kind of frame-based multiplexing is a common pattern in network protocol design, and can be used for arbitrary framed protocols quite easily.

---

[6]The eagle-eyed reader will note that Twisted sets no upper limit on the size of the data passed to `write()`, which means that this data chunk may be larger than the HTTP/2 maximum frame size. If this happens, we will have to do a memory copy anyway; it's unavoidable.

The building and maintaining of this priority tree are handled by the third-party `priority` library. This library builds and maintains the priority state as sent by the client, and provides an iterable that incrementally instructs the Twisted implementation which stream should be served next. It also includes information from the Twisted application about whether each stream has any data available to send. Streams that have no data to send are considered *blocked*, and the fractions of the TCP connection that would normally be assigned to those streams are instead split among the streams that are child dependencies.

The need to run all data through a loop around the priority tree adds a wrinkle to the data sending pipeline that doesn't exist in the HTTP/1.1 implementation. For HTTP/1.1, all writes of the response data can be passed directly through to the underlying TCP connection object, which can be responsible for handling buffering and sending data. For HTTP/2, we don't want to do that because we need to interleave the writes according to the relative stream priorities.

Even more importantly than that, the implementation needs to be responsive to changes in the stream priorities sent by the client: if the client increases the priority of a stream, we want that to be reflected in the data as soon as possible. If the implementation eagerly writes all stream data to the TCP connection object it can lead to a large buffer of data waiting to be sent that is allocated according to the *old* stream priorities, rather than the new ones. For situations where the TCP throughput on the connection is much lower than the rate data is generated in the Twisted application, this can lead to multiple-second delays before the priority change is reflected in the actual data: clearly unacceptable.

For this reason the Twisted HTTP/2 implementation needs to do its own internal buffering of data and to send data asynchronously to the calls to `transport.write`. This is done by repeatedly using `IReactor.callLater` to schedule a function that will send the highest priority available chunk of data.

The use of `callLater` allows us to avoid overfilling the send buffer by paying attention to backpressure from the TCP connection (see the next section for more details), as well as to ensure that we send all available data without blocking any calls to `write`.

The core of the data sending function looks like this (with error handling and some edge cases removed for clarity):

```
class H2Connection:
    def _sendPrioritisedData(self, *args):
        stream = None
```

```
while stream is None:
    try:
        stream = next(self.priority)
    except priority.DeadlockError:
        # All streams are currently blocked or not progressing. Wait
        # until a new one becomes available.
        self._sendingDeferred = Deferred()
        self._sendingDeferred.addCallback(self._sendPrioritisedData)
        return

# Wait behind the transport. This is managed elsewhere in this class,
# as part of the implementation of IPushProducer.
if self._consumerBlocked is not None:
    self._consumerBlocked.addCallback(self._sendPrioritisedData)
    return

remainingWindow = self.conn.local_flow_control_window(stream)
frameData = self._outboundStreamQueues[stream].popleft()
maxFrameSize = min(self.conn.max_outbound_frame_size, remainingWindow)

if frameData is _END_STREAM_SENTINEL:
    # There's no error handling here even though this can throw
    # ProtocolError because we really shouldn't encounter this problem.
    # If we do, that's a nasty bug.
    self.conn.end_stream(stream)
    self.transport.write(self.conn.data_to_send())

    # Clean up the stream
    self._requestDone(stream)
else:
    # Respect the max frame size.
    if len(frameData) > maxFrameSize:
        excessData = frameData[maxFrameSize:]
        frameData = frameData[:maxFrameSize]
        self._outboundStreamQueues[stream].appendleft(excessData)

    # If for whatever reason the max frame length is zero and so we
    # have no frame data to send, don't send any.
```

```
            if frameData:
                self.conn.send_data(stream, frameData)
                self.transport.write(self.conn.data_to_send())

            # If there's no data left, this stream is now blocked.
            if not self._outboundStreamQueues[stream]:
                self.priority.block(stream)

            # Also, if the stream's flow control window is exhausted, tell it
            # to stop.
            if self.remainingOutboundWindow(stream) <= 0:
                self.streams[stream].flowControlBlocked()

        self._reactor.callLater(0, self._sendPrioritisedData)
```

This function can be broken into four logical parts. The first checks whether there are any streams that are considered "able to progress" (that is, that have data available to send and space in their flow control window[7] to send it). If there aren't then we don't have any data to send, so we set up a Deferred that will be called back when a stream becomes unblocked for any reason.

The second part checks whether we have space in the send buffer. This is another bit of signaling done by a Deferred: if there is a Deferred in self._consumerBlocked, then Twisted has signaled to us that the send buffer is full and that we should avoid writing. Again, we return without doing any work and ensure that when the Deferred fires, this function will be called. In both of these cases the function will not be recalled until the situation that blocked its progress has been resolved.

The third and fourth sections have to do with the sending of actual data. In this case, we have a stream that has data available to send and room in the send buffer to send it. We then pop a chunk of data (previously written in a call to write) off a deque. If that object is the _END_STREAM_SENTINEL, then the body is complete, and we need to complete sending the stream. Otherwise, we create a data frame that can send the data, and optionally do some other state management.

As a final step, if we sent any data, we schedule this method to be recalled using callLater, as noted earlier.

This approach, while dramatically more complex than the logic required to send data for HTTP/1.1, is the core of the HTTP/2 multiplexing approach. This added

---

[7]For more on flow control windows, see the next section on backpressure.

computational complexity makes HTTP/2 slower in Python code than HTTP/1.1, but vastly improves the network performance of the protocol.

The above approach is a model for how to handle complex multiplexed data sending or any kind of buffered sending logic: a single function that can be repeatedly called each step of the way and that can be rescheduled easily if for any reason it is unable to do any work (e.g., because the transport cannot accept more data, or because there is no data to send).

Backpressure

A frequent mistake made by novice programmers when working with asynchronous systems like Twisted is to not consider how they will handle overload conditions. Asynchronous networking frameworks like Twisted vastly increase the amount of network traffic an application can potentially handle, but the application code written by developers using the framework may not be able to keep up with the amount of data that Twisted and the operating system can process.

All networked applications are at risk of encountering a situation where work is entering the system faster than it can be processed. A simple example of this is a web application that can process a single request in 10 ms running on a single CPU core. If this application is exposed to a constant load of less than 100 requests per second, then everything is fine.

What happens when this exact same system is exposed to a level of load that exceeds 100 requests per second? There are many possible answers to this question, but the standard behavior of most Twisted applications in this system is that they will buffer the data.[8]

This approach is often reasonable for "spiky" load: if the load on the system only briefly exceeded 100 requests per second and then dropped back below that level, then the requests will briefly see higher latencies (the time taken to respond to the request) due to them sitting in the buffer for a while before they get processed, but the Twisted application will serve the data out of the buffer faster than the new data arrives and so the buffer will slowly become empty.

However, if the load exceeds 100 requests per second for a sustained period of time or *substantially* exceeds that level (e.g., by hundreds or thousands of times), then the buffering represents a problem. The latency seen by each request will climb, potentially

---

[8]Well, mostly. It depends on what the 10 ms is spent doing. If most of this 10 ms is spent waiting for other things to happen (e.g., database queries), then Twisted will buffer. If that 10 ms is spent entirely doing computation on the CPU, then the behavior will be different. For now, we assume that the former situation is what occurs.

to a level that makes it indistinguishable from failure (most users will not wait more than a second or two for a response to a request, so a 20-second request latency is equivalent to request failure for these users). Worse is the fact that if the overload persists the buffer will continue to grow, and if left unchecked will eventually consume all of the memory in the system. The best possible outcome of this is that the operating system will kill the process: in the worst case, the process will begin to swap, which will vastly slow down its computation and reduce the processing speed of the application, making it even harder for the application to handle the overload.

As a result, scalable Twisted applications need to be prepared for overload. The most common way to handle this is to create systems that propagate *backpressure*. Backpressure is a signal from one system to another that says "you are submitting work faster than I can complete it, please slow down." Correctly propagating backpressure through an asynchronous application allows that application to communicate how much work it can process through to the portions of the system that ingest work.

A good example of propagating backpressure is, ironically, blocking I/O. When sending data over TCP with blocking I/O, if the remote peer is not reading data fast enough, a call to send will eventually block until the remote peer consumes enough data to allow your OS to continue sending. This forcibly slows down the sending application such that it sends data no faster than the remote application can read it from the socket.

Backpressure in Twisted

Currently, in Twisted, backpressure is propagated by having transports and protocols implement two interfaces: IPushProducer and IConsumer. In general the Transport implements IPushProducer and the Protocol implements IConsumer, though in more complex systems (such as the HTTP/2 implementation in Twisted) the same object may implement both IConsumer (for inbound data) and IPushProducer (for outbound data).

These two interfaces are very simple:

```
class IPushProducer(IProducer):
    """

    A push producer, also known as a streaming producer is expected to
    produce (write to this consumer) data on a continuous basis, unless it
    has been paused. A paused push producer will resume producing after its
    resumeProducing() method is called. For a push producer which is not
    pauseable, these functions may be noops.
    """
```

```
    def pauseProducing():
        """

        Pause producing data.

        Tells a producer that it has produced too much data to process for
        the time being, and to stop until resumeProducing() is called.
        """

    def resumeProducing():
        """

        Resume producing data.

        This tells a producer to re-add itself to the main loop and produce
        more data for its consumer.
        """

class IProducer(Interface):
    """

    A producer produces data for a consumer.

    Typically producing is done by calling the write method of a class
    implementing L{IConsumer}.
    """

    def stopProducing():
        """

        Stop producing data.

        This tells a producer that its consumer has died, so it must stop
        producing data for good.
        """

class IConsumer(Interface):
    """

    A consumer consumes data from a producer.
    """

    def registerProducer(producer, streaming):
        """

        Register to receive data from a producer.
```

This sets self to be a consumer for a producer. When this object runs out of data (as when a send(2) call on a socket succeeds in moving the last data from a userspace buffer into a kernelspace buffer), it will ask the producer to resumeProducing().

For L{IPushProducer} providers, C{pauseProducing} will be called whenever the write buffer fills up and C{resumeProducing} will only be called when it empties.

@type producer: L{IProducer} provider

@type streaming: C{bool}
@param streaming: C{True} if C{producer} provides L{IPushProducer}, C{False} if C{producer} provides L{IPullProducer}.
@raise RuntimeError: If a producer is already registered.

@return: L{None}
"""

```
def unregisterProducer():
    """
    Stop consuming data from a producer, without disconnecting.
    """

def write(data):
    """
    The producer will write data by calling this method.
```

The implementation must be non-blocking and perform whatever buffering is necessary. If the producer has provided enough data for now and it is a L{IPushProducer}, the consumer may call its C{pauseProducing} method.
"""

The most-important parts of these interfaces are IPushProducer.pauseProducing, IPushProducer.resumeProducing, and IConsumer.write. The rest are administrative, relating to telling the consumer about the producer and telling the producer that the consumer can no longer accept data.

When an IConsumer is experiencing too much load, such that they would like data to stop coming in to them, they can call pauseProducing on their registered producer. When they're ready to accept more work, they call resumeProducing. At this point, the consumer's registered producer will start calling write again until the IConsumer calls pauseProducing again.

Backpressure in HTTP/2

HTTP/2 has two signaling methods for backpressure, both using flow-control algorithms. The first one is shared with HTTP/1.1, becuase it's actually built into TCP, which both HTTP/1.1 and HTTP/2 use. TCP maintains a receiver window that communicates a receiver's capacity back to the sender. If one end of the TCP connection stops reading from the socket, the other end will eventually find that it is not allowed to send further data.

Additionally, HTTP/2 maintains four further flow-control windows of its own: two for the connection as a whole (one for data sent from the client to the server, and one for data from the server to the client) and two for each stream (again, one for each direction). These flow-control windows limit how much data each peer is allowed to send: the stream windows manage how much data may be sent on a given stream, while the connection window controls how much may be sent on the connection as a whole.

Each of these windows can also be used to propagate backpressure: letting any of these window sizes go to zero will force the remote peer to stop sending some or all of its data. This means that we want to be able to propagate these backpressure signals sent from the client to the Twisted server. We also want to be able to propagate backpressure signals from the Twisted application to the client: if the web application is processing data more slowly than the client can send it, we should slow down data delivery appropriately.[9]

The strategy for this is twofold: add support for the Twisted servers to both emit and consume backpressure, and manage our HTTP/2 flow-control windows appropriately. Let's talk about emitting and consuming backpressure first.

---

[9]Note that this is distinct from the case where a peer no longer wants the data *at all*. If a peer simply no longer wants the HTTP/2 stream to continue any longer, it can outright cancel that stream by means of a specific HTTP/2 frame, called RST_STREAM. This is not directly related to backpressure, but is worth noting.

One key wrinkle of the IConsumer/IPushProducer interface is that these two interfaces are one-to-one. This means that each consumer can have only one producer, and each producer can be producing for only one consumer at once. This is problematic for HTTP/2, when we have multiple streams of data, each of which can propagate backpressure individually.

The easiest way to work around this is to define a HTTP/2 connection in terms of two objects, not one. The first object owns the underlying TCP transport, and registers itself as both a producer to and consumer of that transport: in the code, this class is twisted. web._http2.H2Connection.

When new streams are initiated by the client, this object creates a new object to handle the stream data and to be both a producer to and consumer of the application code: in the code, this class is twisted.web._http2.H2Stream. Between these two objects we use a custom interface that exists only for HTTP/2 to allow the connection to tell the stream when it should pause its producer because that stream can no longer send (H2Stream.flowControlBlocked) and when the window size has been changed (H2Stream.windowUpdated). The H2Stream converts these calls into calls to pauseProducing & resumeProducing on its application. Similarly, the H2Stream allows the application to call pauseProducing to prevent the stream from delivering more data. When called, this will cause the H2Stream to begin to buffer data rather than deliver it to the application.

This rather confusing relationship is diagrammed in Figure 11-3.

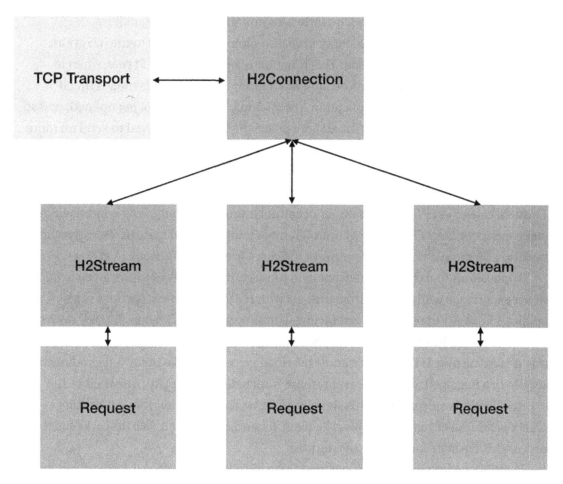

Figure 11-3. *The producer/consumer relationships between the various objects in a HTTP/2 connection. Each line represents a single producer/consumer relationship. Note that these relationships are not always implemented with the* `IProducer/IConsumer` *interfaces, as discussed in this section.*

A stream may become "blocked" if any of the flow-control windows associated with it is zero. That is, if the TCP stream blocks (the transport calls `pauseProducing` on the `H2Connection`), all of the `H2Stream` objects owned by that connection will call `pauseProducing` on their applications. Additionally, if the connection flow-control window goes to 0, all of the `H2Stream` objects will call `pauseProducing` on their applications. Finally, if a stream-specific window goes to 0, the `H2Stream` object associated with that stream will call `pauseProducing` on its application, but the others will not.

This buffer is not unbounded, however. It's bounded by the stream flow-control window. You see, the H2Connection also offers another API to the H2Stream: H2Connection.openStreamWindow. This function is called by the H2Stream when it has *delivered data to the application*, and not a moment before. This means that if production is paused by the application, the stream window will not get opened, and so will eventually be exhausted by the remote peer, which will be allowed to send no more data on that stream until the application starts processing the backlog.

It is important to note that even if the application is unable to process more data, the H2Connection does not prevent the client from sending more data on the TCP connection. This is because HTTP/2 uses a number of control frames to manage flow-control windows and connection state. These extra control frames cannot be used to cause excessive data buffering, so there is no reason to prevent the client from sending them.

Applications that appropriately opt in to propagating backpressure are given a much richer experience with HTTP/2 than they get with HTTP/1.1. Slower portions of the application, or portions that are interacting with slower clients, can happily slow down without limiting the overall concurrency of the system. This also ensures that applications that serve data over HTTP/2 can handle overload gracefully and carefully, degrading their service in a managed way that prevents them from being completely overwhelmed.

Applications can opt in to this signaling by ensuring that their request handler registers an IPushProducer for each Request it handles. twisted.web.http.Request provides IConsumer for exactly this purpose.

It should be noted that the IConsumer/IPushProducer interface is limited and does not necessarily offer all of the richness that a backpressure-propagating API should do. To see an example of a better interface that may eventually supplant IConsumer/IPushProducer, take a look at tubes.[10]

Current Status and Future Expansion

The Twisted HTTP/2 implementation was shipped in Twisted 16.3, which was released in July of 2016. The implementation is gated behind a number of optional dependencies that must be installed to enable it, as well as some requirements on the OpenSSL version that Twisted is using. These gates effectively place the HTTP/2 support in an ongoing "beta" state.

---

[10]https://twisted.github.io/tubes/

Since the initial release, a number of enterprising users have opted in to the support and have helped track down bugs and report issues. The result is that Twisted's HTTP/2 stack is now running on an enormous number of machines with few to no problems. This is an enormous success, and a very positive sign for the ongoing health of the project.

There are a few natural directions for expansion of this work. The first and largest is to tackle writing a HTTP/2 client that transparently shims into the current HTTP/1.1 client. This is a substantial chunk of work that has not yet been seriously attempted, though some of the precursor work has been laid down.

The other major focus for work is to start exposing APIs for taking advantage of HTTP/2's features. In particular, HTTP/2 enables server push, which allows servers to optimistically begin sending resources that a client may need to render a page. An interesting future enhancement would be to allow Twisted applications to programmatically emit pushed resources by exposing an appropriate API. This could be extended with Link header parsing to support pushes from traditional WSGI applications.

Finally, an API that allowed more configuration of the HTTP/2 stack would be a useful extension. Currently there is no support for allowing Twisted applications to modify the HTTP/2 configuration, either globally or on a per-connection basis. Adding this support is a necessary evolution toward providing a fully feature-complete HTTP/2 implementation.

Summary

In this chapter, we introduced the HTTP/2 protocol defined in RFC 7540. We discussed the extension of `twisted.web` to support this protocol, focusing on the goals of the design for that integration, as well as some of the specific concerns that arose during the implementation. We also covered the importance of backpressure in concurrent programming, as well as the importance of interface design to the extensibility of interfaces. Finally, we summarized the current state and future direction of Twisted's HTTP/2 support.

CHAPTER 12

Twisted and Django Channels

Introduction

The following sections will dive into the structure of Django Channels and the technologies used in building it, and will try to tease out useful design details that can be used whenever you're building complex multi-tier distributed applications intended to scale horizontally.

Python was one of the earliest programming languages to define a standard interface between web applications and web servers that wasn't based on CGI, the Common Gateway Interface. CGI, while effective, was not particularly fast or high performance, so a need was identified to develop a richer interface between servers and applications, ideally one that took advantage of language primitives and features.

In 2003 the Python core development team adopted PEP 333, which defined the Web Server Gateway Interface (WSGI). WSGI is an API specification that allows web servers that are capable of creating Python objects and calling Python functions (either from Python or via the C API) to invoke web applications in a standardized way. The goal of WSGI was to decouple web application frameworks from web servers, such that any web server can run any Python web application.

From this perspective, WSGI was enormously successful. Most readers of this book will not remember a world before WSGI, and so the above description will seem perplexing: How could there be a world where web frameworks and web servers were not decoupled? In the post-WSGI world the Python community has seen a proliferation of great web application frameworks (such as Django and Flask) and great web servers (such as uWSGI, gunicorn, and Twisted) build on top of WSGI's flexibility.

365

© Mark Williams, Cory Benfield, Brian Warner, Moshe Zadka, Dustin Mitchell, Kevin Samuel, Pierre Tardy 2019
M. Williams et al., *Expert Twisted*, https://doi.org/10.1007/978-1-4842-3742-7_12

However, it is not a perfect protocol. In particular, a WSGI server invokes a WSGI application by calling a synchronous Python function and blocking execution until it returns. This fundamentally synchronous invocation of a Python application in WSGI means that WSGI applications cannot easily be written in an asynchronous manner. At the surface level, this causes programmers some inconvenience: they can't use Twisted or the `async` and `await` keywords. At a more foundational level, however, it makes Python web applications somewhat inefficient: each concurrent web request they handle requires a brand new operating system thread to process. The inefficiency of this approach is well-understood: after all, it's part of why Twisted exists!

Django Channels represent an attempt to allow Django applications to be written in a more concurrent manner, while retaining backward compatibility with WSGI applications. This is quite a substantial chunk of work, and so "Django Channels" actually cover a wide range of related technical projects. These include a new interface for server-to-application communication, the Asynchronous Server Gateway Interface (ASGI); a reference web server that implements the server portion of this interface (Daphne); and a Django application that enables Django to handle ASGI requests.

The net effect of Django Channels is to refocus Django away from requests and responses and toward "events." This allows Channels-based applications to handle not just HTTP requests and responses, but things like WebSockets or even plain TCP/UDP data. This is achieved by dividing the complete web stack into three parts:

1. An ASGI server. This server is responsible for accepting the incoming connections and translating from the write protocol (e.g., HTTP) to ASGI messages, placing those messages into queues ("channels"), and receiving messages from those channels and translating them back into wire protocol data. In the reference implementation, this is Daphne, a Twisted-based web server.

2. A "channel back end," which is basically a data store that can be used as a message broker. For trivial applications this can just be some shared memory, but in larger applications this will usually be a Redis deployment.

3. One or more "workers." These workers listen on some or all of the channels and run relevant code when there are messages to process. The workers may be sequential and threaded but also may not be. This is where the traditional Django application code will run.

Of these three parts, both 1 and 3 can integrate with Twisted. However, most Django users will stick with regular synchronous Django code for their worker code, at least for the foreseeable future, so there is relatively little of interest to say on that point.

The more interesting thing to focus on is Daphne and the design of the Channels system. Channels represents a useful worked example of how to structure complex multi-layer distributed systems using Twisted and message brokering. This chapter will use Channels in exactly this way. It will also discuss Channels as it relates to Autobahn, a WebSocket implementation for Twisted.

Channels Building Blocks

The fundamental components of Channels are a collection of well-known and trusted software tools. This is a major advantage in the design of Channels. For software as important and widely used as Django, it is important to favor reliability and certainty over the "cool" factor of a software component.

As discussed earlier, Channels is divided into three components. Each of those components is built on top of a single piece of core software.

The first component, Daphne, is a web server built on top of `twisted.web`. Daphne's operation goals also include supporting WebSockets, a protocol that is not supported in Twisted core, so Daphne makes some modifications to twisted.web in order to also use Autobahn to provide WebSocket support. It should be emphasized here that Daphne is a surprisingly small chunk of code that is mostly responsible for translating the HTTP and WebSocket protocols into Channels messages on queues, and handling reading from queues to write data back to connections.

The third component, the Channels "workers," are Python processes running the Django web framework and the Channels application. This application is responsible for listening on and sending to appropriate queues and generally hiding the Channels abstraction from the application code. The magic here is that the regular Django-using code base can be used almost without change, allowing for seamless upgrade from non-Channels-using Django deployments.

The second component is the only non-Python component in the stack: Redis. Redis is an open source in-memory key-value database that supports a number of data structures. While its primary function is as a database, it has a number of properties that make it useful as a message broker, including the ability to safely manage queues.

Each of these components can be deployed independently from the others, and implements a different part of the Channels topology. Taken together they form the complete web application, with Daphne handling the protocol support and talking to clients, Django handling the business logic, and Redis providing its services as a message broker between the other two services.

Message Brokers and Queues

A key design feature of Django Channels is that all regular Django applications need to continue to work as normal when running with Channels, but with one added feature: the ability to scale horizontally independent of the web servers serving the HTTP traffic. Essentially, regular Django applications that previously blocked the serving of web traffic must suddenly become asynchronous, allowing the web server to avoid blocking while it waits for the response to be delivered. How can this be achieved without changing any lines of code?

The key is the addition of a message broker. A message broker, or queueing system, is a common component in distributed systems. Its purpose is to route messages from a number of message producers to a different number of message consumers, without requiring those producers or consumers to know anything about how to find each other.

Generally message brokers use a FIFO *queue* as their core abstraction. Components of the system that produce work do so by adding work items to the back of the FIFO queue. These items are pulled off the front of the queue by one or more "worker processes" that are responsible for taking some action based on the submitted work. This system has many advantages: it can be used as a service discovery tool, and it also provides a useful decoupling between the sender of a message and the receiver of that message.

The advantage of a message broker like this is that it separates the runtime of the different components. In WSGI, the web application is tightly coupled with the execution model of the web server, because the web server is required to call a Python function that will block until execution completes. This tight integration means that the web server and the web application cannot have different approaches to concurrency: both end up being required to run single-threaded synchronous code.[1]

---

[1]This is not *quite* true: `twisted.web`, an asynchronous webserver, is somehow able to run synchronous blocking WSGI applications. It does this by invoking the WSGI application in a background thread and using a `Deferred` to communicate the result of that invocation back to the server. This does work, but it still means that the core of the business logic is being dispatched to a synchronous pool of background threads: not ideal from the perspective of scaling!

With the addition of a message broker between the web server and web application, each can have a different paradigm for execution. More than that, they can use whatever paradigm will still allow them to submit work to and receive work from the message broker. In this case Daphne, a Twisted-based asynchronous web server, can interact with the message broker using its asynchronous programming model, while traditional single-threaded synchronous Django handlers can run in the workers without getting in the way.

More importantly, we can now have vastly more worker processes than web servers. This greatly improves the performance of traditional web applications: rather than taking up precious time holding Python's Global Interpreter Lock, each invocation of the application can be done in a separate process.

This allows Django applications to become synchronous but parallel. Each Django request handler can be a regular synchronous blocking Python function, but the entire application can run as many of these as necessary in as many processes as they like in parallel. More importantly, the number of worker processes can be scaled dynamically and independently of the number of web servers. This allows independent horizontal scaling of each component of the application based on where bottlenecks are, which grants much more efficient use of resources.

Message brokers are a commonly used tool to add asynchrony to fundamentally synchronous programs. By allowing multiple instances of single-threaded synchronous code to run at once in separate processes or threads, it becomes possible to increase the amount of asynchrony in an application without needing to fundamentally rewrite it.

On top of that, message brokers allow you to avoid worrying about how to coordinate these multiple parallel workers. Each worker acts as though it's in its own little world, adding and removing data from queues without worrying about where that data comes from or goes. The message broker is responsible for ensuring that as many workers as needed are able to access data and process it appropriately.

While message brokers are not a panacea, they are a great tool for enabling scale and concurrency in non-concurrent programming models.

Distributed Multi-Layer Systems in Twisted

Django Channels is not just a useful tool for deploying horizontally-scalable web applications, it is also a useful example of a common construction of a distributed multi-layer software system.

A distributed multi-layer software system is a system that is constructed by separating the responsibilities of the system into "layers" that communicate among each other using some kind of messaging bus. In the case of an application using Django Channels, this will typically be a 3-layer architecture of Daphne, Django, and whatever database is used to persist the Django models (e.g., MySQL or PostgreSQL), but the idea of a multi-tiered architecture is substantially more general.

Asynchronous networking frameworks like Twisted are frequently a key component of multi-tiered systems. This is largely because multi-tier systems inevitably incur latency due to their use of either formalized or ad hoc RPC ("remote procedure call") mechanisms. As each node in a given tier in the system will want to use system resources as effectively as possible, multi-tier systems that use asynchronous programming techniques are vastly more scalable and efficient than those that do not.

The canonical multi-tier architecture divides the application into three tiers, each responsible for a separate aspect of the application. Typically this involves one tier devoted to storing data (a database), one tier devoted to performing application or business logic, and one tier devoted to presentation. This kind of pattern is very common, and in fact the very common "model-view-controller" pattern is closely related to this canonical construction.

When writing multi-tiered applications in Twisted, it is necessary to define the communication mechanism between the tiers. However, in all cases what ends up being built is a form of RPC to allow the individual tiers to request that the other tiers do work. Given that these applications require an RPC layer anyway, you'll save yourself a lot of time and effort by relying on some kind of standard RPC mechanism.

The most common choice for RPC is REST, an excellent choice given Twisted's excellent support for HTTP, but depending on your application any number of different RPC mechanisms may be sensible choices. The key to this kind of architecture is to know that the nature of Twisted application design lends itself very nicely to writing RPC-based applications: once your core application expects asynchrony, adding more layers of asynchrony is often relatively simple. With careful RPC choices and application design, it becomes possible to allow arbitrary horizontal scaling of your application. The world's largest web projects are all built in this style, and it's useful to know that Twisted gives you plenty of tools to embrace it yourself.

Current Status and Future Expansion

On September 9th, 2016, Channels was adopted as an official Django project. This means that it is managed under the auspices of the Django project and the Django Software Foundation, but it is not part of the core Django repository. The project remains under active development and is production ready.

It now also supports most of the major features. HTTP/1.1, HTTP/2, and WebSockets are all fully supported, though much like with core Twisted, some HTTP/2-only features are not yet supported. Redis is supported as the primary channel back end, but in-memory back ends are also supported for smaller deployments.

The future directions for Django Channels are many and varied. As a complex framework for deploying concurrent web applications, there are multiple possible directions for expansion. Additional channel back ends, alternative ASGI servers, and even compatibility layers for different web frameworks: all of these and more could be fruitful directions of enhancement. Wider support for alternative protocols would also likely be of some value to the project.

Of course, the ideal long-term future would be to adopt the Channels model in Django core as the default execution model. This would provide default support for highly scalable application design in Django, helping ensure that developers build their applications for future scalability from day one.

Summary

In this chapter we introduced Django Channels, a framework that allows developing web applications using the Django web application framework in a concurrent, asynchronous programming model. We discussed the basic architecture of Channels and introduced its building block technologies. We then discussed how these building blocks can be repurposed for arbitrary multi-level distributed system design, and how such a system could be designed to use Twisted to its fullest. Finally, we discussed the future growth of Channels.

Correction to: Expert Twisted: Event-Driven and Asynchronous Programming with Python

Mark Williams, Cory Benfield, Brian Warner, Moshe Zadka, Dustin Mitchell, Kevin Samuel, Pierre Tardy

Correction to:

Chapter 7 in: M. Williams et al., Magic Wormhole,
https://doi.org/10.1007/978-1-4842-3742-7_7

The original version of the book was inadvertently published without incorporating the author's proof corrections. The chapter has now been corrected and approved by the author.

The updated version of the chapter can be found at
https://doi.org/10.1007/978-1-4842-3742-7_7

© Mark Williams, Cory Benfield, Brian Warner, Moshe Zadka, Dustin Mitchell, Kevin Samuel, Pierre Tardy 2019
M. Williams et al., *Expert Twisted*, https://doi.org/10.1007/978-1-4842-3742-7_13

Index

A

Access Control Lists (ACLs), 248
AccountFileChecker class, 244
AccountURLChecker, 242
aiohttp, 312
Allocator state machine, 268–270
asDeferred helper function, 313
assertNoResult, 278
async / await constructs, 288
Asynchronous exception handling
    callback method, 66–67
    deferred implementation, 70–71
    encounter exceptions, 68–69
    Errbacks, 68
Asynchronous Message Protocol
        (AMP), 128, 214
    commands, 218
    custom plugin, 216–218
Asynchronous programming, 3, 63
Asynchronous Server Gateway Interface
        (ASGI), 366
Asynchronous testing, deferreds, 277
asyncio package, 305
asyncio and Twisted
    event loops, 306
        asyncio.get_event_loop, 307
        asyncio.set_event_loop, 307
        epoll, Linux, 307
        event loop policies, 307
        kqueue, macOS, 307

reactor, 307
        reactor selection, 307
        system event triggers, 308
        twisted.internet.reactor, 307
    PEP 3156, 305
    promises, 306
asyncio.Future class, 306
asyncio.get_event_loop_policy, 307
asyncio.set_event_loop_policy, 307
Async services, Buildbot's code
    addService, 325
    AsyncMultiService, 325
    ClientService class, 326
    disownServiceParent, 325
    IService, 324
    IServiceCollection, 324
    MessageQueueConnector, 326
    orthogonal problem, 324
    serialization, 324
    setServiceParent, 325
    startService, 324
Autobahn, 259, 286–287
Automat, 268

B

Biased coin toss, 215
Buildbot
    defined, 317
    history
        async build steps, 322–323

373

Printed in the United States
By Bookmasters